HYMNS OF THE HEART

HYMNS OF THE HEART

DISCOVERING GOD IN THE PSALMS

Adam Faughn

ISBN-10: 1941972543
ISBN-13: 978-1941972540

Library of Congress Control Number: 2014954980

Published by Start2Finish Books
PO Box 680, Bowie, Texas 76230
www.start2finish.org

Printed in the United States of America

Cover Design: GlideArt Design

To Leah

Contents

Foreword

Adam Faughn is one of the finest young preachers among us. He is a strong Christian who knows, loves, teaches, and lives the Scriptures. He has accomplished much for the Lord wherever he has been at work in the Kingdom. He has blessed the lives of all who have heard him preach and who have read his writings. Adam has favored us in writing *Hymns of the Heart*. This book is not simply another book on the Psalms. It is a well-researched and carefully-written book that is characterized by fresh insight and depth of understanding. It is not designed to cover each one of the 150 chapters in Psalms; rather the author's purpose is to promote a deeper understanding of and appreciation for the ancient songs.

The reader will notice that each Psalm treated in this book is discussed in an easy-to-follow manner in which the Psalm is divided and explained under bold headings according to the subject being treated. Preachers will find the book to be helpful in preaching from the Psalms. Bible class teachers will find it to be a useful tool in teaching classes on these songs. And all Christians will benefit from studying these *Hymns of the Heart*. I heartily recommend Adam Faughn's book to every student of the Word of God.

— Dr. Jay Lockhart
Whitehouse, Texas

Strong Roots in the Lord

PSALM 1

The Psalms, composed over five centuries, constitute the longest book in the Bible. Its length, however, acts as no deterrent to contemporary readership. Only a rare few attempt to gloss over or avoid it because the Book of Psalms offers wisdom and comfort, but also a unique human perspective on our relationship with God.

We often refer to them as the "the Psalms of David," although he only authored about half of them. Moses, Solomon, and the sons of Korah wrote many of the others psalms. A few, however, remain anonymous, but all were borne of divine inspiration. It is that fact, I think, that draws many people to the psalms. They display a wide range of emotions, which we have all experienced at one time or another. They declare praise to God, but they also reassure us that He is there, regardless of whether we receive a response.

These poems, regardless of subject, are in the Bible because God wants them there. He inspired them; they are His messages to His flock. He understands the turbulence of our thoughts, doubts, and reservations. By inspiring the faithful with these words, He acknowledges and approves of every possible emotion we might experience in order to help us through life.

In reflecting on the psalms, I want to start at the very beginning. I do not make this choice simply because it is the first, but because of its subject matter, and because it is here that the tone for the entire book is established. Psalm 1 is a series of contrasts between what is righteous and good and what is sinful and weak. In reality, it deals with godly wisdom, a topic which the remainder of the psalms attempt to work through both intellectually and emotionally.

In separating and studying the six verses of Psa. 1 one at a time, we can gather more insight into how we might better live our life for God. As you read and study along, you will probably find more applications than those I propose. Ultimately, I hope that these few verses will assist you in starting to understand the overall message of the Book of Psalms, as well as help you grow stronger in your walk with the Lord.

THE SEDUCTION OF SIN (v. 1)

Psalm 1 begins with a reminder of what it means to be blessed. The original Hebrew word was actually an interjection or exclamation—Blessed is the man! We are not being introduced to any old topic, but the path to being blessed!

There is a clear progression found in this verse that shows how sin can seduce us. It draws us in slowly, making us think that wicked actions are no big deal. We are, all of us, vulnerable to walking "in the counsel of the wicked." He who listens to what God's enemies are saying may begin to think that it is good advice. Many Christians, young and old, find themselves in this position by simply watching the nightly news, talk-shows, and other public entertainments that espouse their ideas as gospel. So many of these figures, however, have no regard for God or His ways. Their position and money convince us that they are competent, perhaps even wise, until finally we begin to believe that their advice is right. In this way, we risk walking with them in wickedness and sin; we risk walking away from the Lord.

If walking with the wicked does not seem bad enough, this verse details a downward progression to standing "in the way of sinners." The wicked begin by listening, but are soon standing near the path of those who have forsaken God. Standing too long in the company of a sinner distorts the truth. We may begin to dress like the sinner, adopt his/her mannerisms, or beliefs. They are no longer ashamed of certain sins or even aware that they are wicked. Avoid such persons, warns this verse, unless you are willing to expose yourself to social pressure.

If we do not attend to these first two warnings, we risk sitting "in the seat of scoffers." The wicked are now unashamed, the sinners without morality, as they sit among those who scoff at God's ways. They carry on conversations and never think of standing for what is right or true. Instead, they judge how Christians conduct themselves and mock sin itself.

Do you see the seduction of sin? Do you understand the ease with which we might tumble into inequity and depravity? When is it that we realize what we are doing is wrong? Perhaps we know all along that our actions are wicked, but we quiet our conscience. After all, we are only listening or just thinking about things; this does not make us ungodly. We know we are happiest when we stay true to God's Word, but nonetheless we can so easily succumb to sin's seduction. It is the truly happy and blessed person who avoids the lure of sin and recognizes this downward progression before it even begins. Blessed only is he who does not walk, stand, or sit among the wicked.

THE SATISFACTION OF SCRIPTURE (v. 2)

In the previous verse, the interjection "Blessed!" describes one who finds satisfaction in the Scriptures. It is he who avoids the ungodly and the sinners, whose "delight is in the law of the LORD," that attains the ultimate happiness. These persons fill their minds throughout the day and night with moral and righteous thoughts.

When we think of law, we imagine the amendments of the Constitution and the tedious litigation seen on television and in movies. It is difficult to consider these laws as inspiring "delight." Psalm 1:2, however, refers to divine law, not a simple rulebook. It is torah, "instruction" on how to live and not merely a set of rules to be followed in order to be a good citizen. More importantly, this is the law (or instruction) "of the Lord." The One who created us and knows everything about us is He who has passed down these rules for us to follow. He knows that if we follow His tenets, we shall bring true delight into our lives.

Satisfaction also comes through constant meditation on God's law. The word "meditation," however, often conjures up strange feelings and ideas because of its modern association with New Age religions. It is an integral element of yoga and other transcendental practices, which we usually interpret as phrases muttered with our eyes closed and without any particular meaning. You may find it interesting that the Hebrew word hagah in Psa. 1:2, which we translate as "meditates," does in fact carry an added nuance of muttering or even growling. The term implies that a person is so saturated with God's law that it is constantly on his lips, whether he is talking to someone else or himself. God's instruction becomes a fundamental part of that person, because it constantly fills his mind.

God knows us. He knows what will bring happiness and joy into our lives. The torah or Divine law is His gift to us—by following it, we can bring true satisfaction to our lives. All He asks is that we allow it to fill our thoughts and words, body and soul.

THE STRENGTH OF THE STUDENT (v. 3)

Imagine you are by a clear brook or a mountain stream. Shading you from the midday sun is a towering tree, whose roots go deep into the earth, drinking up the rich nutrients from the soil and stream. The roots cannot help but grow deep; they are strong and thick in order to provide for every branch, leaf, and limb. Whoever planted this tree knew how to care for it, how to keep it secure and nourished into maturity. The tree is strong, swaying but not bending in the strongest winds, sending forth its seed and enduring the long, hard winter.

This is the most famous verse from this psalm; possibly because it was used as the foundation for the song "I Shall Not Be Moved." It presents a picture of something solid and strong; it is a representation of the blessed man, who cannot be felled by wicked counsel or turned away from God's path. The one who is strong in faith can only prosper, like a tree with roots grown deep.

In late October 2013, a strong storm system hit Britain. The major problems were caused by strong winds, which toppled dozens of trees. Cars and buildings were destroyed, while four people lost their lives. In the following days, people noticed that the roots of the felled trees had not grown deep enough because of their proximity to city streets and sidewalks. Phone and electric companies had cut through other roots in order to access wiring and cables. The need for strong, deep roots to secure these trees against storms had been disrupted, leaving them easily brought down.

Our faith in God needs similarly strong roots, or it will be prey to the blustering of the immoral and unjust. God's Word is our nourishment; just as the tree drinks from the soil, so we drink from God's glory. We cannot claim to want to be more like God yet forsake His Word. In doing so, we weaken ourselves to the scoffers and sinners (discussed above), who would turn us from righteousness. David writes that this nourishment impacts every aspect of our lives, and the greatest prosperity will come only through the wisdom and instruction of the Lord.

THE SEPARATION OF THE SINNER (v. 4)

He who is firm in his faith and obeys the Word of God will prosper, but not so the ungodly. Verse 4 supplies the counterpoint to the glory of the blessed man by describing what will happen to the one who follows the seduction of sin. These are the wicked that, instead of being strongly rooted, are like chaff carried away by the wind.

In ancient times, harvested grain—especially wheat—was manually removed from the husk. It was taken to a great covered space where a large rake-like implement was used to throw the grains into the air. The useable seeds would drop back to the floor, while the evening breeze would carry away what was called the "chaff." What blew away was the refuse; those unusable and foreign elements that men cannot eat.

David employs a familiar image here. Even modern readers can easily envision a steady wind blowing about leaves and seeds. The wicked are just like these bits of chaff; they might look substantial, but they are merely husks—their insides empty of anything significant. They are dead on the inside, and this emptiness denies them the strength needed to withstand the difficulties of life. The chaff may settle again upon the earth, but it will never grow or mature. It will idle there until it decays into nothing.

The storms of life are divine tests that separate the righteous from the wicked. In these moments, it becomes clear who has embraced God's Word and who has not. This is not to say that the righteous will not struggle, but they are rooted in faith, which gives them strength to persevere. The wicked and blessed ask the same questions in times of trial, but the godless receive no answers. Moreover, they have no hope—no expectation of ever receiving an answer. The righteous may not always have a perfect solution to their every woe, but God blesses them with the fortitude to believe in brighter times. As the song explains, "We will understand it better by and by."

Do not be the chaff! Do not allow a strong gust to blow you away from the righteous path. Stay strong by remaining near the Word of God and gaining the spiritual nourishment it provides.

THE SUBMISSION OF THE SCOFFER (v. 5)

When this life ends, we will see a great separation. The wicked, who might have appeared to have it all together and everything figured out, will realize that they are not able to stand alongside the righteous. The storms of life will reveal the course of the wicked as incorrect, just as the ultimate judgment will show that God has seen their true ways. Eddie Cloer explains: "Life will eventually break [the wicked], for their approach to life is flawed. It follows then that if they cannot stand up under the blazing light of the judgment of life, they cannot even begin to find approval before the bar of God."[1]

The wicked will see the error of their ways because God will show them to be nothing more than chaff. Whatever guise they hid behind in life will be torn away, their souls laid bare, and God will censure them. They will not stand among the righteous.

In the NT, Paul reminds us of the final judgment and fate of the wicked. In Phil. 2:9, we are told that God highly exalted Christ "and bestowed on him the name that is above every name." Then Paul wrote, "So that at the name of Jesus every knee should bow, in heaven and on earth and under the earth, and every tongue confess that Jesus Christ is Lord, to the glory of God the Father" (Phil. 2:10-11).

Paul explains that it will not be a few who bow or confess before God. No, he assures us that every person will kneel on that Day of Judgment, regardless of what they did or did not do in this life. No one will pass through judgment freely. The righteous will be vindicated and the wicked condemned by the power and truth of God's ways.

---

1. Eddie Cloer, Psalms 1–50 (Searcy, AR: Resource Publications, 2004), 40.

THE SEEING OF THE SOVEREIGN (v. 6)

God is omniscient. He sees all, knows all, and misses nothing. The previous verses have expounded on the truth that God will not stand for those who have lived a wicked life. He is not blind to your dabbling in sin or your slow progression towards wickedness. Verse 6, the final verse of Psa. 1, forgoes the poetic imagery of the earlier verses to reveal the blunt truth of our fate, righteous and wicked alike.

Look back at the structure of this psalm. It began with a regression that attends the following of sin: first we might only walk with the ungodly, but before we know it, we are standing and sitting among them. The psalm ends with a word of warning to those who would stray from the righteous path: God will see your actions and, should you continue in them, your path will end in death.

The prophet Jeremiah said, "I know, O LORD, that the way of man is not in himself, that it is not in man who walks to direct his steps" (Jer. 10:23). Solomon comments on the fate of the wicked in Prov. 14:12: "There is a way that seems right to a man, but its end is the way to death." This is exactly what David is trying to reinforce with Psa. 1. When we start down the path toward sin and fail to see the strength and nourishment of God's Word, we face spiritual death. We cannot hide our actions from God, for he is ever aware of our movement away from Him.

There is, however, good news for the one who exalts in the Law of the Lord. Verse 2 assures us that the one who is blessed studies God's doctrine daily, absorbing it and living by it. It is in v. 6 that we learn the glorious end of the blessed: "The Lord knows the way of the righteous." God sees when someone drifts away from Him, but He also knows those who find delight in, meditate on, and find strength in His Word. We cannot avoid all negative experiences in life, but our strong roots in the Lord will allow us to weather them safely. God knows us, and we who are right with Him will receive His protection.

CONCLUSION

John Rippon, a simple man who served in a single congregation for 63 years, wished to provide that congregation with a hymnal. He took it upon himself to make one and, in the process, came across this poem. Originally seven stanzas, he fitted it to music and published it under the title "Exceedingly Great and Precious Promises."[2] The promise made is most notably found in Isa. 41:10: "Fear not, for I am with you; be not dismayed, for I am your God; I will strengthen you, I will help you, I will uphold you with my righteous right hand."

The first verse of Rippon's song is a powerful reminder that echoes the sentiment of Psa. 1. It prompts us to find strength and nourishment for the storms of life in the Word of God. So, we sing:

> How firm a foundation, ye saints of the Lord,
> Is laid for your faith in His excellent Word!
> What more can He say than to you He hath said,
> To you who for refuge to Jesus have fled?

This hymn has remained a favorite among Christians since it was first published in 1787. Its popularity resides within its biblical promises or, more specifically, in that God will protect His children. Its seemingly simple concept has been adopted into hymn and inarguable belief. God's people find their refuge and strength when they are faithful to Him. He has promised to remain near to us at all times if we keep to His path, blessing us with His glory when we do. Our task is to look upon our lives and honestly answer one simple question:

Am I blessed?

---

2. Robert J. Morgan, *Then Sings My Soul* (Nashville: Nelson, 2003), 83.

The Lord Is My Shield

PSALM 3

Have you ever felt down? Have you ever felt defeated? Have you ever had this sense that you are all alone, and the world is closing in? These are the emotions David suffered as he wrote Psa. 3.

Most modern editions of the Bible contain a note above this psalm that reads, "A Psalm of David, when he fled from Absalom his son." The background of this event is found in 2 Sam. 15-18, when Absalom, the son of David, rebelled against his father and stole the hearts of the people of Israel. Second Samuel 15:1-6 tells us that Absalom created the image of himself as a leader by sending a chariot, horses, and fifty men running before him. He would sit at the city gates and stop people who had come to the city for King David to settle their disputes.

Absalom would ask these people, "From what city are you?" and when the answer came, replied, "See, your claims are good and right, but there is no man designated by the king to hear you" (2 Sam. 15:3). In other words, Absalom was telling these people that the king held a low opinion of them and their homes, which was why he never appointed a local official to settle their disputes. "Oh that I were judge in that land!" Absalom would exclaim. "Then every man with a dispute or cause might come to me, and I would give him justice" (2 Sam. 15:4). Absalom promised that, unlike David, he would have both the time and energy to decide every case throughout the entire kingdom!

The political finesse demonstrated by Absalom is marred only by its inherent dishonesty. He could make no promise of this magnitude and intend to keep it. The goal was power, and he wooed the people however he could to win their hearts. He hugged and kissed them and "stole the hearts of the men of Israel" (2 Sam. 15:6). Four years of this passed, with Absalom constantly winning over the trust of the Israelites while concocting his plan for a rebellion.

Finally, David learned of his son's intentions, though we must wonder where he was for four years and how he did not know what Absalom was doing. Regardless, 2 Sam. 15:13 tells us that a messenger warned David, "The hearts of the men of Israel have gone after Absalom." This is the context of Psa. 3. David would not fight his son. He responds, "Arise, and let us flee, or else there will be no escape for us from Absalom. Go quickly, lest he overtake us quickly and bring down ruin on us and strike the city with the edge of the sword" (2 Sam. 15:14).

David fled. Instead of fighting his own son, he ran from his kingdom and a rebellion based on lies. What must he have felt during this exile? Betrayal? Hurt? Anger? A longing for home? This episode also illuminates David's weakness as a father, which was a regular occurrence during his life. Now, however, he must contend with the power of his son and his fears that Absalom might kill him to claim the throne.

The third psalm, attributed to David during his time in exile, clearly expresses his despair and sense of loss. It is remarkable, however, that the true message of these verses is of peace and comfort. David's words reveal a deep, abiding trust in God during a turbulent season of life.

PROBING YOUR FAITH

The number of enemies overwhelmed David. Absalom had declared war on him, forcing him to flee his kingdom. All alone and far from home, despair is understandable. Thus when David writes, "Many are saying of my soul, there is no salvation for him in God" (v. 2), we appreciate what he is feeling. This is his greatest fear, which speaks directly to his soul, to his inner self. These words discourage him deeply because they threaten his very relationship with God.

Has anyone ever questioned your faith? It is never easy to stand firm in the face of doubt. It is even harder to do so when times are already difficult. This is what David went through upon fleeing his kingdom. In addition to Absalom's rebellion and David running for his life, people tried to chip away at his faith in God. Had the Lord stopped listening to David? Maybe God was not strong enough to deliver him from this particular trial. Maybe God no longer cared. These were David's doubts, all of which we can identify with on a very personal level.

PROTECTION IN GOD

David pauses and considers this problem, rather than quitting altogether. At this point in time, he has the wonderful revelation that he will not allow these thoughts to eat away at his faith. He was not going to turn his back on the Lord who had protected him so many times before. Instead, he wrote some of the most beautiful words found in the Book of Psalms about the protection of God: "But you, O LORD, are a shield about me, my glory, and the lifter of my head" (v. 3).

When reading this verse, do not focus on the word "shield," but rather on the preposition "about." When men went into battle, they carried a shield in front of them. We can all conjure up an image of an ancient or medieval warrior, garbed in some sort of armor with his shield before him. It was good protection from arrows, spears, and face-to-face combat, but only against what was in front of them. The warrior was still vulnerable to attack from behind or the sides; if his speed and agility failed him, the shield would do little to thwart any threat. Not so the protection of God. He is the shield that protects David against attackers from all directions. God offers constant, all-encompassing shelter from danger, and it is this that David recalls in these dark moments.

God was also David's "glory." Any accomplishment, victory, or great deed David achieved in life he directly attributes to God. The throne upon which he sat, the kingdom over which he ruled—these were glorious because God gave them to him. Yet David no longer sat upon that throne when he wrote these words; he wore no royal robes or jewels, and he certainly was not sleeping safely in his citadel. He was beyond his capital city and battling for his very life against subjects once loyal to his name. Despite this, he still paused to honor God as the great Provider and without complaint of his current situation.

Finally, David calls God the "lifter of my head" (v. 3). This is one of my favorite phrases in the Bible because it is so true to life. We have all felt our heads droop as if the weight of the world is on our shoulders. There are those moments when we struggle to put one foot in front of the other, and we have experienced times when we were unsure if the malaise would ever lift. Oftentimes, we find support and comfort in the people around us, but they cannot lift our spirits the way we truly need them to—the way God can. Their help is temporary; in the end, we still find ourselves struggling as we had before.

God can lift our heads. There are times when He alone can put energy in our soul and elevate our spirits. He is the Lifter of our soul. It may take time for us to get back on our feet, but we know God is walking with us through every storm. He is always there to lift up our head and provide us with strength for the journey ahead, even when the steps are difficult.

After this verse, David adds a reminder that God always hears his children: "I cried aloud to the LORD, and he answered me from his holy hill" (v. 4). Have you ever done this? Have you ever felt so defeated or downtrodden in life that you just cried out to God? We might have done so in the past, and it is possible we will do so in the future. We need to understand what David did and why, but more importantly, we must acknowledge that God will hear our prayers. God does not always reply, "yes" to our requests, but he does answer every prayer for His people. It is only in those instances when God says "yes" that we exclaim, "God answered my prayer!" David understood this, but despite his trials, he still wrote that God answered him; He did not remove David's difficulty, but rather provided protection so that he might survive it.

How will you respond to God's answers? Will you trumpet His glory only if you hear a "yes" in response? Or will you do as David did before you and know that God stands beside you, regardless of His answer?

PEACE IN BELIEF

We have all experienced the traumatizing effect of nightmares. As children, our imaginations ran wild, conjuring up scenarios so horrifying that they startled us from our sleep. Most, if not all, of us would then run to our parents' room seeking comfort. Only with the reassuring presence of our mother or father by our side could we again find peace in sleep.

In Psa. 3, David is living his nightmare. He is hunted by his own people, betrayed by his own son, and exiled into the unknown chaos of the world. Like a waking child, he calls out to his Father for solace and, also like a child, to find comfort in sleep. Here he was, alone and fleeing death, yet he said, "I lay down and slept." Let that image fill your mind for a moment. In the midst of personal chaos, when people sought to move him away from the Lord, when he was filled with doubts, David simply lay down and slept. How beautiful is that! How remarkable this proof of trust in his heavenly Father!

David has no proof that he will wake in the morning, only the belief that God will see him safely delivered. He wrote, "I lay down and slept; I woke again, for the LORD sustained me" (v. 5). It seems such a simple thing, to wake up, but we cannot forget that David was being hunted; had his enemies found him while sleeping, they would have killed him. This is a far more terrifying reality than having a mere nightmare. David did not put his trust in the people around him, in those who told him that God's silence meant He did not care. He knew that a night of sleep and the ability to wake up in the morning came only from God Himself.

When London Bridge was rebuilt in the 1600s, the homeless and destitute, once accustomed to sleeping along the banks of the Thames River, transitioned to sleeping over it. A writer named William Gurnall remarked upon this, invoking the names of safer and more secure neighborhoods in London better suited to these poor men and women living on the streets. Take note of what he said: "Do you not think that they sleep as soundly who dwell on London Bridge as they who live at Whitehall or Cheapside? For they know that the waves which rush under them cannot hurt them. Even so may the saints rest quietly over the floods or trouble or death, and fear no ill."

Gurnall succinctly captures the sentiments expressed in Psa. 3. Storms will come into our lives, but we can still rest soundly and wake unafraid because we know that God is overseeing it all. This is a peace that, to use Paul's words, surpasses all understanding.

The peace David found in these words rebuilds his failing courage. He next writes, "I will not be afraid of many thousands of people who have set themselves against me all around" (v. 6). Some translations specify the number of his enemies at "10,000 people" (NIV, KJV), but *rebâbâh* is simply translated as "myriads." The sense, however, is the same: David will not allow any size army to lure him from his trust in God. Cloer eloquently comments, "We must remember that the gravity of a situation should not be assessed by counting the number of fierce attackers standing around in battle array. Our condition can only be evaluated by whether or not we have invited God's power into it."[1]

There will always be people against us, seeking to disturb our peace in faith. Allow me, however, to reassure you with truth: if we walk with God, no one can ever truly stand against us. They may seek to harm or intimidate us, and we may cower and wail, but that is because we are looking only to our own limited strength. We must remember that they who are against us also stand against God and His power. They work not to undermine us, but the Lord Himself, and this cannot be done. This is what David tells us in his psalm. We too can be emboldened like David and fearlessly declare, "It does not matter how many there are or what they do; I will not leave God!"

PRAYER, THE MIGHTIEST WEAPON

The psalm ends with a prayer. Perhaps it is the same one David mentioned in v. 4, when he cried aloud to the Lord. It may simply be a new prayer, calling upon God for help. But it is without a doubt the victorious culmination of David's mental battle against his doubts.

Tradition taught the Jews that if they remained faithful, Jehovah would fight their battles and deliver them from harm. This promise has led scholars to read the phrase "Arise, O Lord!" as part of a battle cry typical to ancient Israel. The rest of the psalm's language—the image of the shield, the repeated mention of enemies

---

1. Cloer, *Psalms 1–50*, 62.

surrounding him, the personal attacks by non-believers—all suggest a physical and spiritual battle. David even rages against himself, defending against his own doubts in God and his present situation.

We can choose to read these lines as some type of formal war cry or as a simple prayer, but the critical meaning behind these words remains the same. David is clearly praying with newfound boldness, which is directly attributed to his renewed trust in God. We might ask, why would he not pray? Why does he not realize that this is the simplest and most obvious answer to his troubles? We cannot fully understand what David was thinking without sharing directly in his experience, but we can be certain that his struggles reaffirmed and strengthened his faith.

In v. 7, he foretells God's reaction to the persecution of His faithful ones. First, He will "strike all my enemies on the cheek." This phrase expresses total control over the situation; God is the ultimate power and needs only shame the wicked into submission. When God enters into battle, there are no partial victories: enemies are removed completely. He will also break "the teeth of the wicked." The enemies of the faithful are likened to animals in these lines, for what weapon does the beast have beyond fangs and claws? David beseeches the Lord to tame the enemy, but He does not merely defeat the wicked; he removes their bite so they will never fight again.

CONCLUSION

David's enemies spoke to his soul, saying, "There is no salvation for him in God." After further reflection and consideration, David rebuilds peace and confidence in himself before writing, "Salvation belongs to the LORD" (v. 8). It no longer matters whether David finds safety from Absalom or escapes this predicament alive: salvation still—and always—belongs to the Lord. David emphasizes that it does not matter how his deliverance manifests because God can and will provide it.

The deposed king ends the psalm with words for his kingdom and its people: "Your blessing be on your people!" (v. 8). David is not ruling from his throne in Jerusalem; he is not among his people, but is, in fact, running from them. Still, he takes time to wish blessings upon them. I think it is in this one action that David proves he can always trust in God; his thoughts were not always on himself. He wanted God's blessing, of course, and has written about the many he has already received. Now, he thinks of others, even those who have risen against him, and prays for them despite their transgressions.

Let us end this chapter where we started, with a question. Have you ever felt down or defeated? Have you ever felt that the world was closing in on you? In these moments, realize that you are not alone, God is always with us. His children were promised His protection; He will come to your aid and fight the battle for you. He is the One who lifts your head in times of strife. He is the One who delivers you.

"You, O LORD, are a shield about me, my glory, and the lifter of my head."

The Majesty of God

"In the beginning, God created the heavens and the earth" (Gen. 1:1). Look about you. Look at all of creation, from the vastness of the universe to the amazing complexity of the atom. Seeing such wonders makes it impossible to miss the glory of God, for both the beauty and design of it cries out to His glory. "For his invisible attributes, namely, his eternal power and divine nature, have been clearly perceived, ever since the creation of the world, in the things that have been made" (Rom. 1:20).

In Psa. 8, David composes a hymn of praise. In the superscript above the psalm, it notes that this psalm was intended for a choir-master, according to (or "on") the Gittith. Scholars are not agreed as to what a Gittith is, debating between two valid theories. The Hebrew word is closely associated with Gath, which means "wine-press." This has led some to suggest that the Gittith was an instrument or common melody from contemporary Palestine. Conversely, the possible linguistic association with Gath implies that a Gittith was performed either during the harvest of grapes or to celebrate the completion of the season's work.

Regardless of the Gittith, this was clearly a psalm of praise and most likely sung aloud. The first half of v. 1 is repeated verbatim in v. 9, the repetition framing the multitude of reasons why God should be praised. It is the majesty of God and how that relates to mankind which David emphasizes. We need to understand what David was thinking when he wrote the words of Psa. 8—namely, what is God's majesty?

THE SUPREMACY OF THE CREATOR (vv. 1-2)

"O LORD, our Lord, how majestic is your name in all the earth! You have set your glory above the heavens." Thus begins Psa. 8 and David's praise of God. The simplicity of this opening in fact stresses the magnanimity of the Lord; so overcome with awe, David can barely articulate God's glory. His name alone, David continues, is majestic in all the earth, which begs the question: how much greater must the Lord's entire person be?

In using the reference of a name, David accomplishes two things. First, and most obviously, David makes it clear that the name of God is to be held in high esteem. Whenever we speak the name of God, we need to do so with the utmost reverence. Many people do not, treating the name of the Lord with disrespect as if He were common. He is not. He is the Creator and Judge of all things, and His name deserves the highest respect.

Second, David was not only writing about the name of God, but about His person. In Hebrew, when you mentioned someone's name, you were in fact speaking about the total character of that person. David exclaims that God's name is glorious, but also that everything about God is majestic. It is all of Him that is glorified throughout the earth, not merely His name.

There are many things on earth that inspire awe. Natural wonders, exotic animals, and the sheer versatility of mankind: all of this makes us marvel at the power of the Lord. Yet, when we look to the heavens, our minds are blinded by its vastness, unable to comprehend its magnitude. David, however, says that people might be in awe of the heavens, but God's glory is greater, more wondrous than all else. It is on display through the beauty and inner workings of all that we see above us. If we cannot fully comprehend the earth and heavens, how could we ever hope to understand the full consequence of God? We are fortunate to see Him in every little detail of our world, from soil to stars, all of which exhibit His omnipotence.

Verse 2 further emphasizes the splendor of God. Instead of writing about His majesty as exhibited in the grandeur of the overall creation, David turns his attention to smaller and, we might even say, weaker parts of creation. God, he declares, has established His strength "out of the mouth of babies and infants" (v. 2). Jesus repeats this statement in Matt. 21:16 when expressing that the seemingly weakest part of creation can still testify to the greatness of God. Only someone with a closed, disbelieving mind can watch an infant or toddler learning to do so many new things and still fail to see the glory and creative power of God.

We consider infants and children as vulnerable and weak because of their dependency on others for survival. There is great power in youth, however, both in its resiliency and unaffected innocence. David is alerting us to the influence even the youngest child can hold over us when inspired by God. Each man and woman begins life in this weak state, dependent on others and vulnerable to a multitude of dangers. Yet these same defenseless creatures grow into heroes of the faith. Moses was a baby when cast adrift into the Nile; he was raised by the enemy of God's children, but delivered them from Pharaoh and slavery.

We must also think of the birth of Jesus. God could have sent His Son into the world full-grown, but he chose to bless Mary with a baby and allow him to mature among mankind. In this helpless child, however, rested our salvation. It is a fitting threat God makes, using infants "to still the enemy and the avenger" (v. 2), for Satan influenced the child-like Adam and Eve toward sin. How apt that one of their descendants should be the Devil's downfall!

This is how God often works. Sometimes, we see Him in the mighty and grand parts of nature; at other times, His hands move through the smallest or weakest beings. God is supreme over all. It is little wonder, then, that David declares the very name of the Lord as majestic!

THE SIGNIFICANCE OF THE CREATED (vv. 3-4)

As the psalm continues, David looks again and again at God's creation. He beholds the majesty of the heavens, but also man. This is the big picture of creation, because God made everything around us, from the heavens to the earth, from the visible to the unseen. We should be amazed by creation in its many diverse forms, but we must be more awed by God, its Creator. This is what David is expressing when he mentions "the work of your [God's] fingers, the moon and the stars, which you have set in place" (v. 3).

No matter how grand creation might be, it is just the work of God's fingers. David is awestruck by how God wove everything together, by how detailed and intricate His work is. Again, we are reminded of Psa. 19:1: "The heavens declare the glory of God, and the sky above proclaims his handiwork." He is in everything, from the air we breathe to the heart that beats within our chests. These thoughts led David to the other end of the spectrum: mankind. He thinks about himself and his insignificance in comparison to God's many creations, which leads him to ask that famous question: "what is man that you are mindful of him, and the son of man that you care for him?" (v. 4).

Compared to the vastness of creation, man is just a tiny, inconsequential speck. God, however, does not compare us to His other works; He cares for man and is mindful of his spiritual needs. Adam betrayed God's trust in the Garden; he and his descendants were punished to walk in suffering and exile. Despite all this, God still cares for us. He still sent the Holy Spirit to educate us on sin and judgment; He gifted us with His Son and the ultimate redemption.

We can easily become lost in the vast grandeur of the universe, and I think this is a good thing every once in a while. Too easily, we forget how small we are in comparison to the world around us. Worst of all, we forget just how awesome the power of God is while we toil away in our day-to-day lives. He made all we can see, and even that which we cannot, simply by speaking it into existence. Think of the infinite power that demands—He says, "Let there by light," and then there is light. Think on this: a large nuclear reactor, which takes us many years to build, can consistently generate only about one gigawatt of power. By comparison, the sun consistently produces about 386 billion gigawatts of energy.

How minuscule are our efforts in comparison to the effortless creations of God. He but spoke, and the sun came into being. All that power, however, does not blind God to your existence. Indeed, He cares for you. We are special to Him, and He loves us. Is it not the greatest privilege to know that the Creator and Sustainer of the universe cares for us!?

THE STATUS OF THE CREATED (vv. 5-8)

The next section of this psalm is crucial to understanding our place in the created order. Both testaments of the Bible make it clear that God has placed man in a very special position. It is not to inflate our ego, but to remind us that we are made in the image of God; He cares for and expects great things from us.

Verses 5-8 helps us better comprehend where we stand among God's creations. First, David writes that man has been made by the Lord to be "a little lower than the heavenly beings" (v. 5). There is a debate over the translation of the phrase "heavenly beings" as other versions say, "You made him a little lower than God" (NASU).

Other translations replace God with "angels" (KJV, NIV) or "heavenly beings." The Hebrew term, *elohim*, is often translated as "God;" for example, "In the beginning *elohim* created the heavens and the earth." Here, however, *elohim* appears in the plural and, as there is only one God, it must refer to distinct personalities within the godhead, namely the Father, the Son, and the Holy Spirit.

In Psa. 8, David is saying that man is a little lower than God Himself, akin to the angels and other heavenly beings. We come from God, like these other entities, but are favored above them. Even if you read this as "lower than the angel/heavenly beings," man is still sovereign on earth. We are as amazed by angels as any other of God's creations, perhaps more so because they serve by His side. We are only lower than them because we walk the earth, while they dwell in heaven. Only man, however, is made in the very image of God. Only man is given a Redeemer and only man can be considered both servant and friend of God.

However we interpret *elohim*, God has set mankind, though insignificant when compared with the rest of creation, in a lofty place of respect. As David writes in vv. 6-8, God has put man in dominion over the rest of creation. When He made us on the sixth day, He said: "Be fruitful and multiply and fill the earth and subdue it, and have dominion over the fish of the sea and over the birds of the heavens and over every living thing that moves on the earth." And God said, "Behold, I have given you every plant yielding seed that is on the face of all the earth, and every tree with seed in its fruit. You shall have them for food. And to every beast of the earth and to every bird of the heavens and to everything that creeps on the earth, everything that has the breath of life, I have given every green plant for food" (Gen. 1:28–30).

David repeats God's command in his psalm, although more briefly: "You have given him [man] dominion over the works of your hands; you have put all things under his feet" (v. 6). *Mashal*, Hebrew for "to reign, have dominion over, " is an interesting term, because it also carried with it the idea of "assimilation." Subduing an enemy might win a battle, but assimilating him into your culture will ensure peace.

God has given us sovereignty over creation because it provides us sustenance. The food we eat, the air we breathe—all of it comes from God's bounty. Ruling over the creatures of the world, however, demands responsibility. Jesus told his disciples, "Everyone to whom much was given, of him much will be required, and from him to whom they entrusted much, they will demand the more" (Luke 12:48). We may hunt and fish, but must not drive animals to extinction. We may use natural resources for fuel and construction, but we must not burn down acres of forest; this is not in God's plan. We are to rule over creation responsibly, for we are managing it for the glory of God.

Consider again David's amazement. Among the stars and planets, trees and mountains, animals, both great and small, He has put all things under our feet (v. 6). God truly loves mankind and holds a special place for him in the created order. What is man then? He is not God. He is not divine. He is not the ultimate power in the universe or even on earth. This truth should keep us from developing inflated egos, but it is true that we are special among God's creation. We have been given the task of glorifying God through the supervision of His creation. Thus, we should feel a special sense of joy in knowing our God-ordained place within the created order, while always deferring to His will and way.

THE SHOUTING PRAISE TO THE CREATOR (v. 9)

David closes this psalm with the repetition of verse one: "O LORD, our Lord, how majestic is your name in all the earth!" (v. 9). At first, it appears formulaic, reusing the same phrase at the beginning and end in order to frame the psalm. However, you must understand that this great shout of praise comes after David has considered the relationship between God and man. He has shown us how we should ideally see ourselves in the greater scheme of things: keepers of God's trust.

Whenever I consider where we stand in the created order, I pause and praise God over and over again. Eddie Cloer succinctly summarizes David's point: "Considering anew God's created world and God's concern for mankind will inspire us to think deeply about the greatness of God; and such meditation can only cause us to repeat his sentence with greater understanding and deeper emotion."[1] Too many people focus on the phrase "What is man" in this psalm, when the emphasis is not on man, but on God. The opening and closing lines clarify that, even when I consider where I belong in the world, it should always lead to the praise of God. I cannot improve upon the glory of His name—I can only hope to reflect it in my life.

CONCLUSION

God is truly majestic. Both the most brilliant star and the tiniest baby house His glory. Our incredible and intimate relationship with Him is shared by none of His other creations; it is a gift, but it is also a sacred trust.

Sometimes we forget just how amazing and majestic God is, and how fortunate we are to be favored by Him. We have all, at one time or another, spoken with customer service representatives. In the morning, they are more lively and willing to help, but by the end of the day, they are exhausted, and their responses are made in tones of bored insincerity. At these times, the phrase "have a nice day" becomes cynical and insincere. If we are not careful, our praise of God can come across the same way. Saying "God is awesome" or "God is great" serves no purpose if we do not allow our minds to understand exactly what that means.

---

1. Cloer, *Psalms 1–50*, 115.

We will never fully understand the majesty and glory of God, but our goal in life should be to love and praise Him without losing sight of His awesomeness. He deserves not only our words of praise, but also the commitment of our hearts and minds to those words. Remember to look around you, both near and far, and accept the majesty and glory of God. Let the wonder of His power and creation fill your mind, and let that wonder lead you to reverent praise of Him who is truly worthy of all you can offer.

Take Refuge in God

4

D avid accomplished many great things in his lifetime, but we must remember that he was not perfect. There were a few stretches where his life was peaceful, especially once he became part of the royal household. Yet he spent a great amount of time in exile, even after he was king. On more than one occasion, Saul tried to kill David due to anger and jealousy because he had the hearts of the people (1 Sam. 19). David played music in an attempt to soothe Saul, but the harmful spirit would always return and torment the king (1 Sam. 16:23). Twice, Saul even tried to pin David to the wall with a spear (1 Sam. 18:11; 19:10).

Besides Saul, there was David's suffering due to his sin with Bathsheba (2 Sam. 11). It was this act of adultery that brought God's wrath, spoken through the prophet Nathan: "I will raise up evil against you out of your own house" (2 Sam. 12:11). Thereafter, his son Absalom rises up against him, and infighting among his children continues for the remainder of David's life. These experiences do not include the many battles David fought as King of Israel and Judah (2 Sam. 8:1–14). At times, he led his armies into battle, but even when he did not, the decisions and stresses of war plagued him.

These trials and tribulations, however, are why we relate so well to David. He was a king and a man of great faith, but the Bible also depicts his humanity. He faced all sorts of stresses and difficulties but was no more than a man. Even when David sinned, his mind and heart remained with God. When confronted with his sin, he repented and sought the Lord (e.g. 2 Sam. 12:18–24). No matter how dire his situation, he knew God would hear his plea for help: "He sent from on high, he took me; he drew me out of many waters. He rescued me from my strong enemy, from those who hated me, for they were too mighty for me. They confronted me in the day of my calamity, but the LORD was my support. He brought me out into a broad place; he rescued me, because he delighted in me" (2 Sam. 22:17-20).

REFUGE IN GOD (vv. 1–3)

The tone and language of Psa. 11 makes it clear that David was either in exile or, at the very least, reflecting upon that time. Most likely, it was composed when he was somewhat younger and running from Saul's forces (1 Sam. 21–2 Sam. 1). Enemies were all around him; at any moment he could be captured and killed.

David's enemies (or friends; we cannot be certain which) tell him to flee from Saul's wrath. The King of Israel has sought to subdue David through demonstrations of physical strength and the strength of his army. Saul, who has forsaken the Lord, kills everyone indiscriminately. Run, David is being told, "Flee like a bird to your mountain, for behold, the wicked bend the bow; they have fitted their arrow to the string to shoot in the dark at the upright in heart" (vv. 1-2).

These advisors, whether friend or foe, exclaim, "If the foundations are destroyed, what can the righteous do?" (v. 3). Saul was disobedient and thus rejected by God (1 Sam. 13:8-15). He became a poor leader, was tormented by an evil spirit (1 Sam. 16:14-23), and even lost the favor of his own son, Jonathan, who acknowledged David as the rightful king (1 Sam. 18:1-4). He was overcome with jealousy and paranoia and had devoted himself, not to the worship of the Lord, but to the destruction of David.

When that happens, what can the righteous do? When our leaders turn from the moral path in order to worship money and power, what hope do we have in remaining faithful to the Lord? We have all felt pressured by the crowd, forced to adapt lest we be made outcast. David was told to give up and flee. He ran, but he did not forsake hope. Even as Saul's army closed in, David kept to God's Law and spared the king not once, but twice (1 Sam. 24, 26). Such was David's faith that he did not succumb to the fear and mania all around him. He remained virtuous and strong before ultimately reconciling with Saul.

We live in a nation that repeatedly turns its back on God. We Christians look to our politicians for guidance, willing them to reinforce a focus on faith, but time and again we are left without their support. Like Saul's kingdom, our country's foundation has become unsound; Satan has corrupted our leaders, urging them to turn from God's Law for the temporal pursuit of campaigning and fundraising. As Christians, we look around and wonder where can we turn? If our own leaders will not stand by us and defend our shared beliefs, then what hope is there for the righteous to survive?

The fact of the matter is, we need to be like David. We must take refuge in the Lord and commit ourselves to Him. It does not matter what happens in society, or that its foundations are crumbling; if we keep ever closer to our Lord, we will find salvation. Does David not say to Saul after sparing his life for the second time, "The LORD rewards every man for his righteousness and his faithfulness" (1 Sam. 26:23)? Despite his tribulations, David is made king of Isarel and achieves great glory so long as he is faithful to God's Law.

GOD IS SOVEREIGN (v. 4)

In the second half of Psa. 11, I want you to focus on the three traits of God that David lays out in this difficult time. These are the qualities that led him to trust in the Lord, and they are the same three reasons why we need to trust God, regardless of what is happening around us.

Verse 4 contains a well-known phrase: "The LORD is in his holy temple." He is still there; He has not forsaken the faithful or abandoned David to Saul's fury. The terror that has infused others has not overcome David, because he is secure in his belief; he knows that God will protect him, even if he must hide for a time. This belief is affirmed with the rest of David's response to his advisors: "The LORD is in his holy temple; the LORD's throne is in heaven; his eyes see, his eyelids test the children of man" (v. 4). God is sovereign. He is above all things. Even David running for his life was a part of God's greater plan.

Discussing the sovereignty of God sometimes opens up a can of worms. There are people who teach that God orchestrates everything that has or ever will happen. The birth of a beautiful new baby, the marriage of a man and woman, a man entering an elementary school and killing children indiscriminately: if God is sovereign, then each of these events must be planned by him, right? No. A million times, no. This is not the sovereignty of God at work.

Too often, people view the world around them in extremes. God either causes everything or else does nothing. He does rule supreme; He sees and knows all, but mankind is rebellious. Bad things happen, not because of Him, but because of us. God can work all things together for good: "And we know that for those who love God all things work together for good, for those who are called according to his purpose" (Rom. 8:28). This verse does not tell us that all things are good; it does not tell us that God makes every situation good. It teaches us that God can bring about good from bad, no matter how rebellious we are.

There are those detractors who argue that believing this only proves that God is not omnipotent. How can He be all-knowing, all-seeing, and yet fail to stop men from wicked acts? Is He incapable of controlling us? Does He not have the ultimate power to keep our actions in check? God gave us the gift of free will; He is not a puppeteer, but the Creator of all things. How can we earn our eternal reward if we are never tested? Challenges and trials throughout our lives, whether small or great, allow us to mature in the Lord. They give us the opportunity to build a relationship and prove our worth.

Do I trust that? Do I trust that God has an ultimate plan for this world, for my life, even if I cannot see or comprehend it? Think of David. He ran for his life from a man who once treated him like a son, who allowed a mere boy to wear his armor (1 Sam. 17:38-39), and who gave his daughter to David in marriage (1 Sam. 18:20-29). David fled and hid because he was afraid, but he never lost faith in God. Saul's betrayal did not cause David to throw up his hands and admit defeat. He trusted that God had an ultimate plan and took refuge in Him. I, too, will trust that God is sovereign, and I will take comfort in the fact that He truly is Lord.

GOD IS RIGHTEOUS (v. 5)

God tests the hearts and minds of men. He challenges our fortitude so as to prove our faith in Him. "He disciplines us for our good, that we may share his holiness. For the moment all discipline seems painful rather than pleasant, but later it yields the peaceful fruit of righteousness to those who have been trained by it" (Heb. 12:10-11).

Such ordeals are commonplace in the Bible; God tests us so that we might better know ourselves and revel in His glory. He tests Abraham by demanding Isaac as sacrifice (Gen. 22:1-18), He tests Solomon (1 Kings 3:1-15), He tests Israel (Judg. 2:20-22; 3:1-6), and, most notably, He tries and retries Job by allowing Satan to torment him (Job 1-2).

Psalm 11 reminds us that no person, good or bad, and no matter how powerful, is beyond the scope of God. David is one of many who must pass God's tests and prove his faith, but he understands this and writes, "The LORD tests the righteous, but his soul hates the wicked and the one who loves violence" (v. 5). He is living in extreme circumstances few of us will ever experience. He is fighting for his life, surrounded by enemies, and betrayed by a man who once treated him like a favored son. These trials, however, occur because he is righteous, not because God has forsaken him (cf. Psa. 17:3; 26:2; 139:23-24). The Lord will allow certain things to happen to us in order to test us, but not because He is vindictive or cruel. He has promised to help us if we put our trust in Him (Prov. 3:11-12).

David, however, also avows that God hates the wicked and those who love violence. This truth is critical to David's faith, because it assures him that, despite his suffering, Saul will suffer more. After all, if the suffering of the faithful can be so acute, how much worse will the torment of sinners be? The wicked, we are told, are abominations in the eyes of God (Deut. 25:16), and thus we must share this same hatred for sin. We must never excuse sin as if it is no big deal, because this merely allows sin to continue (Heb. 10:26).

Today, we bemoan certain issues that seem to be attacking the moral fabric of our nation. How often, however, do we focus on the "big issues" while completely overlooking sin in our own lives? How many Christians will "amen" when their preacher speaks out against homosexuality, only to go home and watch TV shows where women are objectified in immodest clothing? How many will speak out against abortion, but "adjust" numbers on their tax return? How many would condemn sex outside of marriage, but watch movies where that very topic is the central theme?

God does not look at a few, larger issues, but at every element of our lives. He knows our position on national sins just as he knows what we do in our private day-to-day lives. God hates all sin, because every sin is an affront to His holiness. Thus, to excuse sin is to ignore Divine Law itself. As much as He abhors the wicked and sinful, the Lord rejoices with the righteous and upright (Prov. 3:32-35). He sees everything you do, both large and small. As Paul told his readers: "Therefore, my beloved brothers, be steadfast, immovable, always abounding in the work of the Lord, knowing that in the Lord your labor is not in vain" (1 Cor. 15:58).

GOD IS JUST (vv. 6-7)

David knows that he is not alone in his flight from Saul and that his enemies, while many, cannot overcome God's faithful. In the first half of the psalm, David is told by his advisors, "Flee like a bird to your mountain, for behold, the wicked bend the bow; they have fitted their arrow to the string to shoot in the dark at the upright in heart" (vv. 1-2). Although David faces death, he understands that he has not transgressed against God and, therefore, will not be abandoned to Saul's rage.

It is this perfect knowledge that leads to perfect justice, for David knows he is safe from the wicked's bows. He replies to these warnings, proclaiming the power of the faithful: "Let him rain coals on the wicked; fire and sulfur and a scorching wind shall be the portion of their cup. For the LORD is righteous; he loves righteous deeds; the upright shall behold his face" (vv. 6-7). Fire and sulfur will burn up the bows and arrows of the wicked; the upright will behold God's glory, not fall beneath the darkness of the scornful.

The ESV's use of "coals" in this translation is not entirely accurate. God is not raining coal upon the heads of the wicked, but traps (Hebrew *pach*). This translation adds to the poetic language of the psalm, balancing the traps set for David with those set by God. Moreover, a *pach* describes a bird trap. Did David's advisors/ enemies not tell him to "flee like a bird"? The imagery of their words has been made impotent, for God's judgment supersedes their own. It is the wicked that will be ensnared like helpless birds.

The punishment of the wicked, however, does not end with mere snares and traps. They have violated the holiness of God, and He will not abide such faithlessness. David writes, "Fire and sulfur and a scorching wind shall be the portion of their cup" (v. 6). "Fire and sulfur" (or brimstone) recalls Gen. 19 and the destruction of Sodom, Gomorrah, and the cities of the plain: "Then the LORD rained on Sodom and Gomorrah sulfur and fire from the LORD out of heaven" (Gen. 19:24). This is not a slap on the wrist, but the complete and utter destruction of cities. Scorching winds, quite common in ancient Israel, were symbolic of great suffering blowing into the lives of the wicked. These winds became a metaphor for the judgment of God, which David employed to show how seriously He would punish His enemies.

Let me ask you this: does God really punish sin? We have never seen Him drop fire from heaven on an evil city or nation as He did with Sodom. We have seen wicked people succeed in life, while those with pure hearts suffer. These discrepancies sometimes lead us to think that God is just sitting back, waiting for time to end. Does he see the injustice in the world? Does he care for what happens in human affairs at all? Of course He does: "I love those who love me, and those who seek me diligently find me" (Prov. 8:17).

God may not appear to us the same way as He once did, He may not rain fire upon the corrupt or send plagues upon the wicked. He is still present, however, and He will not stand for evil. "Nothing will ever change about God's character. We will not find that one day, especially during the day of our trials, God has changed and defends evildoers. However, only the righteous heart will have the benefit of His blessings and the companionship of His presence."[1]

As David said, God loves the righteous. He loves righteous deeds.

---

1. Cloer, *Psalms 1–50*, 149.

If we remain true to Him, follow His commandments, and live righteously, then He will protect and reward us with a glimpse of His face.

CONCLUSION

A very obvious question should arise when you seek to apply this psalm to your life: Is God my refuge? When everything seems to be moving away from God and the foundations of society are crumbling, do you run away in fear, or to the Lord in hope? More personally, when struggles occur in your own life, do you find your refuge in Him? Are you living the life of one who is righteous and completely trusts in the Lord? He rules over all, He knows all, and He will judge all perfectly. Knowing this, how can we help but run to Him and find refuge in Him?

David assures the naysayers, "For the LORD is righteous; he loves righteous deeds; the upright shall behold his face" (v. 7). Jesus echoed these words in His famous Sermon on the Mount: "Blessed are the pure in heart, for they shall see God" (Matt. 5:8). Is this not what we all want, to walk so closely with God that we see His face? David is not simply promising some future reward of heaven. I think what David has in mind is that, when we walk with God and take our refuge in Him, our fellowship grows with Him, and we know Him better and better.

Dwelling in God's Presence

PSALM 15

ach week, Christians gather to worship their Creator and Lord. Each week, many of them struggle with a lack of motivation, which dissuades them from attending service. There are countless reasons why we are tempted to skip that one sermon, that one morning of church: sleepiness, boredom, or a multitude of other distractions that keep our mind occupied on personal issues.

Worshipping the Lord is not about us, however, but about Him, about worshipping Him "in spirit and in truth" (John 4:24). How many moments of boredom and distraction would be solved if we simply recalled why we entered the church in the first place? In order to better focus our minds during worship, we need to think less of ourselves and more of the Lord. If we place our minds and hearts on Him and what He has done for us, how could we ever be bored? We must realize that worship is directed toward Him, for He is truly worthy of all we can give.

Each time we come together to worship, it should be with a sense of awe. We are standing before the Almighty! There should be a sense of wonder as we marvel at His wisdom and love, a sense of reverence, because He is higher and greater than all else. We should fear His disappointment, for He will not accept half-hearted worship, but we should also feel gratitude. God has done so much for us already, but also because He allows us the glorious privilege of coming before Him in worship.

In Psa. 15, David asks himself who can worship the Lord. He is not focused on why we worship, because he understood that our knowledge of God is a gift. David answers his question by listing the attributes of a good, faithful Israelite and, ultimately, a Christian. Moreover, he reminds us that not everyone is deemed worthy to worship in God's temples or churches. Worship is, after all, a blessing—something earned by how we live our lives. It is not our right, but our reward.

THE PONDERING WANDERER (v. 1)

In v. 1, David asks the question, "O LORD, who shall sojourn[1] in your tent? Who shall dwell on your holy hill?" The repetition of his question emphasizes the depth of his desire for its answer. The tent David refers to is in fact the holy tabernacle, a migratory temple carried about by priests for worship (Exod. 36:8-39:43; 1 Chron. 15:1-2). The holy hill refers to Mount Zion, where the Ark of the Covenant finally came to rest (2 Sam. 6:12,16; 1 Kings 8:1; 1 Chron. 15:1-2, 29; 2 Chron. 5:2). David's question, then, seeks to understand who can be a true member of His church and who will receive eternal glory.

There are those scholars who speculate that this psalm was composed when the Ark of the Covenant was taken from Jerusalem (also known as Zion). It was the illustrious King David who was attempting to retrieve it. If this is true, then both Psa. 15 and 24 would have been written around the same time. Psalm 24 focuses on a similar subject (the return of the Ark) and contains expressions comparable to those in Psa. 15. Regardless of its composition date,

---

1. It is because of the word "sojourn" (Hebrew *guwr*) that we call this section "the pondering wanderer." David is longing to be near God, but is often running for his life in exile. He wants to be certain that he can prove his worthiness to the Lord when he cannot worship regularly.

David is asking a timeless question: who can worship God as a true member of His church? How often do we reflect on our worthiness? God is perfectly holy and all-powerful; He has made, and dwells within, everything. What are we in comparison? Why would God even allow us to be near Him?

God allows us into His presence in worship so as to express our gratitude and praise Him for the bounty He provides. When we consider this, it should cause us to think about how we approach worship. We are just wanderers here on the earth, all of which belongs to God: "For every beast of the forest is mine, the cattle on a thousand hills" (Psa. 50:10). He is Lord over all, including us. We, as lowly as we are, can still stand before Him in worship. While we may not go to a "holy hill" as those in the Old Testament did, we still enter His holy space and marvel at His glory. The church building is not sacred in and of itself; it is what happens therein—worship of and communion with Him—that is most blessed and holy.

THE PURE WALK (v. 2)

David writes an inspired answer to his question between vv. 2 and 4. All told, there are eleven qualities mentioned in this psalm. It is not meant to be an exhaustive list, nor can we check off all eleven qualities and be perfectly qualified to come before God. David is in fact trying to give an overall portrait of what defines those truly faithful to the Lord. He divides the list into two parts: five qualities of what the righteous must do and six that they must not. David then weaves these together in poetic balance to answer his question at the beginning of the psalm.

He begins his exposition on the key elements of the truly righteous in v. 2: "He who walks blamelessly and does what is right and speaks truth in his heart." Herein lie three unique qualities. First, we must walk blamelessly (Hebrew *tamiym*), which can also be translated as "with integrity" or "in accord with truth." David is not telling us that we must be perfectly sinless to come before God in worship. If this were so, none of us would ever qualify. God knows we are imperfect; He made us. The point David is trying to make is that the blameless are those who seek the Lord's will, not their own, and thereby maintain true devotion to God.

He who is right with the Lord must also do "what is right" (v. 2). This seems like a more-obvious-than-not quality, but it follows the first point perfectly. Someone who walks with integrity cannot help but do things that are right, just as someone who does things that are right cannot help but walk with integrity. This is not a type of "works salvation" where someone is better than someone else in the eyes of God because they do more good works. David is simply saying that whoever walks closely to the Lord will demonstrate this in everything he does.

There is a familiar adage that says "actions speak louder than words." When we commit ourselves to righteous deeds, we are proving our worthiness in God's sight. Words and actions, however, can hide someone's true character, leaving us uncertain of their true motives. Such truth is not, however, hidden from the Lord. He knows and sees all, and he who "speaks truth in his heart" (v. 2) will be rewarded, just as he who is false will be punished. This is a key phrase in David's answer, but it simultaneously recognizes and forgives our imperfections. What we cannot express through word or deed is still visible to God. He knows whether what resides in our hearts matches the life we live.

My words—my innermost self—will speak truth. My heart will want to speak the truth, and that will manifest itself, not just in what I say to other people, but also in what I say to myself and to the Lord. Listen to these wise words from Charles Spurgeon: "Saints not only desire to love and speak truth with their lips, but they seek to be true within; they will not lie even in the closet of their hearts, for God is there to listen; they scorn double meanings, evasions, equivocations, white lies, flatteries, and deceptions."[2]

How often do we speak in partial truths? How often do we omit details in order to present a better picture of ourselves? How often do we do that, even in our own hearts? Someone who seeks a life of purity in order to stand before God is one who speaks, lives, and thinks the truth.

THE PEACEFUL NEIGHBOR (v. 3)

David's first set of qualities looks inward, focusing on what we do, say, and think as individuals. The second set, however, focuses more attention on our position in society and how we treat others therein. The one who can worship in the Lord's temple is one who "does not slander with his tongue" (v. 3). The Hebrew word *ragal* was used to describe those who go around spreading gossip or bearing false tales. James reminds us that our tongues, although small, have the ability to set great events in motion: "The tongue is a small member, yet it boasts of great things. How great a forest is set ablaze by such a small fire!" (Jas. 3:5). A person who wishes to come near to God will not want to share the latest juicy stories about someone else, especially when those stories are hurtful. True Christians control what they say and only speak graciously about, and to, one another (Col. 4:6).

Humans are social creatures. We might need time alone, but few of us seek the hermit lifestyle. God created us to be so and passed down His laws so that we might live peacefully together. Saul had ruined this delicate peace by hunting down David. Is it any wonder that David adds to his list, "does no evil to his neighbor" (v. 3)? David did not want to harm Saul, thus his decision to let the enraged king go on two separate occasions (1 Sam. 24, 26). We do not wish

2. Spurgeon, *Treasury of David*, 1.1.177.

to harm anyone, just as we do not want anyone to harm us. We are, after all, "sons of God, through faith" (Gal. 3:26), and to harm each other would be like harming our brother.

All siblings, however, argue from time to time. We are not passive beings, and there will likely be confrontation and tension between us. Regardless of these trials, the true follower of God will keep the best interests of his neighbors in mind. He might say and do things that are difficult for others to hear, but he says and does them with love and compassion. Christians who worship at the Lord's feet are not those who ignore the feelings and needs of those around them. They do not harm others, but seek to live in peace with all.

Neighbors, acquaintances, or the person standing behind us in line: they all deserve our respect as fellow human beings and children of God. We do not know what is in their hearts, but we know what the Lord wishes of us, and that is to do no evil unto others. Similarly, he who is right with God must not "take up a reproach against his friend" (v. 3). This seems pretty straightforward. After all, why would we shame our friends? It is said that we often hurt the ones we love most. We expect forgiveness from those we are close to; we expect patience and understanding. It is all too easy to ignore the feelings of our friends when attempting to fit into a new situation, because we expect them to overlook our mistakes. Is this not what David did for Saul, who turned against him and hunted him across Israel? David forgave his old friend and was rewarded by God with victory in battle, as well as the throne of Israel (1 Sam. 27:8-12; 30:16-31; 2 Sam. 2:1-7); Saul, who betrayed David, saw his sons slain by the Philistines before taking his own life (1 Sam. 31).

If we want to come before the throne of God, we cannot speak evil of those around us and then bless the Lord with those same lips. Is this not exactly what James taught us? "With it [our mouths] we bless our Lord and Father, and with it we curse people who are made in the likeness of God. From the same mouth come blessing and cursing. My brothers, these things ought not to be so" (Jas. 3:9-10). Even if there is a tidal wave of cruel words against someone, the worthy Christian will always stand for truth and try to say what is good in order to build up others. Anonymity is no excuse, either. What we post on Facebook or Twitter can hurt someone just as easily as the spoken word. How many of us are willing to critique and ridicule politicians and celebrities from behind a keyboard? We do not know these people; we hear only limited details related by gossipmongers and PR personnel. Those who want to worship God in His temple will not use their words or actions to bring reproach.

THE PIOUS JUDGE (v. 4)

In the previous chapter, we discussed God's stance on sin and the sinful. He abhors wickedness, violence, and those who perpetrate either: "All who do such things, all who act dishonestly, are an abomination to the LORD your God" (Deut. 25:16). Thus, we must emulate His disdain in order to worship Him: "In whose eyes a vile person is despised" (v. 4). It seems contrary to put this quality after we are told not to harm our neighbor (v. 3); what are we meant to do if not chastise and reprimand the sinner? This, however, is not what God wants of us. He alone can judge men's hearts and see their true nature, which means we are left to observe men's actions and words. We must love and respect our neighbor, but if we perceive sin, we must seek to introduce correction. It is not love, after all, to allow our brothers and sisters to walk the wicked path: "If anyone among you wanders from the truth and someone brings him back, let him know that whoever brings back a sinner from his wandering will save his soul from death and will cover a multitude of sins" (Jas. 5:19-20).

It is here that David recalls his earlier admonitions: walk blamelessly and do what is right (v. 2); speak only truth, both aloud and in your heart (vv. 2-3); and treat your brothers and sisters righteously

(v. 3). These actions alert others that you are a servant of the Lord and live your life by His laws. Thus, David adds that he who is worthy to worship in His temple also, "Honors those who fear the LORD" (v. 4). Honoring those who walk the way of God reveals that we are also prepared to come before Him. This only makes sense when we consider it in the context of worship. I do not go to church to worship alone, even though it is a very personal experience. It is, in truth, a communal activity. I am with others, and together we praise and glorify God; we are spurring one another on in our Christian life. Whenever I observe someone doing good work in the name of the Lord and maturing in faith, I should honor that person. I should celebrate his achievement and bid him Godspeed, because they are helping to spread the fame and glory of the Lord, just as we should all strive to do each and every day.

Honoring the Lord and those who fear Him requires commitment, honesty, and a lack of self. He who is worthy of worshipping in the temple of God is he "who swears to his own hurt and does not change" (v. 4). This is perhaps the hardest concept to understand. David is speaking of truth and our commitment to promises made. The Bible is clear on the importance of vows sworn to God. For instance, ""If you make a vow to the LORD your God, you shall not delay fulfilling it, for the LORD your God will surely require it of you, and you will be guilty of sin" (Deut. 23:21; cf. Num. 30:2). A vow is a sacred covenant between you and God, and to renege on it is a sinful act.

The crucial point to David's admonition is that a true Christian keeps his word, even if it means he might come to harm. Judges 11 tells the story of Jephthah who vowed to God that, if He helped Jephthah defeat the Ammonites, "Whatever comes out from the doors of my house to meet me when I return in peace from the Ammonites shall be the LORD's, and I will offer it up for a burnt offering" (Judg. 11:30-31). Sure enough, Jephthah returned home triumphant only to have his only child come through the doors of his house to greet him. In grief, he tore his clothes and cried "Alas, my daughter! You have brought me very low, and you have become the cause of great trouble to me. For I have opened my mouth to the LORD, and I cannot take back my vow" (Judg. 11:35). Jephthah sacrificed his only child to honor the promise he made God, though it hurt him greatly.

Promises made to God must be fulfilled, no matter the personal pain. The example of Jephthah is an extreme case, but it also expresses the strength and commitment of the faithful. Jephthah made a rash promise, but such was his unswerving faith that he killed his only child. We are not likely to face choices like this, but that does not mean we do not experience similar regrets. When you sign your name and buy that new car, you make a promise to pay for it. It might be painful a few months later when the first bill arrives, but you would never consider going back on your word. When you say, "I do," before a preacher, you are swearing to your new partner and God that you will remain by that person's side. Marriage is not easy; there will be times when it might be easier just to end it. The faithful will remain true to their covenant and work ever harder to make that union work.

All of this connects to being a person who walks blamelessly and with integrity. David is not telling us that a person must be rigid and inflexible, but rather confident in his convictions. Certain circumstances make us want to break our vows and make it more difficult to keep our promises, but these are just Divine tests. The Lord wants us to prove our faith, to work for the end reward, for this is His way of weeding out the sinners from the true believers.

THE PENITENT SERVANT (v. 5)

David is reminding us of the proper and dutiful behavior of the faithful. We must act righteously. We must treat those who act in accordance with Divine Law righteously. Moreover, we must spurn the unrighteous. It is David's final note, regarding finances, which seems to diverge from his former cautions. He who wishes to worship in the Lord's temple must "not put out his money at interest" or "take a bribe against the innocent" (v. 5).

We must read these lines in two ways: historically and morally. David is not saying—nor does the Bible teach—that it is sinful to lend money or charge interest when doing so. Israelites, under the Law of Moses, could not charge interest to a fellow Israelite: "If you lend money to any of my people with you who is poor, you shall not be like a moneylender to him, and you shall not exact interest from him" (Exod. 22:25; cf. Lev. 25:36-37).

The Israelites considered themselves as family, united by their faith. Any harm, financial or otherwise, committed against a fellow Israelite was the equivalent of a crime against God. They could loan money to a foreigner and charge interest, but to do so to a fellow Israelite was forbidden. David reminds his brethren that the one who would come before God in worship is one who has a heart of compassion. The righteous do not use another's suffering for personal gain. They will not set aside morality for money. We might summarize these final two traits by saying that he who would be near God is one who does not succumb to the love of money.

THE PROMISING WORD (v. 5)

Looking at this list of traits, we might panic and think, "I can't do that!" After all, Rom. 3:23 makes clear that all "fall short of the glory of God." What hope do we have, imperfect as we are, of standing before God in worship? We must remember, however, that these qualities on David's list arise from Divine Law. How we treat one another and how we worship God were all told by God to Moses and then to His people; David is not demanding anything new of the faithful. He is reminding us that we cannot worship in God's temple if we forsake these laws.

David ends this psalm with a great promise: "He who does these things shall never be moved" (v. 5). This is a wonderful avowal. It promises the faithful the ultimate gift: closeness to God. The Hebrew word, *mowt*, translated here as "moved," is better defined as "shaken." This slight change in nuance is actually quite wonderful. In a word, it recalls the very first psalm, where we are told that the one who meditates on the word of God constantly "is like a tree planted by streams of water" (Psa. 1:3), unlike the wicked, who resemble the "chaff that the wind drives away" (1:4). The faithful are sturdy like the great tree; they are immoveable and unshaken in their dedication to God.

These words mark a promise the Lord made long before to His children, and what has David just said about vows? They cannot be broken, for he "who swears to his own hurt and does not change" (v. 4) will be worthy of worshipping in God's temple. David has already proven himself to be righteous; he has served God faithfully and is spared Saul's rage. He did not ask the question of v. 1 out of random curiosity. He wanted to know for certain who could draw near to God and be close to the Lord. Why? Because David wanted that for his life!

Do we not all fail from time to time? What David is telling us is that, if we do live that way, if we do our best to obey these laws, then we might be nearer to God. If we follow these admonitions, we will not be moved, we will not be shaken. If we keep our vows to Him, we will be close to the Almighty in His place. What a glorious promise!

CONCLUSION

When I consider coming before God in worship, I ask myself: Am I fully devoted to Him, or am I distracted by the world? I wonder whether I am prepared to pour all of myself into worshipping him. It is not that I think I must be perfect in order to worship—if that were the case, none of us would qualify to enter His presence in praise. Instead, when approaching God in worship, I reflect on how I live. Does my day-by-day life equate with my lips' confessions in Sunday worship? Am I loving God the Creator, yet ignoring those made in His image? Does my heart want to do right, or am I just glad that the worship hour is over so that I can go back to doing what I want to do?

If I want to be with God on that "holy hill"—the eternal city called heaven—my life and my worship must agree. I cannot praise God on Sunday then live selfishly for the rest of the week. God cannot be drawn from some box only when I need Him. I must always give Him praise and honor in my life. I must dedicate my every word and action to glorifying His name. Thankfully, if I live for Him daily, I know that I will be with Him on His holy hill and, eventually, in heaven. After all, "He gives power to the faint, and to him who has no might he increases strength. Even youths shall faint and be weary, and young men shall fall exhausted; but they who wait for the LORD shall renew their strength; they shall mount up with wings like eagles; they shall run and not be weary; they shall walk and not faint" (Isa. 40:29-31).

Three Books of Praise

God is worthy of praise. We know this to be true and understand it as fact. We also know, however, that sometimes we fail to praise Him as we should. Even when we extol His glory and devoutly worship Him, we do so imperfectly, because we are imperfect. It is our duty to strive towards perfection, however, for only then can we be certain that we offer Him the very best of ourselves. We must remember that He is all around us, in everything, and thus we must praise Him for everything.

Psalm 19, sometimes referred to as "God's Two Books," is a reminder that God is the great Creator. It praises all of creation, as well as the Word of God, for both are worthy of daily exultation. David, the supposed author of this psalm, contemplates both of these wonders. He marvels at God's glory surrounding and infiltrating his life, but he does not merely observe. David reacts. The knowledge that God is in everything—from the air we breathe, to the food we eat, to the very words we speak—causes David to look deep within himself and ask what he can and must do to praise the Creator.

The modern world is not always considerate of personal faith or beliefs. It allows freedom of religion, yet appears to discourage it when it does not coalesce with public opinion or scientific theory. God and science, however, are not mutually exclusive. Over a century ago, Charles Spurgeon wrote these very powerful words in an introduction to Psa. 19:

> In his earliest days the Psalmist, while keeping his father's flock, had devoted himself to the study of God's two great books—nature and Scripture; and he had so thoroughly entered into the spirit of these two only volumes in his library, that he was able with a devout criticism to compare and contrast them, magnifying the excellency of the Author as seen in both. How foolish and wicked are those who instead of accepting the two sacred tomes, and delighting to behold the same divine hand in each, spend all their wits in endeavoring to find discrepancies and contradictions.[1]

We need to understand that God gave us science, just as He gave us the earth to populate, the laws with which to regulate our societies, and the words with which to communicate. Let us approach Psa. 19 as praise for His varied creations. Notice that these two great books—nature and Scripture—are both from God, and it is our duty to add our voices to exaltation of the Almighty. It will be by our hands that a third book will praise the Creator of all things.

The Book of Powerful Stars (vv. 1-6)

"In the beginning, God created the heavens and the earth" (Gen. 1:1). The very first line of the Bible, perhaps the most famous of all, confirms the glory and majesty of the Lord. In a few words, we are told that once there was nothing until He made everything, which we now accept as normal and unremarkable. We expect that there will be sky above and ground beneath us, just as we expect the sun to rise and set each day. How often, however, do we reflect upon the

---

1. Spurgeon, *Treasury of David*, 1.1.269.

wonder of these creations? How often do we marvel at the beauty of His creations? The first "book" of Psa. 19 is David's response to mankind's self-absorption.

As in Psa. 8, his attention is upon the natural world as proof of God's amazing majesty. Nature constantly praises God's gifts; it "day to day pours out speech, and night to night reveals knowledge" (19:2). The opening lines indicate continual action; nature's declaration of God's glory is constant and never ceasing. Each day is a manifestation of His awesome creation and, lest we think the setting of the sun signifies the end of God's power, we are assured that it continues every night, manifested by the millions of shining stars.

David was no stranger to the wonders of nature. Before slaying Goliath, running from Saul, and becoming king, he was a simple shepherd. Unconfined by city walls, he would have been very familiar with the beauty of the sun and stars, the earth and the trees. Daily, he worked among God's creation, not manmade walls and streets. It is little wonder that he was able to glorify God through the sun and night sky. David understood that no part of the earth was untouched by the Lord's hand.

Nature is universal. In vv. 3-4, David explains that everyone, regardless of nationality, language, or economic status, have all marveled at this display of God's glory. At one time or another, everyone has beheld the wonders of the sky, sun, and stars, for the voice of creation "goes out through all the earth, and [its] words to the end of the world" (v. 4). Paul reminds us in Rom. 1:19-20 that although the created order cannot teach us all we need to know about salvation, the many wonders of nature do not allow us to ignore the involvement of the divine hand.

People have long sought to explain the wonders of nature. How was it made? Why is it here? In this psalm, David attempts to explain what he has observed. He refers to the sun as a bridegroom leaving his chamber; it emerges from its tent (nighttime) like a groom prepared for his wedding day. The *chuppah* originally referred to the "chamber in which the bride awaited the groom for the marital union,"[2] only later evolving to a ceremonial canopy held over the Jewish bride and groom. The canopy was symbolic of heaven under which the couple said their vows. David is likening the appearance of the sun with the revelation of a handsomely dressed groom, magnificent and splendorous in his finery. Both emerge from darkness—night and the *chuppah*, respectively—and dazzle all who look upon them. The sun is unwavering in its circuit across the sky, just as a groom strides purposefully to the altar.

On August 23, 1712, a London newspaper called *The Spectator* published a poem by Joseph Addison. Accompanying the poem were these words of explanation, also written by Addison:

> The Supreme Being has made the best arguments for his own existence in the formation of the heavens and the earth, and these are arguments which a man of sense cannot forbear attending to who is out of the noise and hurry of human affairs. [...] The Psalmist has very beautiful strokes of poetry to this purpose in that exalted strain.[3]

In 1798, Franz Haydn took Addison's poem and added music. Congregations continue to sing Addison's words to Haydn's melody, because together they celebrate the unfettered glory of God's creations and remind us all that He is everywhere and in everything:

> The spacious firmament on high,
> With all the blue ethereal sky;
> And spangled heavens, a shining frame
> Their great Original proclaim.

---

2. Huppah, Jewish Encyclopedia. http://www.jewishencyclopedia.com/articles/7941-huppah.

3. http://cyberhymnal.org/htm/s/p/spacious.htm.

The unwearied sun, from day to day,
Does his creator's power display
And publishes to every land
The work of an Almighty hand.

Soon as the evening shades prevail,
The moon takes up the wonderful tale;
And nightly to the listening earth,
Repeats the story of her birth.
While all the stars that 'round her burn,
And all the planets in their turn,
Confirm the tidings as they roll
And spread the truth from pole to pole.

What tho, no real voice nor sound,
Amid their radiant orbs be found
What tho in solemn silence all
Move round this dark, terrestrial ball
In reason's ear, they all rejoice,
And utter forth a glorious voice.
Forever singing as they shine,
"The hand that made us is divine."

Nature is the ultimate proof of God's power and glory. Addison's poem and even David's psalm, though beautiful, still fail to fully illustrate the true wonder of God's creation. Nature is a mere testament to something greater, which we are privileged to see day after day, night after night. David sought to caution us against taking our surroundings for granted. The sun, he reminds us, passes overhead every day "and there is nothing hidden from its heat" (v. 6). None of us are immune to the sun's gaze, just as none of us are veiled from God's sight.

The Book of Perfect Scripture (vv. 7-11)

In the beginning, God created the heavens and the earth, but this is not all He did. When He made mankind, He gifted us with words and understanding. Communication is a crucial element among humans; it is how we share ideas and emotions, how we govern and pray. It was "by the word of the Lord the heavens were made, and by the breath of his mouth all their host" (Psa. 33:6). He is not only a God who communicates, but also a God who loves. His Word is proof of affection for His creations and His gift to guide us through life.

After remarking on the glory and wonder of nature, David turns his attention to God's Word and its perfection. He divides this section into six couplets—two per verse—each describing an innate virtue of God's Word and the positive results of accepting and following His testimony. As with the previous "book," David seeks to remind us of the infinite glory of the Lord by pointing out the multitude of creations and gifts He has given us. We are surrounded by nature, but we are also imbued with the very Word of God. These are the two proofs of His existence and love of us.

Verse 7 begins with the couplet, "The law of the Lord is perfect, reviving the soul." *Tawmeem*, the Hebrew word for "perfect," can also be translated as "whole" or "innocent," both of which suit David's point. Certainly, God's law is perfect—it comes from the perfect Source, after all. What David is telling us is that, should our soul not revive under God's law, we cannot blame the law itself. God is perfect; therefore, His law is perfect. If we have the wisdom and fortitude to follow His law, our souls will be revived. Our inner being will be moved, motivated, and strengthened in the Lord.

The second couplet of v. 7 continues, "The testimony of the Lord is sure, making wise the simple." This line recalls the first part of the psalm, wherein the "heavens declare the glory of God" (v. 1), and provides those who may not be educated ("the simple") in His glory with a foundation upon which to build their knowledge of the Lord. Solomon said, "The fear of the Lord is the beginning of knowledge; fools despise wisdom and instruction" (Prov. 1:7).

If I want to be wise, I need to spend time considering the ways of God. If I want to accept Him into my heart, I must seek Him out and embrace His law. God's testimony, however, is not only for the simple. David is reassuring us that God's ways are not difficult to understand. We may never grasp the meaning of every word of Scripture, but the fact that God "exists and that He rewards those who seek Him" (Heb. 11:6) is a simple enough message for anyone willing to let Him into his/her heart.

Where v. 7 reaffirmed the truth and saving grace of God's teaching, v. 8 attests to personal revelation in His statutes. The first couplet of v. 8 begins: "The precepts of the Lord are right, rejoicing the heart." "Precepts" are those things we are obligated to do, those specific commands we must observe. Many rebel against this concept. Who enjoys having to do anything? As children, we throw tantrums and count the days until we are old enough to make our own choices without our parents telling us what to do. Then as adults, we choose not to do certain things anyway. David, however, is reminding us that God only requires things that are right, not only in His sight, but for our own good and joy. The Lord does not demand we brush our teeth or go to bed on time; He asks that we educate ourselves in His law so as to live fulfilled lives.

When we do as God asks, it brings joy to our hearts. Think of the saddest or most frustrated people you know; how many of them are striving to find joy in all the wrong places? One reason is that they have no true foundation. They just keep looking, thereby diverting their focus from the Lord who waits patiently for them to find Him. Those who remain true to the ways of God, however, know that He asks us to do what brings about our ultimate joy and fills our heart with rejoicing. As Paul said to the Philippians: "Rejoice in the Lord always" (Phil. 4:4).

First, David assures us of joyful hearts if we follow God's precepts, then reminds us of how to achieve it. Verse 8, couplet two, continues: "The commandment of the Lord is pure, enlightening the eyes." The "commandment," the singular unity of God's will, is our instruction manual towards joy. There are dozens of commands to follow, but they are all from God and, thus, a single precept to follow. David's stress here, however, is that nothing false enters into what God would have us do: "The commandment of the Lord is pure" (v. 8). The standards of men are always changing; God's are not. We can water down or intensify our rules and laws, but God's are always consistent and pure. We can rely on His Word to enlighten us with what we must do or avoid doing. People desire truth and consistency, even as they struggle with achieving it. If you are looking for a consistent, pure, unchanging standard to follow, look no farther than the commandment of God.

Verse 9 begins with the couplet, "The fear of the Lord is clean, enduring forever." Over the previous eight verses, David has sought to instill in his reader the appreciation of the Lord and His many works. Has He not given us our laws? Has He not given us all of creation? We are reminded that He is all around us, in everything, and fear of Him is right and pure. It must be clean, that is, morally pure. It is "clean in itself, and cleanses out the love of sin, sanctifying the heart in which it reigns."[4] This reverent fear also endures forever. We are accustomed to things coming to an end; we are taught as children that nothing lasts forever. It is not so with God. His love for us is eternal and He is always worthy of reverent awe.

Verse 9 ends with a final couplet that reaffirms, "The rules [judgments, NASU] of the Lord are true, and righteous altogether." If ever you second-guess devoting yourself to God and obeying his commands, remember that your fear and reverence of Him is not without reward. Abraham asked the great question, "Shall not the Judge of all the earth do what is right?" (Gen. 18:25) We already know the answer to that question. God always makes proper and right judgments, which come to us through His holy Word. What we see as His

---

4. Spurgeon, *Treasury of David*, 1.1.273.

"rules" (or judgments) are altogether true, unchanging, and without bias. Moreover, He proclaimed them in order to help his creation, namely mankind, achieve unfathomable heights of glory at His side.

Consider for a moment the import of what David wrote in vv. 7-9. He has spoken about commandments, rules, and law, as well as our duty to fear and revere the Lord always. These six couplets are meant as praise for the Word of God. More importantly, they represent the deepest desires of our heart.

God's Word is more desirable than gold (v. 10). The most precious of metals, ultimately, is worthless in comparison to the many gifts given us by the Lord; the value of gold is ascribed by man and can only be held temporarily. Salvation, however, is eternal and measured by the Creator of all things. His Word, moreover, is sweeter than honey, a delicacy that was not only delicious, but life-giving. It was to a land "flowing with milk and honey" (Exod. 3:8) that God commanded Moses to bring His people. Honey represented the Promised Land of the Jews and other sweet gifts of God to His chosen faithful. David, however, is telling us that the very Word of God is sweeter than these promises and gifts. It is the essence of the Lord himself, more wondrous and powerful than all we know, and our privilege to obey.

We need to actively seek the Word of God. Why? His Word changes us, makes us better within our souls. Yes, gold can help us financially, but it can also corrupt us. It is temporary wealth and, eventually, we will leave it behind. Honey is also impermanent. Its taste is sweet and delicious but only for a few moments. Moreover, too much will make you sick: "If you have found honey, eat only enough for you, lest you have your fill of it and vomit it" (Prov. 25:16). The Word of God, however, is permanent. It cannot corrupt like gold, nor can it make us ill like too much honey. Jesus said that if we hunger and thirst after righteousness, we would be filled (Matt. 5:6). God's Word fills us; it changes us, but it does not itself change. It does not leave. It does not lose its power. Instead, it strengthens and renews the souls of those who seek it, forever and always.

David concludes the second 'book' with caution: "Moreover, by them is your servant warned; in keeping them there is great reward" (v. 11). He states that this book of praise—the book of God's Word—helps in ways that are both positive and negative. There is warning in the Word, and God's servant can see it. We know the punishment if His ways are not followed, but that may not be all that David is stating here. It is not merely punishment we should fear, but how our lives will decrease in worth and happiness should we fail to live as our Creator demands. If I fail to maintain my marriage according to the Lord's precepts, how can I expect to have a happy and joyful home? If I fail to run an honest business, how can I expect others to want to work there? If a nation fails to follow the ways of God, how can it expect to stand strong?

When we follow God's Word, David said, "there is great reward" (v. 11). Again, we know there is a reward in heaven, but there are also earthly rewards. Not gold or honey or other inconsistent, material things, but peace, joy, and mercy are among the countless blessings that come to our life when we follow the ways of God each day. The books of the Old Testament contain laws that guide the faithful toward God, which David used to order his life accordingly. How can we, who are blessed with the complete Word of God from Genesis through Revelation, fail to see that this book is a perfect Word that speaks to the glory of our Creator?

The Book of Pure Speech (vv. 12-14)

After David had pondered over the power of creation and the perfection of the Word of God, he ends Psa. 19 with one final "book" in praise of God. These three verses are his own "book," written in contemplation and faith. It is the book of pure speech.

David presents two, key points in his "book." First, having been reminded of his place in comparison to the purity of God, he asks for forgiveness for those times he failed to live up to God's expectations. He begs mercy for his "hidden faults," those things unknown to others or perhaps forgotten by David himself; while unseen, they are still sinful in God's eyes. David wants purity in his actions and thoughts, because that is what he sees in the Word of God.

Purity, however, must be maintained. We can never be perfect, like the Lord, but must always seek it as the ultimate goal. Knowing this, David also asks for protection in the future: "Keep back your servant also from presumptuous sins" (v. 13). There are times, when others or our own laziness influence us, and it becomes easy to commit sins because we have lost our focus on God. David is aware of such dangers, and so he seeks protection. He wants God to lay a staying hand on his shoulder and warn him against sin.

After asking for this cleansing, David then asks for purity in his words and heart: "Let the words of my mouth and the meditation of my heart be acceptable in your sight, O Lord, my rock and my redeemer" (v. 14). Notice David's emphasis on total purity. Nothing can block the power and design of God; He sees and knows all, even what is deepest in our hearts. Eddie Cloer writes, "The psalmist is not asking that God approve of his life as it is, but he asks that the cutting edge of God's Word would make him the sweet-smelling offering he desires to be. He wants God to look at his heart and his lips, the core of his being, and make him fit for worship."[5]

The praise of creation clearly points to the Creator, just as there is no other explanation for the perfection of Scripture other than through divine origin. Nothing in Scripture contradicts itself and causes us to question God's wisdom or knowledge. David wants that for his life. He wants his words and thoughts to have the same impact on others as God's Word had on him. He wants even "the meditation of [his] heart" to be acceptable to God.

5. Cloer, *Psalms 1-50*, 252.

Conclusion

David began this psalm by looking outward toward nature then marveled at how the world itself praises God. Notice, however, that nature only speaks to the "glory of God." The diversity and magnitude of the world tells us a lot about the Lord, but nature cannot tell us everything. It is a testament of divine power, but it is an incomplete picture of the Lord. David, therefore, ponders the Word of God. It is there that he notices the perfection and direction of the Lord. God provides a path for man; it is perfect, true, righteous, and unchanging. Moreover, it is the only way to God's glory.

It is no wonder David marvels at these wonders and seeks change in himself. He concludes his "book" with two words that briefly reiterate the message of his psalm: "O Lord, my rock and my redeemer" (v. 14). God is our rock. While we may recognize this idea from Scripture, rocks are elements of nature that provide protection and strong foundations. Every time we see a mountain or a large bed of stone, we should think of God, because He created the earth and is within it. God is also David's redeemer, a truth found, not in nature, but in the Word of God. The Lord redeems us through the message of His Word and guides us to His side.

God is glorious and true. He is the rock in our lives, perfection itself, who calls us back from sin and offers us the most wondrous of rewards. Knowing this and having read David's example, we might all add our own book of praise, and may it be one of pure speech.

"Lord, Save the King!"

PSALM 20

When the prophet Samuel was an old man, the people of Israel demanded he appoint a king to judge them (1 Sam. 8:4-5). They were dissatisfied with the present leadership and sought greener pastures, specifically, "a king to judge [them] like all the nations" (1 Sam. 8:5). God warned his people that a king would be little more than a thorn in their side, but the desire to be like everyone else had taken hold of their hearts. God spoke to Samuel the prophet and told him, "They have not rejected you, but they have rejected me from being king over them" (1 Sam. 8:7).

God first appointed Saul as king, for he would "save [God's] people from the hand of the Philistines" (1 Sam. 9:16). It is in this choice that we begin to understand what God meant when He warned against the adoption of kings. Saul was chosen because he could deliver the faithful from the wickedness of a heathen enemy through military prowess. But there is no mention of faith when God speaks to Samuel. In fact, it is Samuel who must ask Saul to pause so that he "may make known to [him] the word of God" (1 Sam. 9:27). The history related in the Old Testament describes the coming and going of kings, the vast majority of which did not remain faithful to the will of God.

There were, of course, exceptions to this pattern of inadequate kings. Saul defended the people against the Philistines before he was driven mad by a need for glory and by his jealousy of David (1 Sam. 18-20). It is David who stands above the rest as the greatest model of kingship. Certainly he was not perfect, but through his trials and tribulations, successes and glories, his heart sought the Lord. David's faith was consistent from his days of shepherding sheep through his role as king of the Lord's people.

Good or bad, God's people were expected to respect and honor their leaders. Centuries after David's death, Paul wrote to Christians, "I urge that supplications, prayers, intercessions, and thanksgivings be made for all people, for kings and for all who are in high positions, that we may lead a peaceful and quiet life, godly and dignified in every way" (1 Tim. 2:1-2). Peter simply wrote, "Honor the emperor" (1 Pet. 2:17), the same emperor who would have him crucified because the position mattered more than the man who held it. Peter did add, however, that while we honor kings, we must also "fear God" (1 Pet. 2:17), for He is the ultimate Ruler, Creator of all civil authority, and more glorious than any man, king or not.

Psalms 20-21 are sometimes referred to as "royal psalms," since they both offer up a type of prayer for the king. It is important to note, however, that the emphasis in both psalms is not about the king, but about God. It is separated into three parts: vv. 1-3 were the people's prayer; v. 4 would have been spoken by the high priest; and the remainder would have been David's addition. They were all praying that God would provide direction, strength, and protection, that the king would remain faithful to the ways of God, and that He would provide victory. It is honest supplication for divine assistance in a time of need. Would that we prayed this way for our leaders and that they would always keep their hearts with the Lord!

At first glance, these psalms might seem self-aggrandizing. Was not David king? Was he so inadequate in his role that God needed to hold his hand every step of the way? Yes, David was king, but these were his words alone. Positions of authority and power are not easy to maintain. Think of our own government and the multitude of debates that occur on a daily basis. David understood the trials of his role and wrote what any king, president, emperor, czar, governor, or other earthly leader would write as they consider the strains and difficulties of being a leader. Revolution, anarchy, and uprisings—these occur when the people have lost faith in their leaders and seek a better alternative.

Specifically, Psa. 20 focused on the strains of battle. David was a true warrior fighting political and spiritual wars. This prayer reminds us that God was and is the true King who rallies His people for battle. In walking through this psalm, notice the emphasis on God and how David and his people pray that He will be with the king. Ultimately, it is a psalm of communal trust, a trust we need each time we go into any of life's many battles.

Security (vv. 1-3)

Psalm 20 is a practical prayer. David and his people ask for assistance with topical issues occurring in his kingdom because they need aid against very real enemies. David's role as leader was a lonely one. The responsibility of good and bad decisions, whether his in origin or not, would always be laid at his door. The well-being of his people and the kingdom as a whole was his burden alone. His people, however, have trust in him and offer up their support by seeking four forms of security as he ventures out on a military campaign.

Response. It is worth noting that there is no sugar-coating in this prayer. It was a serious situation, and the people were treating it as such. "May the Lord answer you in the day of trouble" (v. 1), they began, without any flowery introduction. They did not demand constant divine intervention, but rather support on that "day of trouble," when even the strongest and proudest among them might have felt alone and helpless.

Tsawraw, the Hebrew word for "trouble," is elsewhere translated as "distress," "anguish," and even "affliction." It has described the consequences facing those who turned from God (Deut. 31:17, 21-22) and the labor pangs of childbirth (Jer. 4:31; 6:24; 49:24; 50:43). More profoundly, Jehosaphat prayed to God, reminding Him that they had worshipped Him rightly and faithfully with the expectation that He would reward them with security: "If disaster comes upon us, the sword, judgment, or pestilence, or famine, we will stand before this house and before you—for your name is in this house—and cry out to you in our affliction, and you will hear and save" (2 Chron. 20:9).

The affliction, *tsawraw*, Jehosaphat suggests is not a minor trouble, but equal to that of famine, warfare, and disease. Thus, when the people said, "May the Lord answer you in the day of trouble," they referred to life or death situations.

It was a serious request the Hebrews made. They eschewed preamble and flattery in order to intensify this moment of need. The intensity of the opening, however, does not remove the simplicity of the words or the reverence felt toward God. In a time of anguish, such as a military encounter, David's people hoped only that God would hear and answer the prayers of the king. Crucial to this supplication is that for God to answer, a request had to be made first.

David's position as king and leader demanded that he offer a prayer to God. To do so, he had to forgo pride of position and ability; he had to humble himself before God and prove he was worthy of divine aid. We know that David made mistakes, like many of his predecessors. It was this willingness to embrace humility that set him apart. His people trusted that he would turn to God, just as he trusted in the security that would come when God heard His children pray. Thus, his people pray for him and his success.

Regard. The people continued, "May the name of the God of Jacob protect you!" (v. 1). Why Jacob specifically? It is most likely that these words recall Gen. 35:3, where Jacob himself said, "Then let us arise and go up to Bethel, so that I may make there an altar to the God who answers me in the day of my *distress* and has been with me wherever I have gone" (emphasis added). Here, the word for "distress" (*tsawraw*) is the same as in Psa. 20:1. The people are calling out to God in supplication, reminding Him of the assistance He gave Jacob when he faced troubles like David.

When we invoke God's name, we seek His whole being and all of His attributes. When God answers, He offers the faithful His full regard and protection. The people mention Jacob as a testament to God's covenant with His people. It is a constant bond, eternal and unwavering since the time of Abraham. The people beseech Him to maintain this relationship by supporting David, another faithful man of God.

All too often, we forget that we are only a small part of an ancient tradition, created by God and blessed with His love. How seriously we would say these same words in our prayers today? Do we really believe God can and will protect leaders who seek His will? Do we believe that He will show them regard? Or do we accept the secular notion that God is separate from matters of state and that the choices made by governments are not judged by our King and Lord?

Reinforcement. Protection and notice are what the people first asked of God, for they feared what would become of Israel should David fail in his kingly duties. If deemed worthy of success, they prayed that God would further reinforce David's spirit: "May He send you help from the sanctuary and give you support from Zion!" (v. 2).

Mentioning a "sanctuary" (literally, "holy place") in Zion indicates that this psalm was composed sometime after the Ark of the Covenant had been returned to Jerusalem to its rightful place in the Most Holy Place of the tabernacle. It was David himself who captured Jerusalem (1 Kings 11:27; 1 Chron. 11:8); who built the Temple on Mt. Zion (1 Macc. 4:37); who delivered the Ark of the Covenant to the tabernacle (2 Sam.7:1-17; 1 Chron. 17:1-15; 28:2,3);

and who gave the holy city his name, "the City of David."

The people's choice of words was a reminder of what their king had done in God's name, actions that reaffirmed his commitment to the faith. The prayer asked that God, who is worshipped on Mt. Zion, would send help to His faithful servant as he fought battles for the faithful. It was a prayer for God to extend His helping hand beyond the borders of the tabernacle's curtains and walls of Jerusalem, as the king was unable to kneel in His Temple.

Do we not also pray for the same thing when we face times of difficulty and cannot be in a church? We may not be fighting a literal battle, but we ask for God's help and strength to be with us at times when we are not sitting in the pews. We often need His reinforcement, sometimes desperately. Like David, we need reassurance that He will hear us, even when we are not kneeling in a sanctified place.

Respect. The people humbled themselves before God, acknowledging their mortal weaknesses by admitting that their king's victories are ultimately in God's hands. They added to the prayer, "May He remember all your offerings and regard with favor your burnt sacrifices" (v. 3).

God does not celebrate every action that proves our faith; we wish He would, but that is not His way. There are no firework displays each time we kneel in church or commit an act of Christian charity. The simple fact is, we cannot do enough good works to repay Jehovah for all He has done for us. Still, we appeal to the good deeds we have done when we beg God's forgiveness and favor.

The Hebrews mention the sanctuary in Zion because they sought to remind everyone, not just the Lord, that it was David who brought the Ark of the Covenant there for worship. The prayer, however, was not said because anyone feared that God had forgotten what his servant had done. It was a simple request, just like we still make today. The word "remember" does not imply that God might have forgotten. It conveys the idea of recalling the sacrifices of a faithful servant, and as a result of that recalling, granting the promised assistance to a servant who has tried to carry out His will.[1]

God always remembers. Moreover, He understands that our prayers emanate from an inability to fully comprehend His glory. We seek God's blessings based upon the good we have done, believing we do not deserve His favor without that shred of proof.

When we combine these four elements—response, regard, reinforcement, and respect—we understand the people's humility before the Lord and their true desire for security. It was security in the faithfulness of the king, which was glorious in its example to true believers. Moreover, it was a celebration of the security found in God, who was and is all-powerful and blesses his faithful servants.

Supplication (vv. 4-5)

After a pause (selah), the high priest continued with a verse that spoke specifically of trust, between the people and their king, as well as between David and the Lord. He exclaimed, "May he grant you your heart's desire and fulfill all your plans!" (v. 4). David, and maybe his officers or advisors, added: "May we shout for joy over your salvation, and in the name of our God set up our banners!" (v. 5).

Consider this part of the prayer carefully. How often do we have leaders in an arena of life whom we trust enough to say to the Almighty, "Whatever their heart desires, grant it"? We have all witnessed leaders making decisions to satisfy their own needs; power all too often leads to corruption. How then can we trust that David was doing what was best for his people and not looking to please himself?

The answer is trust. God chose David as king and forged a covenant with him (1 Sam. 7:8). God can see deep into our hearts and knows best who we are; thus, He knew David would serve as a faithful servant and king. The trust the people showed in David was

---

1. Cloer, *Psalms 1-50*, 261.

based on their trust in God. The community would pray for the king to accomplish all he needed because his plans were also God's. David made mistakes. Sometimes he lost his way and marred his relationship with the Lord (cf. 2 Sam. 11), but God knew his heart was never in question and sent Nathan to remind the king of his duties. The people (and, more importantly, the Lord) knew David's heart was always for the faith and the faithful.

Proverbs 23:7 famously stated, "For as [a man] thinketh in his heart, so is he" (KJV). We are not necessarily all we project ourselves to be to the rest of the world. As one grows older and seeks to climb the ladder of success, the temptation grows to try and seem stronger and more faithful to those around us. If we are fortunate enough to know our own heart and who we truly are, then the inward and outward man will be in harmony. In turn, we shall become more faithful to the Lord and become better leaders in our own communities. Psalm 20:5 affirmed the promise that, when God provides victory, the people will "shout for joy" and "set up our banners." David and his people promised to recognize that it would be God who brought victory, and that He deserved the praise and credit when that success occurred.

The psalm spoke of joyful praise. It is not reluctantly giving God credit when something good happens, but instead living a life that is constantly looking for reasons to "rejoice in the Lord" (Phil. 4:4). He is worthy of constant praise for what He has done and the many gifts he has given us. According to Spurgeon, "[i]f joy were more general among the Lord's people, God would be more glorified among men; the happiness of the subjects is the honor of the sovereign."[2]

Leaders need people to pray for them, but they also need to be people of prayer themselves. Whether they are leading a home, congregation, business, or a nation, the world would be stronger and better with leaders whose hearts were in harmony with the will

---

2. Spurgeon, *Treasury of David*, 1.1.302.

of God. David and his people's words espoused so much trust between the king and his people, because they were living as a united community dedicated to God. The people trusted David's heart, just as they trusted in the power and blessings of the Lord. They knew victory would occur because their king was right with the Almighty. In this psalm, David reiterated his trust in the Lord, just as his people must have reassured him with theirs: "May we shout for joy over your salvation, and in the name of our God set up our banners!"

This should be true of God's people at all times. We should all remember to confirm our faith in God and trust in His plan for us. We are not waging war like David, but that does not mean we should not give the Lord praise and glory when victory is ours. Even the smallest fight against seemingly insignificant sin is a triumph! Furthermore, we must pray that our leaders find the way to strengthen their relationship with the Lord and petition Him for the ability to do right by His people.

Salvation (vv. 6-9)

The final segment of the psalm is from the priest (v. 6) and David himself (vv. 7-9). The priest avowed, "Now I know that the Lord saves His anointed," perhaps after the completion of a sacrifice typical of such Jewish rites. David would have proven himself a man of God by participating in the prayer and making offerings; literally, he would have humbled himself before God. What is important about this phrase is the first person pronoun. "I know," said the priest, but he spoke not only for himself, but also for everyone who saw David partake in the ritual. Together, they are a single community of faith, serving both their corporate and spiritual kings.

This verse was a statement of trust. The people "knew" that God could save them and thus added, "He will answer him from His holy heaven with the saving might of His right hand" (v. 6) In that one short statement, we are reassured of at least four traits of our God that should comfort us when we fight our own spiritual battles.

Communication. God "will answer." Why would we take the time to pray if we thought God could not hear us? The Lord may not give us exactly what we seek—not in a literal, word-for-word fashion—but the Lord always answers the prayers of His people. When you are struggling with the battles of life, "take it to the Lord in prayer" (Phil. 4:6-7). He wants to hear from His children, and He always answers their prayers in the way that is best for His glory.

Consecration. God answers us from "His holy heaven." He is holy and the only God, but set apart. He is separate from our daily troubles and mortal dilemmas; He is above such petty concerns, but He is not arrogant. The Lord will answer. When we struggle through our private battles in life, we must remember that we are not asking for help from a fallible or (worse!) duplicitous person. Instead, we are seeking counsel and help from He who is completely perfect in every way. He has perfect knowledge and wisdom, perfect justice and mercy to comfort us when we struggle.

Capability. Psalm 150:2 demands, "Praise Him for His mighty deeds; praise Him according to His excellent greatness." God has "saving might." He has the capability of fighting for His people, because He has all power. He is the mightiest and strongest, and for that we must remain humble before Him. Alone, we are not strong enough to fight the battle for our souls; instead, we must lean on His mighty arm and trust in His unfailing power.

Command. God's might is said to come from "His right hand." It is the hand of righteousness (Psa. 48:10; Isa. 41:10) and power (Exod. 15:6). It was considered the hand that could bring life or death (Psa. 21:8; Lam. 2:4). More importantly, it was the seat of royalty and honor. It was Jesus the Christ whom He set at His right side: "And He is the radiance of His glory and the exact representation of His nature, and upholds all things by the word of His power.

When He had made purification of sins, He sat down at the hand of the Majesty on high" (Heb. 1:3).

The power and royalty of earthly monarchs pales in comparison to the power and royalty found in the right hand of the Almighty God! The priests and people can only trust that He will protect "His anointed (...) with the saving might of His right hand" (Psa. 20:6).

After the priest's words of affirmation, the voice of the psalm shifts to David or, at the very least, his officers. David exclaimed, "Some trust in chariots and some in horses, but we trust in the name of the Lord our God. They collapse and fall, but we rise and stand upright" (vv. 7-8). Since the conquering of Jericho (Josh. 6), when the people trusted God's will and followed His plans, they were victorious; if they did not, they failed. Notice again the trust relayed in these words: "They collapse and fall, but we rise and stand upright" (v. 8). They were spoken as if events had already swayed in David's favor, as if he had already won. When the people were truly in harmony with God's will and trusted Him, then the battle was over before it even began! There is an old saying that summarizes this well: "The battle is always won the day before in the closet of prayer."

God is the One who provides deliverance in our lives. All else— weapons, physical strength, money, prestige—are false symbols of power and safety. David, a true warrior and king, verbally bowed before his Lord; he knew that the might of his army was nothing without His blessing. God alone brings salvation and only to the righteous and pure of faith. Another call for the salvation of the king concludes the psalm: "O Lord, save the king! May He answer us when we call" (v. 9). Hear us. Deliver us. These were simple requests, but founded on deep, reciprocal trust. Trust in the king, God's anointed, and trust in the Lord Himself.

Conclusion

It is easy to read this psalm and imagine it was a form of self-ag-grandizement on David's part. It is also easy to use the psalm as motivation for our president or other people in power. These words speak to the heart of a leader, especially in times of difficulty. They offer strength and support from a united community. We should all spend more time in prayer for our leaders, hoping that their hearts are filled with the Word of God and that their desires are to promote the glory of the Lord of heaven.

We must also look inward, however, for we are all leaders. We may not face an army on the battlefield or lead a nation through economic crises, but each of us leads in his/her own way. Each day, you and I fight battles for our homes, communities, and even for our souls. Do we not have a greater enemy than any nation? Is he not more powerful than any number of chariots or horses, soldiers or swords? He is after your soul. He is after the soul of your spouse, children, and neighbor. He hunts for the soul of elders, Bible School teachers, and ministers. He does not discriminate and takes any who leave themselves unprotected.

God, the mightiest and strongest, most glorious and magnificent, has promised to stand beside us and fight! In return, we need only to remain faithful to Him. Pray, then, for our leaders, that they might live for the Lord and serve Him rather than themselves. Also, pray for yourself. Each day, you will wage a battle against sin, but each day, you will be victorious if you trust in God to see you to safety.

He's All I Want

PSALM 23

Once a little girl was asked to quote the famous 23rd Psalm. She worked very hard all week to memorize the verses, and then the time came to recite what she had learned. The other students were nervous as they waited for their turn to quote the verses. When it was her turn, the little girl dutifully stood beside her chair and began. "The Lord is my shepherd; he's all I want."

This story has been told many times. The little girl may have misquoted David's words, but she clearly understood its message. Psalm 23 is one of the most well-known passages in Scripture. Six simple verses have spawned countless books and appeared in so many movies and television shows that even the most devout atheist can recite them with ease. Many Christians have said that these simple words represent their favorite part of the entire Bible. Many of you have likely memorized this poem; even if you have not, I am certain you are familiar with it and love it deeply, cherishing the powerful difference such words can make in a person's life. The psalm has received several nicknames, but "The Pearl of the Psalms" describes it best, both in terms of its popularity and spiritual value.

"The Lord is my shepherd." In that opening line alone resides a world of promises.

- There is singularity, because He is the One.
- There is sovereignty, because He is the Lord.
- There is sustenance, because He IS.
- There is specialness, because He is mine.
- He is the Shepherd.

Considering these truths, it is no wonder the little girl said, "He's all I want." In this chapter, we will walk through these well-known lines and come to understand that the Lord should be all we want. He should be our ultimate goal, regardless of the troubles and trials that come our way.

In Destitute Times. Sheep, like all domesticated animals, have many needs. Also like other domesticated animals, they are rarely able to meet those needs on their own. In his book, *A Shepherd Looks at Psalm 23*, Philip Keller mentions several times that sheep will often eat or drink just about anything, and that this lack of discretion can kill the animal. Sheep are also infamously timid, and the rush of a stream can be enough to spook them. They require protection from predators, their wool to be sheered, and food to be abundant. It is the shepherd who tends to them and leads them to "green pastures" and "still waters" (v. 2).

David stated in v. 2 that the Lord "*makes* me lie down" (emphasis added). This seems like a strange choice of words, for the Lord does not force us to do things. Why would lying down in green pastures be a command? When we are fearful, we rarely think straight. It is the same with sheep. Keller wrote about such fear in his book:

> One day a friend came to call on us from the city. She had a tiny Pekingese pup along. As she opened the car door the pup jumped out on the grass. Just one glimpse of the unexpected little dog was enough. In sheer terror over 200 of my sheep which were resting

nearby leaped up and rushed off across the pasture.[1]

He later added:

> As long as there is even the slightest suspicion of danger from dogs, coyotes, cougars, bears or other enemies the sheep stand up ready to flee for their lives. They have little or no means of self-defense. They are helpless, timid, feeble creatures whose only recourse is to run.[2]

Obviously, we are not sheep. Our brains are complex and advanced, allowing us to rationalize and bolster our courage. Sometimes, however, rational thought abandons us, and the smallest surprise can send us running for the hills. In these moments, we feel alone, scared, lost, and helpless.

God is our Shepherd. He knows where to find green pastures and still waters. He knows how to instill us with calm courage and stands beside us as we battle our fears. You and I need spiritual nourishment; sheep do not. God is the only One who can fulfill that particular need. He's all I want when I am alone and destitute.

In Downcast Times. Psalm 23:3 does not lend itself to the sheep/shepherd metaphor as easily as the rest of the poem. It is the most spiritual verse, focusing directly on the soul: "He restores my soul. He leads me in paths of righteousness for his name's sake." Sheep sometimes lose their way and become separated from the flock. A good shepherd is one who is able to bring them home again, sees to any injury, and reassures the animal when it is panicked or scared.

Do you ever get weary? Do you ever feel like you have lost your way? If we are honest, we know that we all do from time to time. In

---

1. W. Phillip Keller, *A Shepherd Looks at Psalm 23* (Grand Rapids: Zondervan, 2007), 42-43.

2. Ibid., 43.

fact, it occurs more often than we think. The littlest thing can make us feel uncertain, downcast, or troubled. We grow weary fighting temptation and dealing with the mundane. We grow weary of struggling through difficult times without receiving any praise. How can we deal with those times? Faith. The Lord is ever our Shepherd, willing and able to guide us through life so that we might find salvation and the rewards of heaven. Whatever path is right and shines light on the good Shepherd, is the path that God will lead us on.

Do not mistake me, God's support does not mean that the path will always be easy. His constant presence, however, does assure us that we shall maintain our way on the righteous and true path of faith. Knowing that the Shepherd walks with us gives us the strength to move forward, even when we are weary and downcast. Cloer assures us, "The follower of God will not want for direction and guidance. His God not only provides sustenance for him, but He also gives him truth."[3] He's all I want when I am weary and downcast.

In Disturbing Times. After the psalm's first line, v. 4 is probably the most well known and most comforting: "Even though I walk through the valley of the shadow of death, I will fear no evil, for you are with me." David had just spoken of the righteous path, the path that leads to a renewed soul. He transitioned suddenly as if to remind us of our fate should we stray from God's side. It is dark, inundated with the shades of death and wickedness. Valleys themselves are depressions in the earth, typically bordered by hill- or mountainsides. Imagine standing on such a valley floor, looking up at the earth pressing in around you.

The paths of the shepherd are not easy and contain many dangers, particularly in autumn when they lead their flocks back home. The changing weather lowers the temperature and increases the rain. It can cause flooding, as well as mud and rockslides. Every step could be treacherous, and the specter of death would hang

---

3. Cloer, *Psalms 1-50*, 301.

over the shepherd and his herd. David understood these dangers; he was once a shepherd, too. When he wrote this psalm, his flock had turned from sheep into people, and he sought to lead them safely, just like the Lord.

Regardless of the perils, the sheep would "walk through the valley" (v. 4) because they trusted in the shepherd. Even when things looked worst, the flock continued to follow their leader as if he alone could bring them through their difficulty. The reason behind this obedience was simply because the shepherd was there. David said, "You are with me" (v. 4). A shepherd leads the herd, but in trying times, he walks with his flock. When danger surrounds them, the shepherd walks among the sheep, beside them, gathering up strays and returning them to the path that will lead them home.

David was reminding us that, yes, there are times in life that are completely disturbing or terrifying. Yes, we sometimes feel overwhelmed, trapped, or lost like that lone sheep separated from the flock. In these moments, we must recall that God is still present, though we cannot see Him, and He will guide us safely home. It is this portion of the psalm that is often heard at funerals; it is a benediction that the Lord will come to us at the end of this life and lead us safely into the next.

What a wonderful picture this is! When we face life's valleys, when we are mired in depression and despair, we must remember that God is not simply out in front of us. He is right beside us. He does not blaze a trail and then idly look back, expecting us to follow blindly. He leads us and walks with us. He's all I want in those dark, disturbing times.

In Directionless Times. Have you ever felt lost at times and not known where to turn? It was as if you did not know which direction to take, though you tried to seek out every possible path. In these moments of confusion, remember that the shepherd knows the way. David declared, "Your rod and your staff, they comfort me" (v. 4).

These are the tools of the shepherd, the instruments he requires to protect and lead his flock.

The distinctive Hebrew terms for rod and staff are significant. *Shaybet* or "rod" also describes a scepter or implement of power (Gen. 49:10; Num. 21:18; Psa. 60:7). It is also a term for the club used by shepherds to protect their sheep from predators: "Shepherd your people with your staff, the flock of your inheritance, who dwell alone in a forest in the midst of a garden land" (Mic. 7:14). This is the symbol of his trade and authority, as he leads his flock through dark and treacherous valleys. Phillip Keller shares this insight:

> I used to watch the native lads having competitions to see who could throw his rod with the greatest accuracy across the greatest distance. The effectiveness of these crude clubs in the hands of skilled shepherds was a thrill to watch. The road was, in fact, an extension of the owner's own right arm. It stood as a symbol of his strength, his power, his authority in any serious situation. The rod was what he relied on to safeguard both himself and his flock in danger. And it was, furthermore, the instrument he used to discipline and correct any wayward sheep that insisted on wandering away.[4]

The rod was often kept in the belt, much like a hunter's knife today, for convenience when fending off any enemy attack. It was a formidable weapon that young shepherds learned to use effectively before tasked with guarding their flock.

The shepherd's "staff," *mishaynaw*, is a less common term in the Hebrew Bible, occurring in only two other places: Isa. 3:1 and 36:6. The *mishaynaw* was the support of the shepherd, which he leaned upon when tired and weary. The staff was what we now associate with shepherds: a stick with crooked or hooked top used to

---

4. Keller, *A Shepherd Looks at Psalm 23,* 112-113.

gently push sheep back into the fold. It could also be wielded as a powerful weapon, but was most often used in a gentle way. In fact, sheep learned to walk under an outstretched staff, with the staff lightly grazing their backs, so that shepherds could count them. Together, the rod and staff kept the flock safe from danger and becoming lost in the wilderness.

You might be wondering why we are discussing rods and staffs after asking if you have ever felt lost. The answer is simple: God is our *shaybet* and *mishaynaw*. He is our Protector and Support. He is our Shepherd. He will not stop us from going through valleys of darkness (for at times, we must), but He will be there with us, guiding us along the path to safety. He will offer comfort when we become lost and lead us back into the fold. No predator can harm us while the Lord stands beside us; no darkness can enfold us and obscure our sight. He is our guide and compass. He's all I want in directionless times.

In Dangerous Times. Verse 5 does not overtly follow the shepherd/sheep allegory. There are no rods or staffs or pastures. Instead, it describes a very picturesque scene: "You prepare a table before me in the presence of my enemies." I doubt the shepherd set up an actual table for his sheep, but the message is consistent with the previous lines of the psalm. Enemies might surround the flock and threaten harm, but the sheep will remain safe because the shepherd is watching. In our weakest, most vulnerable moments when we might be taken by surprise, our Shepherd will be beside us. He will stand watch so that we might eat in peace and safety.

The shepherd's first priority is always the overall health and well-being of his flock. He considers their basic needs and ensures that they are met. There is courage in the shepherd as he places himself at risk for the betterment of all. He prepares a "table," meaning that he took the time to look over the lay of the land and assess it for threats, all while maintaining his flock.

Is that not just like God!? We live in a world filled with dangers to our soul, but God does more than just "keep His cool." He does not sit back and watch how we handle threats to our souls; He prepares for our well being; He warns us of our enemy and how to defeat him. If we remain with our Shepherd, our enemy will find no victory because He gives our souls nourishment, the type that only comes through the pages of Scripture. The Lord provides us with communication, so that through prayer we might calm and reinforce our souls.

Our Lord does not tell us that dangers are non-existent. These trials are tests of our faith and endurance; each victory strengthens our souls and prepares us for Him. In Psa. 78, the doubters asked, "Can God really spread a table in the wilderness?" (Psa. 78:19). Yes. He can and will for those who believe in His glory and grace. We must trust the Shepherd, for He will provide all we need in the midst of our enemies, even if we are unaware of the peril.

He's all I want in dangerous times.

In Damaged Times. The shepherd has led his flock to green pastures. He has kept them along the righteous path, safe from harm, with his crook. He has seen to their daily needs of nourishment and rest. He must also tend to their wounds and other maladies. After the sumptuous banquet, held in the haven of God's protection, David said to his Shepherd, "You anoint my head with oil" (v. 5).

In connection with the previous line, the oil, *shehmen*, takes on a symbolic purpose as, by anointing David, God showed him favor and honor (Psa. 45:7; Luke 7:46). It was also a part of king-making: "Then Samuel took the horn of oil and anointed him in the midst of his brothers. And the Spirit of the Lord rushed upon David from that day forward" (1 Sam. 16:13). Oil was also used to anoint priests (Exod. 20:7; 30:22-38; Lev. 8:10, 12; 21:10, 12). To be anointed with oil was to be blessed by God and set apart as His chosen vessel.

David was praising God for making him king, but also for seeing to his continued good health. A good shepherd personally attends to those things that irritate his flock. Oil was used to soothe pain and discomfort (Isa. 1:6; Jas. 5:14). Sheep can easily become injured by predators or natural accidents when out to pasture. They also suffer from parasitic nasal bot flies that—and I say this as gently as possible—lay their eggs in the noses of sheep. When the eggs hatch, the larvae crawl into the nasal passages and irritate the animal until it purposefully bangs its head against trees or the ground to be rid of them. Sometimes, these parasites cause malnutrition, septicemia, and death. Shepherds must be aware of these little flies and their flock's behavior, anointing the sheep's head with oil in order to prevent any harm befalling their charges.

A true shepherd cares for his hurting sheep. He is not stingy with his care, but tends to the flock carefully and lovingly. It is no wonder, then, that David exclaimed, "My cup overflows." He has reflected upon the goodness of God as his Shepherd and realized that he has been given every blessing and advantage. His life was not always perfect, but David's needs were fulfilled by the perfect Shepherd who led him through difficult moments. Thus did God soothe his pain, heal his injuries, and calm his anxieties.

I ask you now, do you ever feel injured or hurt? Are you ever irritated? Do you feel as if you are beating your head against the wall in desperate need of soothing and comfort? We all feel that way at times and often look for our own solution instead of asking for help. Instead, we need to look to God. It is He alone who can soothe our very souls and provide the healing we require.

He's all I want in times of damage.

Conclusion

David concluded this psalm with a simple, but profound benediction: "Surely goodness and mercy shall follow me all the days of my life, and I shall dwell in the house of the Lord forever" (v. 6). Do not mistake this as an assumption of constant purity on David's part;

it was a hope that he would continue living righteously, as well as find favor with God. He was reflecting, not on a perfect life, but on a perfect Shepherd. At times he had strayed from the path, but God redirected him towards righteousness. At times he felt lost and desperate, but God tended him, calming his fears and soothing his wounds.

The Shepherd will lead his flock to green pastures and still waters. When they are destitute, the Shepherd will provide. When the flock becomes confused, irritated, or sad, the Shepherd will restore their souls. When they are downcast, the Shepherd will provide. When the flock travels through perilous places and the threat of death is very real, the Shepherd will lead them with courage and comfort. When they are disturbed, the Shepherd will provide.

When they are lost and don't know where to go, the Shepherd will guide and protect them with his rod and staff. When they are directionless, the Shepherd will provide. When enemies are all around and the flock is defenseless, the Shepherd will ward off danger and see to their basic needs. When they are in danger, the Shepherd will provide. When the flock is injured or harmed, the Shepherd will care for their wounds. When they are damaged, the Shepherd provides.

Looking back at these verses, how could David have claimed anything other than that the Shepherd had provided goodness and mercy? He was blessed by God for his good deeds and faith, so he knew a continuation of those things would mean an eternity by His side. David was not special. He was simply a man who lived by faith and, because of that, the true Shepherd provided. It was in a tone of comfort and satisfaction that David added, "I shall dwell in the house of the Lord forever." Where else would David want to be than with the Shepherd who provided for his every need, removed all danger, and cared for every member of His flock indiscriminately?

When we first memorize v. 6, we are told that the first word is "surely." I want you to consider, however, an alternative translation of the Hebrew word ak: "only goodness and mercy shall follow me all the days of my life" (emphasis added). It is this distinction that summarizes this psalm best. If I live according to God's laws, commit myself to His glory, and live each day for the Lord, then only one outcome can arise. The little girl had it right all along: "The Lord is my Shepherd; He's all I want!"

The Shelter of the Lord

PSALM 27

I have a friend who started blogging when it was the "new" thing. His posts were somewhat irregular, but I always enjoyed reading what he wrote. Eventually, he gave up blogging, finding new pursuits and passions. But the name of his site, "From Calm to Chaos," has always stuck with me. When explaining his choice of titles, he would say that times of calm, as well as chaos, are what make life memorable. I completely agree.

We have all experienced those calm, slow times. Inevitably, we become bored with the day-to-day tedium and crave change. There are also those moments when everything seems to go wrong, and we feel completely out of control. There are extremes of calm and chaos, as well as times of great strength and fear when we walk with the Lord. Everyone has vacillated between doubt and faith. We may want to "walk by faith, not by sight" (2 Cor. 5:7), but we will stumble and let fear grip our souls many times before reaching our destination.

Psalm 27 reflects on both ends of the spectrum. David, the presumed author, wrote about a time when his faith was strong (vv. 1-6), and then when he was overcome with fear as the chaos of the world threatened to overwhelm his faith (vv. 7-12). Thankfully, by the end of the poem, his faith had held strong, and he offered up a final, positive prayer (vv. 13-14). Ultimately, the psalm exemplifies tried, tested, and successful faith in the Lord.

Scholars do not know the exact event or season of life that led David to pen these words. Some suggest the two halves were written at separate times; vv. 1-6 during a time of peace and vv. 7-12 while he fled from Saul or Absalom's treachery. Personally, I prefer the mystery because it allows the psalm to be applied universally. Anytime we feel fear grip our souls, we can read Psa. 27 and see that these moments happen to everyone. In the end, if our faith is in God, we will find peace and comfort; we can always find shelter in Him.

Faith (vv. 1-6)

Two things define the first six verses: strength of faith and confidence in God. David clearly described a dangerous situation. Enemies assailed him, and an army had encamped near him. His faith in God, however, remains undiminished. These verses mark words of praise to God that are clear, strong, and confident of personal faith.

Shelter. Several times, David referred to God as shelter in Psa. 27. In the first verse, He was David's *mawoze* or stronghold. In God, we find refuge, but here David took it a step further: "The Lord is my light and my salvation; whom shall I fear? The Lord is the stronghold of my life; of whom shall I be afraid?." These words exhibit glowing confidence due to the strength of the Lord and David's trust in Him. In God's embrace, no enemy may harm us; He guards us with His love because of our devotion to Him.

God's power, wisdom, and glory surpass all things human; therefore, why would we fear man when God is our stronghold? At the end of v. 3, David exclaimed, "I will be confident." He would be confident in his faith and confident in the Lord, because "He will hide me in His shelter in the day of trouble; He will conceal me under the cover of His tent; He will lift me high upon a rock" (v. 5). This expectation echoes the final lines of Psa. 23: "Surely goodness and mercy will follow me all the days of my life, and I will dwell in the house of the Lord forever." How could anyone be afraid with so glorious a protector? Who would fear the perils of the world when commitment to God could assure such wonders? David's confidence and faith promised him the greatest of allies; he would be untouchable, no matter the danger, so long as he lived for the Lord.

David did not trust in his own strength because he knew men were easily weakened. Instead, he found strength and protection in the stronghold of the Lord's care. The longing of his heart was to be in the shelter of the presence of the Lord "all the days of [his] life" (v. 4). What is the longing of your heart? Where do you run for protection from the chaos of the world? Do you have the confidence to seek out God and give yourself over to His protection?

Beauty. There is beauty in the purity of faith. David wrote that he wished to "gaze upon the beauty of the Lord" (v. 4). It is only when we are near the Lord that our minds are truly able to perceive how beautiful and glorious He is. Where He is, there is true beauty. What He makes is truly beautiful. However, the Hebrew word for "beauty," *no'am*, can also describe the "favor" shown to someone. Psalm 90:17, for example, declared, "Let the favor (*no'am*) of the Lord our God be upon us, and establish the work of our hands upon us; yes, establish the work of our hands!" The beauty of the Lord is not merely a physical attribute, but of His generosity to the faithful. All that He is and does is perfect, yet he favors us with his gifts. It is the giving of His love, however, that is the most beautiful of all.

Safety. In the New Testament, Peter wrote the famous words, "Casting all your anxieties on [God], because He cares for you" (1 Pet. 5:7). It is a comforting sentiment to know that He will help bear the burden of your worries out of love. Peter also told us how to find the strength we require in order to cast our anxieties on the Lord. It is not found in us, but in Him: "Humble yourselves, therefore, under the mighty hand of God so that at the proper time He may exalt you"

(1 Pet. 5:6). Peter was telling us that we must place ourselves under the protective hand of God, for only then could we find the strength to cast our burdens onto Him.

Long before Peter, David attempted to share the same idea. He said that God "will hide me in His shelter in the day of trouble; He will conceal me under the cover of His tent" (v. 5). The two verbs—hide and conceal—contain deeper meanings than to seek cover. The Hebrew word *tsawfan* ("hide") is also used to describe hidden treasure or the covering of something precious. God will provide safety because He treasures us. Moreover, He will carefully conceal us, *sawthar*, in order to protect us. God provides safety, but also affection. He favors and guards us from our enemies. Where He is, there is true safety.

Encouragement. Thus far, David has exclaimed that God would conceal him, protect him, and lead him to safety. God "will lift me high up on a rock. And now my head shall be lifted up above my enemies all around me" (vv. 5-6). This is a promise of triumph, for when we follow Him, we are the victors. David was offering encouragement for doubters to find their own confidence and strength in the Lord. When we live for God, we live without fear, because He is our rock and strength against our enemies. The Almighty lifts us up. Where He is, there is true encouragement.

Praise. All of the knowledge David shared in these first six verses culminates in thanksgiving. He wrote, "I will offer in His tent sacrifices with shouts of joy; I will sing and make melody to the Lord" (v. 6). This is an affirmation of David's devotion. He did not expect these divine gifts to be free, but neither does he begrudge the Lord His rightful worship. David is more than prepared to sacrifice in His name and proclaim His glory! Is it any wonder that heaven is depicted as a place of praise (Rev. 4-5)? When God is near, we praise Him. When we consider what He has done, we praise Him. When we think of all He has promised, we praise Him. Where He is, there is true praise.

Does this not sound like a wonderful place of shelter and protection? Why should we fear? Why should we doubt? When we consider all that God has done for us, our desire should be to draw nearer to Him in faith and not fear the machinations of our enemies. He is a refuge of love, beauty, and in the chaotic storms of life, He is our rock and stronghold.

Fear (vv. 7-12)

Most psalms begin with words of fear or foreboding, then add words of comfort and faith. The pattern allows the writer to build the intensity of the poem, his emotive language culminating in a joyful outcry of worshiping the Lord. Psalm 27, as you can see, is different. David opens first by confidently praising God, but then at v. 7, "the mood changes."[1]

Despairing. Do not mistake this mood change as a sign that David was turning from God. If anything, these lines reaffirm how strong his faith truly was. These verses were his expressions of fear as he struggled against many enemies and trials during his life. Feeling fear or doubt does not negate our faith, but it does test it. Thus, David opened with a plea for God to hear and answer in His grace: "Hear, O Lord, when I cry aloud; be gracious to me and answer me!" (v. 7). Once again, he has shown that his heart is dedicated to God.

David was not being arrogant or demanding when he said, "be gracious to me and answer me." He was distressed. He was crying out to God, seeking His face in the midst of a struggle. Adam Clarke, in his commentary on Psa. 27, analyzed the phrase "Hear, O Lord, when I cry," and remarked,

> [t]his is the utmost that any man of common sense can expect—to be heard when he cries. But there are multitudes who suppose God will bless them wheth-

---

1. Cloer, *Psalms 1-50*, 359.

er they cry or not; and there are others and not a few, who (...) listlessly pray and cry not, yet imagine God must and will hear them! God will answer them that pray and cry; those who do not are most likely to be without the blessings which they so much need.[2]

We cannot know what was happening when he wrote this particular section, but we can all relate to his sense of desperation. If we find ourselves in a similar situation we should model our pleas on his, emulating both his humility and sincerity.

Searching. In his moment of despair, David cried out, "You have said, 'Seek my face.' My heart says to you, 'Your face, Lord, do I seek'" (v. 8). God does not wish to hide from us; He wants us to find Him! In Deuteronomy, we are told, "But from there you will seek the Lord your God and you will find him, if you search after him with all your heart and with all your soul" (4:29; cf. Jer. 29:13; Isa. 55:6). Psalm 105:4 similarly exclaimed: "Look to the Lord and his strength; see his face always" (cf. 1 Chron. 16:11).

David accepted God's command and was drawing on it to bring himself comfort. Why? Those who take up God's invitation are closer to Him, and the closer we come, the more we might glory in His awesomeness. Interestingly, the Hebrew word, *bawkash* or "seek," is plural; God summoned all His children to seek Him out. David's response, however, is in the singular: "Your face, Lord, do *I* seek" (v. 8; emphasis added). It is as if David was saying, "You have given this command to everyone, yet I am one of the few to follow it." In faithful obedience, he sought the Lord's blessing.

Embracing. The language of the psalm becomes even more frantic in v. 9. There David sought out God, obeyed His commands, beseeched Him for aid, and then panicked that He would forsake his servant: "Hide not your face from me" (v. 9). It was a promise

---

2. Adam Clarke, *Commentary with Critical Notes* (Nashville: Abingdon, n. d.), 3:308.

God had made to His faithful: seek Me and you will find Me. We cannot imagine what trauma had occurred in David's life that made him think God might go against His own words. It must have been something terrible indeed, for he continued, "turn not your servant away in anger, O you who have been my help" (v. 9).

David knew that God was benevolent, but also that He could become angry and act upon that anger. The wrath of God is real and it is an attribute of His that we cannot fail to remember (e.g. Deut. 9:8; 29:24-28; Josh. 23:16; Isa. 13:9). His wrath, however, was only turned upon the faithful when they had broken the covenant (e.g. Deut. 11:17; Ezra 8:22; Neh. 13:18), and David readily clarified that he had done no such wrong: "Your face, Lord, do I seek! (...) Turn not your servant away in anger."

What did David fear most in this moment but loneliness? He begged God not to cast him off, not to forsake him. This concern appeared more than once in David's writing. Consider, for example, Psa. 51:11: "Cast me not away from your presence, and take not your Holy Spirit from me." In these words, we again see straight into the heart of David. To him, and to all who live for the Lord, being cast away or forsaken by Him was and is the most horrifying punishment of all.

In Psa. 27:10, David continued with his reasons for his fear: "For my father and my mother have forsaken me." It is unlikely that his biological parents had cast him off, but he was separated from their guidance and protection when Samuel anointed him as king of the united Israel and Judah (2 Sam. 2:1-7; 5:1-10). Here, David referred to the temporary nature of man in the world. His "father and mother" represent all people, anyone David had ever associated with, all of whom would pass from the earth at one time or another.

God, however, is permanent. God is reliable, the rock upon which we lean in times of despair and hopelessness. David understood this and kept its truth in his heart. Thus, after he had lamented over his lonely state on earth, he added, "but the Lord will take me in"

(v. 10). Even though there was great fear in David's life, he begged the Lord for comfort and protection because he knew the Lord would always be with him. God would bring shelter, safety, and solace when He embraced His faithful servants. Temporarily hidden by fear and panic, this was the truth in David's heart all the time: "the Lord will take me in."

Guiding. God is benevolent and caring; loving and constant. David knew this and, although his courage faltered, he offered up a prayer to the Lord for renewed strength. He ends this section of the psalm with one, final benediction that recalls his earlier verses: "Teach me your way, O Lord, and lead me on a level path because of my enemies" (v. 11). Notice the humility in David's words. Teach me your way, he asked. Lead me. David did not see himself as a standard of excellence. He did not try to solve all the answers; he did not even presume to know them. David understood that God asks for things to be done a certain way and was patiently awaiting His commands.

Sometimes, God leads us through dark valleys (Psa. 23:4); usually, we seek the easier path, and God often obliges. David did not ask for an easy path, but a level one. *Meeshore,* Hebrew for "level place/plain," also describes a place of uprightness: "Your throne, O God, is forever and ever. The scepter of your kingdom is a scepter of uprightness (meeshore)" (Psa. 45:6; cf. Psa. 67:4; Isa. 11:4). Lead me, David asked, in your (God's) path. Guide me, lest I stray from righteousness and true faith. This was not an empty request either, for David sought refuge from his enemies, mentioned in v. 11 and again in v. 12: "Give me not up to the will of my adversaries; for false witnesses have risen against me, and they breathe out violence."

Where are enemies easier to spot than on a clear, level path? Who these enemies are, we cannot know for certain, but they were formidable enough that David—a tried and tested warrior—fears for his safety. David asked God to guide him to a place where he would be able to discern his enemies, who have become "false witnesses" against him. Lies and violence were being cast upon David, thus he sought the pure and righteous path of the Lord, whereupon his enemies could not walk.

It may seem strange to see these words of fear after such a strong opening, but David's heart never strayed from God. He was fearful, but continued to seek after God because only in Him could David find the security he most needed. When we find ourselves at our lowest, despairing as our world turns upside down, we must recall David's words and call out to the Lord, for He will take us in.

Foundation (vv. 13-14)

At the end of the psalm, David's faith was renewed, and he exulted in the Lord. His spirit wavered under challenges and trials, but returned to faith in God and His divine plans. He doubted no longer: "I believe that I shall look upon the goodness of the Lord in the land of the living!" (v. 13).

The opening of v. 13 varies between different translations of the Hebrew. The Hebrew reads, "unless I had believed that I would see the goodness of the Lord in the land of the living" (NASB). Unless what? Several editions attempt to respond to this by including phrases like "I had fainted" (KJV) or "I would have despaired" (NASB). These do not come from the Hebrew, but from translators attempting to evoke David's message more clearly in English. He was not questioning, but rather acknowledging that he would have failed had he not held a foundational faith in the Lord.

David could have turned away from God. Verses 7-12 suggest he came very close to losing all hope; his enemies were very real, very deadly, and they were closing in around him. He was afraid. He was lost. He was near despair. David's faith in the Lord, however, kept his eyes where they needed to be: looking on the goodness of the Lord.

It is a testament to his enduring faith that David was able to end the psalm with the foundational truth that God is in control. We must submit to His will and trust in Him to see us through the dark times.

In the final verse, David stated three things he (indeed, all of us) must do in order to show his submission to and trust in the goodness of the Lord: "Wait for the Lord; be strong, and let your heart take courage; wait for the Lord!" (v. 14).

Be Calm. Twice in v. 14, David said, "Wait for the Lord." This is easier said than done, but consider David's situation when he wrote the poem. He mentioned his enemies several times, first in regard to his being protected from them by God (vv. 2-3), and again when his fear overwhelms him (vv. 11-12). It was a real and pressing threat that led to words of despair. It would be far easier to lash out against those who oppose us, but David realized that waiting for the shelter of God was best. Wait patiently, he cautioned, for the Lord's plan will come to fruition and He will be there beside you.

Be Capable. David also wrote that we need to "be strong;" literally, "to have resolve." We do not need to be strong for our own actions, but rather for the Lord. Our strength is in Him. We are strongest when we commit all of ourselves to the Lord and trust in His guiding hand. If we do this, then we shall have no need of fear.

Be Courageous. Finally, David advised that we let our "heart[s] take courage." God is able to restore a weakened heart with courage, but only if we open it up to Him first as our guide and protector. Human courage is not durable and falters easily in the face of certain challenges. God, however, is courage. He is strength. If we put our trust in Him, we can withstand anything. He will be our courage and strength, unfailing and formidable.

Conclusion

David's foundation was always in the Lord, just as ours must be, too. In Him, we shall find the hope, courage, and strength to fight the many battles to come. Consider again the structure of this psalm. Several times, I mentioned how it seems to be written backwards. Instead of starting with a problem and walking closer to the Lord, Psa. 27 begins with strong words of faith, only to have hope give way to despair. David never turned from God; he doubted himself, not the Lord.

It is possible that David wrote this psalm "backwards" on purpose because it better exemplifies how our walk with the Lord can be. We often speak of the thrill and deep motivation that comes from knowing the Lord. We are on fire to serve Him, and our faith in Him is strong! But challenges then arise. Enemies might cause us to question our beliefs. They might press in on us and tempt us to leave the Lord because faith is too hard. Can He hear us? Does He care that we struggle?

Of course He does, for He is all that is true and pure. He tests us, refusing to move obstacles from our path, yet all the while wills us to succeed. If we continue forward, however, with the Lord in our hearts, He will bless us tenfold. If we walk with the Lord and trust in His protective hand, we will be strong with encouraged hearts because of Him and His love for us. In fact, the message of Psa. 27 is quite simple. Do not lose faith, no matter what life might throw your way. Stay true to the Lord by trusting in His divine presence and protection. Wait on Him, and He will deliver.

I would like to end this chapter with a non-biblical poem that embodies the message behind David's psalm and life itself. There are good and bad experiences in life, but each of those moments are opportunities to strengthen yourself in the Lord. After all, no matter how low we feel, He is always there to take us in and lift us up.

> The wind's not always at our back,
> The sky is not always blue.
> Sometimes we crave the things we lack,
> And don't know what to do.

Sometimes life's an uphill ride,
With mountains we must climb.
At times the river's deep and wide,
And crossing takes some time.

No one said that life is easy,
There are no guarantees.
So trust in the Lord continually,
On calm or stormy seas.

The challenges we face today,
Prepares us for tomorrow.
For faith takes our fears away,
And peace replaces sorrow.[3]

---

3. Anonymous, "Trust in the Lord."

After the Trouble

O ne of the most interesting aspects of the psalms is that the poets—in our case, David—wrote from real life experiences. They did not sugarcoat life or faith and make it seem as though nothing bad will ever occur. Instead, the writers chronicled their loneliness, fear, and heartache as they faced the many struggles inherent to life.

Thus far, we have read the famous words of Psa. 23: God, the Shepherd, walks with us "through the valley of the shadow of death." We have also heard that God "will take [us] in" when we feel forsaken by everyone else (27:10). But what about when the storms have passed? What do we do when peace is finally ours and the proverbial sun shines brightly upon our lives? These times can be just as difficult on our faith. After successfully navigating the challenges and trials, we can still fail to be thankful to our Lord and walk away from Him by thinking that we triumphed without His help. Gratitude and humility, however, are just as important as prayer.

When we face a time of peace after the storm, we must show our thanks for God's assistance. In Psa. 30, David wrote after a horrible experience had passed. We cannot be certain which struggle David spoke of here, but some scholars suggest that it was after the experience of "numbering the people." In 2 Sam. 24, David demanded a census be taken of both Israel and Judah. Pride goaded him into measuring his power by the number of fighting men under his dominion, possibly with the intention of expanding his borders. Foolishly, David tallied his strength and confidence in the size of the nation, rather than in the size of his faith in God.

God offered David the choice of three punishments on account of his sin: three years of famine, three months pursued by his enemies, or three days of pestilence. Regardless of which he chose, two things were certain: (1) the punishment was going to be harsh and severe, and (2) there was no way out of it. God was not going to let this presumption go unpunished. Ultimately, David chose to have the hand of God bring pestilence over the land: "Let us fall into the hand of the Lord, for his mercy is great; but let me not fall into the hand of man" (2 Sam. 24:14). Even after he had sinned against God, David trusted Him; even in His wrath, the Lord is merciful. Some 70,000 Israelites died before He stilled the hand of the death angel and ended the punishment (2 Sam. 24:15-16). When the pestilence had ended, David built an altar to the Lord and offered sacrifices for forgiveness and praised the mercy of God.

We cannot be certain that this episode was the background to Psa. 30, but the humility and praise within the poem certainly reflect just such an experience. David had obviously come through a harrowing experience, like the one in 2 Sam. 24, when he wrote Psa. 30. He described not only success after awful circumstances, but how his faith had to remain constant in order to weather the storm.

The psalm is David's reflection on an experience that led him to doubt, struggle, and return his heart to the Lord. First, David was nearly overwhelmed by enemies, only to be saved by God. His subsequent prosperity blinded him to the Lord's glory as he began to rely on worldly wealth and prestige, instead of divine power. In punishment, God brought forth challenges and troubles until David realized his error and prayed for forgiveness. Restored to divine favor, he promised to give thanks to the Lord forever after, as it was only through the grace of God that he found true strength and, finally, peace.

Restoration (vv. 1-3)

The opening lines of the psalm explain that David had overcome some trouble with the help of the Lord. God had "drawn" David up from a place where his enemies would have rejoiced over his failure and suffering. In response, David assured the Lord, "I will extol you" (v. 1). It is important to note that David was giving all the praise for his salvation to the Lord. He kept none of it for himself, though he was king over hundreds of thousands of people. Whatever his situation when writing this psalm, David acknowledged it was the Lord's hand that brought true deliverance.

In vv. 2-3, David described his restoration, praising and admiring God for the salvation He afforded His servant. Again and again, he returned to this theme, first by explaining that he had lost his way, and then how God helped him. David said, "you have drawn me up" (v. 1); "you have healed me" (v. 2), "you have brought up my soul (...); you restored me to life" (v. 3). Four times, he remarked on his salvation. God provided whatever David needed for him to come through his troubles in a nourished and healthy way. The Lord delivered him and brought him back to the path of faith, for the Lord was his Shepherd and provided for His ailing sheep.

These expressions of salvation are generic, in and of themselves, and do not relate any great suffering. If we look at the rest of David's language, however, we begin to see that it was not merely a simple poem, but an exclamation of gratitude. We already know that his enemies were upon him (v. 1) and that his faith or health (or both) had weakened (v. 2). But in v. 3, we get a stronger image of despair: "O Lord, you have brought up my soul from Sheol; you restored me to life from among those who go down to the pit."

The origins of the term *sheol* are uncertain, but its synonyms—grave (*abbadon*, *shahat*), pit (*bor*)—make it clear that it describes a place of the dead. This "underworld" is described as beneath the earth (Gen. 37:36), a "land of darkness and deep shadow, land of gloom like thick darkness, like deep shadow without any order, where light is as thick darkness" (Job 10:21-22). It is the antithesis of heaven, where the Lord is the Shepherd of the righteous: "Like sheep they are appointed for Sheol; death shall be their shepherd" (Psa. 49:14). It is a place that always hungers for more souls (Prov. 30:16; Isa. 5:14) and traps its inhabitants with ropes (2 Sam. 22:5-6; Psa. 116:3). Sheol represented finality; no one returned from its dark embrace (Job 7:9-10, 10:21; 2 Sam. 12:22-23).

The dark despair that defines Sheol, however, is no match for the glory of God. David wrote that the Lord restored his life and brought him back to the world of the living. He lifted up David's head and imbued him with renewed energy and vigor. How severe were David's troubles that he compared his situation to being among the dead? The imagery associated with Sheol would have served to intensify God's mighty power and benevolence. The darkness and bonds of the underworld, after all, are nothing compared to the Lord's shining omnipotence. God restored and continued to sustain David's life, giving him purpose and hope. It was not a one-time "pick-me-up," but rather constant support of His faithful servant so that David could reengage in life and remain strong in his belief.

As we ponder these words, we need to remember an important point: God is still in the work of restoration! When we read words like those in Psa. 30, we must remember that He does not participate in partial restoration; He does not restore once and only once. He continues to give us the energy, strength, and life to face the world's many struggles. He continually gives us help, because He provides full restoration.

Response (vv. 4-5)

If we understand the Lord's restoration of David, then we need to respond as David did and joyously sing His praise! David's cry is for all the saints of the Lord to "sing praises to the Lord" and "give thanks to His holy name" (v. 4). David calls for singing and thanksgiving, two forms of praise we still use to offer thanks to the Lord for what He has done in our lives. The translation of the Hebrew word *khawseed* as "saints" might confuse some, as it does not refer to sainted men and women of the Christian faith. Here, *khawseed* has a more generic meaning and describes "faithful, pious, or godly" people (cf. 2 Chron. 6:41; Prov. 2:8; Psa. 4:3, 16:10, 37:28, 50:5). David is calling upon those who are faithful—godly men and women—to remember what God has done for them and to thank Him with praise.

Verses like Psalm 30:4 can help shape how we think about worship. Notice that David clearly stated that our praise is for "the Lord," not for us. When we worship, God must be the center of our every thought and word; He must be the only recipient of our praise. All too often, we focus on what we have done, giving God credit as a minor player in our success. We need to remember that He is the Author of life and the giver of every good and perfect gift (Jas. 1:17). Any good thing that comes to us in fact originates from Him. Any success we experience is His, first and foremost, and we must praise the Lord for sharing victories with us.

David specified that any thanks we offer is in God's "holy name." There is a time and place for showing gratitude to others, and we should be thankful to those who help us through life. Our ultimate praise, however, should always be centered on the things that God has done for us. Paul wrote, "Do not be anxious about anything, but in every situation, by prayer and petition, with thanksgiving, present your requests to God" (Phil. 4:6). All our worship should be an offering of praise to God, for He blesses us daily with gifts and wonders without asking for recompense.

Let your mind consider all the good things God gives us on a regular basis. How glorious is the earth and its many forms of life? Should we not praise and thank Him for these creations? Now, think of those times when He has helped us through trials and tribulations. How much more glorious is He then? How much greater should our thanks and praise be? We should respond as David did, calling upon everyone of faith to praise the Lord and thank Him for what He does for His children. Whether anyone joins us or we give our thanks alone, we must always and continually offer up our sacrifice of praise (Heb. 13:15).

The Lord is always good. He will always bless and strengthen us when we are in need. It is in this context that David wrote v. 5, the most well-known line in the psalm: "His anger is but for a moment, and His favor is for a lifetime." If anyone understood this characteristic of God, it was David! David had felt the anger and wrath of God several times during his life (2 Sam. 11, 24), yet lived in the full favor of the Lord until his dying day (1 Kings 1-2). Although God's wrath often brings about severe punishment, for the truly faithful it is the briefest of moments when compared to the glorious blessings God constantly pours out.

God's punishment is momentary, just like the troubles that discourage us in life. David continued this verse by writing, "Weeping may tarry for the night, but joy comes with the morning." Nighttime is often used to represent evil, fear, and despair, but David's words here were only positive and uplifting. This verse reminds us that, while fear and sadness are natural parts of life, something greater is on the horizon for the faithful. By balancing "night" and "morning," David invoked the Jewish custom of marking days. In Gen. 1, the first six days of creation were marked by the phrase, "there was evening and there was morning" (vv. 5, 8, 11, 19, 23, 31). The "day" starts with darkness, which can evoke fear and sadness, but it ends with light, hope, and joy.

Such is the way of God. There will be fear and darkness in our lives, but "joy comes with the morning" (v. 5), and the morning will always come. Something better is on the horizon, shining down upon the faithful and banishing despair. Our response to these many promises and gifts is simple: praise. Praise God! Remember to hold His hand while walking through the "night," for these moments are inevitable. Remember also that dawn will come, so thank Him for the morning and His constant blessings.

Realization (vv. 6-7)

As David arrived at the middle of his poem, he offered words of personal realization that were truly humbling. David was a man of great wealth and power. As with anyone who has money and privilege, it is easy to forget the temporary uncertainty of such riches. Wealth cannot be trusted (1 Tim. 6:17). In v. 6, David reflected on his time of prosperity and recalled that he once said, "I shall never be moved." David's life was so blessed that he had begun to trust in the temporal and forgot that "night" comes to all of us. As Spurgeon aptly said, "No temptation is so bad as tranquility."[1]

It was at that moment that David came to a powerful and all-important realization. It was not his wisdom or power that brought him success, but the Lord's generosity. He wrote, "By your favor, O Lord, you made my mountain stand strong" (v. 7). It was God who made David king, who strengthened him for battle, and brought glory to Israel. Thankfully, David's faith allowed him to look beyond his own self-importance and acknowledge God as the true, Almighty King. As only He can, the Lord helped David become like a mountain, strong and immoveable in his faith.

David's self-importance did not go unpunished. God hid His face

---

1. Spurgeon, *Treasury of David*, 1.2.45.

from David, turning from his servant who had failed to acknowledge where his success had derived: "you hid your face; I was dismayed" (v. 7). David sinned, and the Lord rebuked him. It is here, however, that we see the true heart of David. All God had to do was hide His face, and it was enough for David to write, "I was dismayed." The Hebrew word *bawhal* suggests a more intense reaction; David was afraid, terrified, alarmed that God had hidden Himself because in that moment, David felt truly alone.

We should all respond this way when we realize God has revoked His favor or is chastising us for our sins. It should cause us great fear when we realize that we have thought too highly of ourselves and forgotten the Lord. He may reestablish us as He did with David, but God will not let such arrogance go unpunished. Dismay and fear will be part of our future (if not our present) should we realize that we have succumbed to pride in our own actions, rather than the Lord's. If that time should come, think back to David and this particular psalm. His heart was always strong, and even though he made a mistake, he still sought a close fellowship with the Lord. The purity of his faith and trust is why he despaired when God hid His face, because David knew what he had lost.

When we realize God is punishing us, we should ask ourselves if it would be better if He were no longer in our hearts? I think we would all agree that the answer to this is a resounding no. We seek atonement because we long for fellowship with Him, not out of guilt or embarrassment for our mistakes. We need only compare our daily accomplishments to the wonders of the universe to realize how glorious He is and how insignificant we are in comparison.

Request (vv. 8-10)

Alone and afraid, David cried out to the Lord and pled for mercy (v. 8). Once again David's focus was on God. He did not seek answers from others—or even from himself—for the problems he faced. He did not make excuses or blame anyone for his poor decisions. Instead, he went to God, the correct source and solution, to seek forgiveness and make reparations. David's plea for mercy was made through three rhetorical questions, each building to a single truth: if God takes David's life as punishment, David could no longer seek and praise the Lord.

The first question is straight to the point: "What profit is there in my death, if I go down to the pit?" (v. 9). David was not appealing in arrogance, but honestly asking how his death would serve God. Spurgeon summarizes this question as, "Wilt thou not lose a songster from thy choir, and one who loves to magnify thee?"[2] David proved his faith countless times, living and leading according to Divine Law. This question is a natural human response to suffering. There is no anger or judgment in David's words, even though it seems impertinent. When Jesus cried out on the cross, "My God, my God, why have you forsaken me" (Matt. 27:46), he was asking a similar question, not condemning the Lord. What purpose do we fragile, mortal creatures serve to the Almighty?

David's second and third questions continued his original point. He asked, "Will the dust praise you?" (v. 9). We are no use dead, David was saying. From the grave, he could not offer God praise or glorify His name. He reiterated this important fact in his third question: "Will it (i.e. the dust) tell of your faithfulness?" Cloer summarizes these last two questions as, "If I died, I could not tell others how faithful You have been to me, could I?"[3] Obviously, the questions are rhetorical and expect the answer to be "no." If God allowed David to die (or killed David Himself), then one less person would be on the earth to give God the glory and praise.

Scripture repeatedly tells us that we are meant to glorify God:

2. Ibid., 1.2.46.

3. Cloer, *Psalms 1-50*, 401

"Ascribe to the Lord the glory due his name; worship the Lord in the splendor of holiness (Psa. 29:2); "It is he who made us, and we are his; we are his people, the sheep of his pasture. Enter his gates with thanksgiving and his courts with praise; give thanks to him and praise his name" (Psa. 100:3-4); and, "So, whether you eat or drink, or whatever you do, do all to the glory of God: (1 Cor. 10:31). David's questions are, in many ways, attempting to make sense of how our struggles can benefit our faith and ability to praise God. How often have people asked what is God's plan? What does He want from us? What good can we really do?

We are all of us lost from time to time, just like David when he was blinded by prosperity. It is David's regret, however, that leads him back to the path of faith. His heart is for God, regardless of his confusion and blindness. Thus, David made his plea: "Hear, O Lord, and be merciful to me! O Lord, be my helper!" (v. 10). There is deep gratitude and humility in these words. David is begging for the mercy of God and appealing to the Lord for help. In this way, he simultaneously admits his weaknesses and proves his undying faith. David knew that God had helped him, but still appealed to the Lord for a clear sign of forgiveness and assurance. If we return to the Lord in penitence, He will hear our pleas and help us through any struggle we might face. Whether we weep through the night or are joyous in the morning, God walks with us always and provides the help we most desperately need.

Rejoicing (vv. 11-12)

David analyzed and reflected, sought restoration and responses for his questions and doubts. In the end, he was left with only one possible conclusion: joy. Joy in life. Joy in faith. Joy in the Lord. Whatever situation David faced, his passionate words express real and serious struggles. Yet, God heard and helped him, leading His servant back to a place where he could seek out the Lord and know His goodness once more.

In v. 11, David joyously exclaimed how God blessed him. First, God turned his "mourning into dancing." This is the first of two parallels where sadness and despair are replaced with joy and hope. David just finished asking God what purpose there would be in his death. Now he is celebrating life! He is a man saved from death, whose sackcloth God exchanged for clothes of gladness. God did not merely remove traditional mourning garb, but cloaked him in renewed happiness, symbolizing both David's penitence and God's forgiveness. Christians can associate this imagery with the change brought about when we put off the old man of sin. After all, we do not replace it with just any old "something." Instead, we put on a new man, because Christ himself replaces that old, rotting garb of sin.

As David ended the psalm, he returned to something he had written earlier. In v. 4, David had appealed to all who were faithful to the Lord to both "sing praises" and "give thanks to His holy name." As David reflected upon God's many gifts, he affirmed that not only was he going to do those things, but he would do them even more intently. Note that David wrote that he would sing "and not be silent," and that he would give thanks "forevermore" (v. 12). It is as if David said, "Even if no one else joins me, I know what You have done, and I cannot stop myself from giving You praise and gratitude." Cloer summarizes this final verse best:

> [David] has learned well the lesson of his trial. God has raised him up that he may praise Him, not so that he may just live for his own pursuits. (...) From that moment forward, David promises to give thanks to God. His new full-time employment will be that of praising and thanking God for what He has done.[4]

---

4. Cloer, *Psalms 1-50*, p. 403.

The same should be true of all our lives. After we face our trials and realize that God is the One who has helped us through, the only true reaction should be rejoicing. Paul declared, "Rejoice in the Lord always" (Phil. 4:4) and his words remind us of David's purpose in writing Psa. 30. The only place there can be true joy is in the One who created and cares for us—before, during, and after our troubles.

Conclusion

Psalm 30, in its very basic form, is a message of hope. David was a man; granted he was a wealthy, powerful king, but still only a man. What marked him as unique was his consistent faith in the Lord. Yes, he struggled with his faith. Yes, he made mistakes and received punishment for his transgressions. Who among us has not similarly struggled and erred?

David repeatedly compared his struggles to death: God drew him up (v. 1); He brought up his soul from Sheol (v. 3); He restored his life (v. 3). The Lord saw no profit in David's death (v. 9), in letting His servant dwell in the pit (v. 9) and become dust (v. 9). David was in mourning until God saved him. Despair, fear, and death—none of these are more powerful than the Lord, and none of them can take hold of us when He is our lifeline. David was extolling his brethren to shake off their complacency and doubt so that they might all "sing praises to the Lord (...) and give thanks to His holy name" (v. 4). God, after all, is joy.

I would like to close this chapter with a short poem from James Rowe. Once a miner in Ireland, he immigrated to America where he worked with various railroad companies until eventually settling into writing greeting cards. Rowe, however, also had a strong propensity for hymn writing and worked with several well-known publishers at the turn of the 20th century. He wrote lyrics for hundreds of hymns, though only a few are still widely used. One of his hymns recalls the most famous line of Psa. 30: "Weeping may tarry for the night, but joy comes with the morning." Even if Rowe did not have those particular words in mind when he wrote this poem, they invoke David's message quite beautifully.

> After the midnight, morning will greet us;
> After the sadness, joy will appear;
> After the tempest, sunlight will meet us;
> After the jeering, praise we shall hear.[5]

Nighttime is real. Struggles are real. Troubles are real. So, too, is joy, and it always comes in the morning. Praise God and do not be silent. Thank Him forever!

---

5. James Rowe, http://www.hymntime.com/tch/bio/r/o/w/rowe_j.htm

The Joy of Being Forgiven

PSALM 32

February 18, 1990 is a date that probably means nothing to you. To me, that date means everything. I don't remember every last detail of that date, but I remember far more about that day than most others for a simple reason. On that day, as the Dexter church of Christ sang "Come to Jesus," I walked to the front of the auditorium, ready to become a New Testament Christian.

I had thought about it for some time, but on that Sunday morning, I knew I needed to have my sins washed away in the waters of baptism. I remember a lot about those few moments, but the one thing I remember more than any other is that, when I came up out of the water, I felt as if a weight had been lifted from me. I know that nothing physical had changed (other than getting wet), but I felt lighter. I felt freer. I was forgiven, and I knew what it felt like to have that burden of sin lifted from my soul. I knew it would be a great thing to be a Christian, but I honestly had no idea how that knowledge would manifest itself in such a powerful way.

Forgiveness is such a powerful thing. When you have wronged a person, and that person forgives, there is a tension that is lifted, and only then can that relationship begin to be truly restored. If that is true between two people, how much greater is it to know that the holy and almighty God has forgiven you?

In Psa. 32, David expresses that beautiful, restorative feeling that forgiveness brings. Even if we did not have the superscription "A maskil of David," we would know these were the words of David. In Rom. 4:6, Paul wrote, "Just as David also speaks of the blessing of the one to whom God counts righteousness apart from works." He then quotes the opening two verses of our psalm.

As is often the case, we are not told specifically when this psalm was written during the life of David, but one event clearly stands out. After David's sin with Bathsheba, he wrote the more well-known 51st Psalm seeking forgiveness from the Lord. It seems as though Psa. 32 was written slightly later, as David's relationship with the Lord had been restored, and he was able to reflect on what forgiveness really meant to his life.

If you know what it means to be forgiven by the Lord, then it should not surprise you that this psalm is filled with joy. When we know what God has done for us, it fills us with joy that sometimes we cannot fully express. Thankfully, we see David's great ability come through in these words to provide us with a voice for our joy.

Covering (vv. 1-2)

Verses 1-2 of the psalm both begin with the word "blessed." In both cases, the word blessed is translated from the Hebrew word ('ashrey), which is actually a plural word. It was a word used to indicate a total cleansing and now had complete happiness. David is expressing the idea of being completely forgiven and feeling that forgiveness in every aspect of his life. He states that one is blessed who has his transgressions forgiven, then restates that in very strong ways in writing that their "sins [are] covered."

The word picture presented here was one that was commonly used in business transactions. In ancient cultures, ledgers were kept on stone tablets, and the particulars were engraved in that stone. The picture that David is using is that of someone who owes something (they have a debt), but now that the debt has been paid, wax is taken and poured into those etchings on the stone, and it is as if no debt was ever owed. The wax so fills the engraving that the stone looks smooth and the debt simply no longer exists. That's the forgiveness of God! And that's why, in the next line, David states that God no longer counts that person's iniquity. When God pours that wax over those etchings, it is gone, and there is nothing left for him to count against us. When He forgives, He completely forgives. He covers the sins so that they are forever wiped away.

David ends this first section by reminding himself (and us) that our inner person must match what we are seeking from the Lord. God only covers the sins and stops counting them against the one "in whose spirit there is no deceit." God knows if we are asking forgiveness for the right reasons, or in some half-hearted way (maybe just because we got caught). That person will not be forgiven because the Lord knows the heart. However, if our heart is right and we are truly seeking God's forgiveness, our sins are covered and wiped away.

Cry (vv. 3-4)

After David writes about the aftermath—the forgiveness and what a blessing it is—he returns to what it was like before he was forgiven. It is one of the strongest pictures in the psalms and should cause anyone who is trying to hide sin or keep from seeking forgiveness to change. David writes, "For when I kept silent, my bones wasted away through my groaning all day long."

If this psalm was, in fact, written in the aftermath of David's adulterous affair with Bathsheba, it sheds some light on one word found in that story. Second Samuel 11 speaks to the sin itself, and David's attempted cover up. He must have thought that he had gotten away with this terrible series of sins. However, 2 Sam. 12 begins with "And the Lord sent Nathan to David." The word "and" does not tell us how long it was between the adultery/murder and when God sent Nathan to confront the sinful king. Our psalm may help us see, however, that some time passed, and David was miserable.

By speaking of his bones wasting away, David is obviously using poetic language, but he is indicating that even his physical body was hurting him in some way from this sin and the guilt of the transgression. That led to a groaning (the word can also be translated "roaring") that went on "all day long." It is possible that this was literal cries of pain, or it could be that David turned to whining about the pain he was in, but not letting on why he was feeling this immense pain. But David knew why. In v. 4, he writes that the hand of God was upon him and even says that hand was "heavy." Over time, David says, "My strength was dried up as by the heat of summer."

Let's be honest. We have all been where David was at this time. We have all sinned and thought we had it covered up. No one knew about it, and we were even a little proud of ourselves for how well we had concealed whatever it was we had done. But we knew, and it ate away at us because we knew that sin was a transgression against our wonderful and holy God. Maybe you are feeling that even now. It is something that no one else knows about, but you know, and you also know that God knows. Learn from David's experience. Don't try to wait it out any longer. Realize what this guilt can and will do to you, spiritually, physically, and emotionally. The crying that you do, even if it is inward, is not necessary—not because sin is no big deal, but because God stands ready to forgive!

Confession (v.5)

Verse 5 may seem simple in its wording, but it is profound in how it changed David's life and how it can change ours as well.

Though this is a brief verse, there are four parts to this verse that speak to how that change came about.

Recognition. David states that he acknowledged his sin to the Lord. For us to be forgiven, we must first recognize and admit that there is something for which we need to be forgiven. While I do not begrudge those who might say something like, "If I've done anything, I pray for forgiveness," we need to be willing to admit the sins we know we have committed. There must be a recognition that we are unholy and stand before a holy God.

Revelation. Upon that recognition, David said, "I did not cover my iniquity." The guilt was too great, and the knowledge was too real for him to try to hide it any longer. The word "cover" (KJV = "hid") here is not the same as that in v. 1. This Hebrew word means an overwhelming concealing. David was finished trying to conceal his sin and opened it before God. Of course, God knew it all along, but we must come to the place where we make that connection and open up ourselves to the Lord—not for His benefit or knowledge, but for ours.

Relation. That change in David led to him saying, "I will confess my transgressions to the Lord." We are calling this *relation* because of what the word translated confess means. The Hebrew word (*yadah*) literally means, "to throw down" or "to cast." Upon uncovering our sin before God, we should be willing to throw those sins before Him, to speak them to Him. That changes our relationship with God because we are no longer trying to be the captain of our lives. Instead, we recognize and admit that God is in control, and we take our faults before Him for forgiveness, rather than continuing to attempt to cover up our sins or chart our own path.

Reaffirmation. As David has already said in this psalm, and will say again, God is a forgiving God. When David recognized his sin, opened it up before the Lord, and confessed it, God "forgave the iniquity" David had. The word "iniquity" here probably could better be translated "guilt" (cf. NASB) since that is what David had been writing about in vv. 3-4. God forgives the sin, but He also takes the guilt away. Any guilt we feel beyond the time God forgives is of our own doing, or it is from the lingering consequences of our sin. It is not because God continues to hold something against us. He reaffirms us as His beloved child and brings new life to us.

Confession is not just mouthing some words. It is a process that involves both our knowledge and our will to be as God would have us to be. But thanks be to God that, when we are willing to confess and change, He always stands ready to forgive!

Call (vv. 6-7)

Reflecting on the joy he is feeling from being forgiven, David spends the next two verses calling for others to realize this same joy, as well. David's words are a clear call: "Let everyone who is godly offer prayer to you at a time when you may be found." Notice in those words, though, that there is a hint of warning: "when you may be found." The words warn that there will come a time when the opportunity is no longer there. This is not saying that God will not forgive. David is saying that we can remove ourselves so far from God, and our heart can be so far from Him, that we cannot find Him because we are no longer willing to find Him.

That thought is reinforced at the end of v. 6: "Surely in the rush of great waters, they shall not reach Him." David is trying to state that, if we wait until there is a flood around us, we will not be ready to come to God. But notice that he is writing to those who claim to be godly. He isn't talking about those who become believers in the midst of a calamity. He is talking about those who would claim with their words to believe in God, but their heart isn't near to the Lord at all. They are not seeking God daily, but are rather living as if they are their own solution. However, when some great calamity hits in their life, it will (at the very least) be difficult to come to God, because they have denied Him in their heart for so long.

As David ends this call to others, he writes about what God has meant to him. He is trying to turn the hearts of those who might be drifting in their heart away from God, back to the Lord by telling of what God has done. Remember, David is writing this after going through a time of guilt and punishment, but now David realizes the wonderful joy of forgiveness. In v. 7, he writes that God gives three things:

Conservation. Notice that David does *not* say God "provides" a hiding place, but David says to God: "You *are* a hiding place for me." God gives a place of conservation for David—a place where David can go to get away and conserve his strength from this world.

Preservation. When those great waters rush into David's life, he writes that God preserves him from trouble. God is able to not only provide a place for us to go, but He sustains us while we are with Him.

Emancipation. God is not just about helping us put one foot in front of the other. He wants what is best for us, so He surrounds us with "shouts of deliverance." I love that David says they are "shouts" of our deliverance. Some translations have "songs," but the word is one of a song, cry, or shout of excitement. Even if the word gives the idea of songs, these are not funeral dirges! God is about celebrating our coming through a rough trial of life. Specifically, God is about celebrating the wanderer who has come back to Him, much like the father of the Prodigal Son.

So, David knows the forgiveness of God, but he doesn't want to keep it to himself. By rehearsing just how wonderful that forgiveness is, he calls upon everyone who might nominally be a follower of God to return fully to the Lord and know that same forgiveness.

Change (vv. 8-9)

After a pause (*selah*), the psalm changes. Although David is still the writer, he begins writing from God's point of view. In fact, as

Spurgeon wrote about this section, "No other than God himself can undertake so much as is promised in the text."[1] Look at what God states He will provide for David.

Instruction. The idea behind this word is one of understanding. God will provide David with insight for how he needs to live.

Teaching. The Hebrew word is one that could mean to "throw" or "set." It was a word that could be used for the shooting of an arrow. God will set teaching before David that is just what he needs. It will be teaching that is like an arrow shot in the right direction. That's why God would say that He would instruct and teach "in the way you should go."

Counsel. This word was sometimes used of meeting together in a council to come up with helpful advice. However, in this instance, God does not need to call some type of council meeting. God always gives perfect advice and does not need our input. We can trust the counsel of God to be right and always for our best.

Protection. The counsel He gives is given "with my eye upon you." He is doing what is best for us, protecting us from sinful ways.

When you consider that God provides all these things, it should cause us to be ashamed when we sin. We are leaving the instruction, teaching, counsel, and protection of an almighty and all-wise Father. To further emphasize that, God pictures for us how foolish we are when we turn from Him and enter a sinful decision. In v. 9, God says, "Be not like a horse or a mule, without understanding, which must be curbed with bit and bridle, or it will not stay near you."

David was not the only psalmist to compare sin with living like an animal. Asaph, in 73:21-22, stated, "When my soul was embittered, when I was pricked in heart, I was brutish and ignorant; I was like a beast toward you." When we sin, we are acting out of rash passions, and we are failing to use our God-given ability to reason and think. That is why God says these words through David, comparing

---

1. Spurgeon, *Treasury of David*, 1.2.97.

sin to being like a horse or mule. Matthew Henry gave these good words of application in writing about this verse:

> Let us not be like [the horse and mule]; let us not be hurried by appetite and passion, at any time, to go contrary to the dictates of right reason and to our true interest. If sinners would be governed and determined by these, they would soon become saints and would not go a step further in their sinful courses; where there is renewing grace there is no need of the bit and bridle of restraining grace.[2]

In these verses, do you see God seeking to change us? Too often, we want to pull away from God, but He shows us what that would mean. We would be leaving His direction and teaching, and we would be following our own rash way of doing things. Instead, we need to heed the instruction and counsel of God and see sin for what it really is.

Contrast (vv. 10-11)

As is so common, David writes a contrast as he closes this poem. However, in this case, he only writes one line on the negative side, then several on the positive side. When we consider again that this is a poem about being forgiven and the joy that forgiveness brings, that should not surprise us.

The negative line is short but clear: "Many are the sorrows of the wicked." When you peel back the glitz and glamour that often accompanies sin, you will find broken and sorrowful lives. They may look happy on the outside, but inside they are empty and breaking because they don't know where to turn, and they do not really have any deep answers for how to handle this life.

---

2. Matthew Henry, *A Commentary on the Whole Bible*, vol. 3 (World Bible Publishers, Iowa Falls, IA), 350.

Notice the contrast: "But steadfast love surrounds the one who trusts in the Lord." I love that word "surrounds." God's love is sure and steadfast, but it also is all around us. It is not just some unknowable entity that is more philosophical than real. God's love surrounds the one who is seeking after Him. Knowing that, David calls for praise as he ends the psalm. There are actually just two Hebrew words in v. 11 that are tied to the idea of joy. The phrase "shout for joy" is simply one for generic shouting in the Hebrew language. The other two words, however, build to a crescendo.

The first ("be glad") was a word that simply means to "exult" or "rejoice." It was a generic word, but one that cannot be anything but positive. The second ("rejoice") was a word that was even stronger and shows how wonderful forgiveness is. This was a word that meant that one was so filled with joy that he or she trembled or danced. It was a word that could mean "to leap with joy." That's what David wants others to feel. If they have sinned, he wants that depth of joy for their lives, but it only comes when God provides forgiveness.

Conclusion

There are many things in this life that bring us momentary happiness. Far fewer bring us real, deep, abiding joy. In this psalm, we see one of those things, and we who are Christians should be filled with joy every day of our lives. Like David, understand the joy that only comes when we know that God has said, "You are forgiven."

On February 18, 1990, I knew that forgiveness for the first time. Unfortunately, I have not always lived the way God would have me to live. Thanks be to the Lord, though, that He has forgiven me time and again, as I seek Him and try to walk in His ways. That joy is inexpressible, and it is that joy that you can know, if you will just allow God to forgive you through His plan of salvation.

Making the Most of My Measured Life

One of the more well-known phrases of the New Testament is from the pen of James when he wrote, "What is your life? For you are a mist that appears for a little time and then vanishes" (Jas. 4:14b). Job put it this way: "Man who is born of a woman [which is pretty much all of us!] is few of days and full of trouble" (Job 14:1).

When we are younger, we feel like we have all the time in the world. But as we grow older, we begin to realize the truth of verses like these from the Bible. Our life really is short. When we wrap our minds around that knowledge, it can cause us to go in one of two different directions. For some, it can be a type of wall that we hit, and we just give up. We don't have all that much time, so we'll just constantly play it safe and not really do anything. While we need to have a certain level of caution in our lives, God has never said that we are to be paralyzed by fear. He will not excuse laziness. At the other end of the spectrum is what seems to be happening in Psa. 39. It is taking the knowledge that life is short and using it as motivation to make the most of the time that we have. It is "redeeming the time," as Paul says in Eph. 5:19.

It's interesting that, in this psalm, David doesn't write about making the most of his time by skydiving, Rocky Mountain climbing, or going 2.7 seconds on a bull named Fu-Manchu. Instead, all of his thoughts have to do with making sure his life is in line with God's will. Often, when we talk about making the most of our days, we focus on doing some outlandish and over the top "bucket list" activity. While there's nothing necessarily wrong with that, we need to place our focus on getting our life right with the Lord and walking in that way. David's key phrase in this whole psalm is the beginning of v. 4: "O Lord, make me know my end and what is the measure of my days."

David wrote this very serious psalm with the intention that it be sung. The superscription states that it was "to the choirmaster," but then it states that this was "to Jeduthun." It is possible that this is the same Jeduthun mentioned in 1 Chron. 16:41. If so, he is mentioned in a section of Scripture dealing with the worship that took place before the Ark of the Covenant. After listing the priests, the text says in vv. 41-42: "With them were Heman and Jeduthun and the rest of those chosen and expressly named to give thanks to the Lord, for his steadfast love endures forever. Heman and Jeduthun had trumpets and cymbals for the music and instruments for sacred song."

In Psa. 39, we are likely reading one of those sacred songs for which Jeduthun was to prepare the music. The subject matter could not be any more important, as David writes about how to make the most of our time. If we follow the four major divisions in this poem, we will also be making the most of our days.

Controlling the Tongue (vv. 1-3)

David was seemingly reflecting on a difficult time in his life, but part of the resolve he made was to control his words. At the end of v. 1, he said he was going to hold his tongue "so long as the wicked are in my presence." Whatever his motivation, David's resolution to control his words was a very important one to make. He began by saying "I will guard my ways, that I may not sin with my tongue; I will guard my mouth with a muzzle."

In fact, David was so serious about this commitment that he wrote, " I was mute and silent" (v. 2) Now, at this point, David writes that this caused him "distress" ("sorrow," NASB), so we are not saying that one should remain completely silent at all times to be pleasing to the Lord. However, if we can make a positive application from David's words, it's that we should be in control of our words. David may have over-applied that and just not spoken at all, which lead to his heart becoming hot, and this fire burning in him (v. 3), but he at least recognized the great trouble words can cause.

Consider two points of application. First, and most obviously, we should always watch what we say, no matter the situation. James 3 compares our tongues to the rudder of a ship, a spark that causes a forest fire, and the bit in the mouth of a horse. Just like those small things control huge things, so our tongue is small in comparison to the whole of our body, but has a lot of control over what we are. Paul would tell us that our words need to always be "gracious" and "seasoned with salt" (Col. 4:16). There is, as Solomon stated, "a time to keep silence, and a time to speak" (Eccles. 3:7). While it may take great wisdom and patience to know when to speak and what to speak, we understand the importance of controlling our words.

For the second application, put these words back in the original context of the psalm. David was not just concerned with what to say, but who to say it to. He would not speak because of his enemies. It seems his concern was that his words would be twisted in a way that misrepresented what he felt or even what he said about God and righteousness. We have all been there and have wondered if it was worth it to speak at all. David realized that by not speaking, something even stronger was burning within him. We need to strike a balance of speaking the right things, and not holding our silence out of fear. We must measure our words and control what we say, but if others twist our words, we can rest assured we have spoken the truth.

If you want to make the most of your life, learn to control your tongue. Speak for the Lord. Speak truth, and also know when to be silent. Represent the Lord with what you say.

Counting the Time (vv. 4-6)

As David continues, he gets to the most well-known part of the Psalm where he writes about measuring our days. In context, David is writing out of the "burning" within him, but he shows a great deal of wisdom and faith because he turns to the Lord and asks for His direction in seeking to know the way of life. For most of this section of the Psalm, David uses seven very picturesque phrases to describe how short life is.

"My end." David writes in a very straightforward manner what few of us want to admit: life will end. But notice that David says "my end." David is not thinking about the whole of humanity at this point. Instead, he wants to consider that his own life will not go on forever. While that may not be a thought on which we want to dwell constantly, thinking about the simple fact that my life will not last forever on this earth is helpful at times.

"Measure of my days." Some translations have "extent of my days." The idea is that life is like a span; it has a definite beginning and a definite ending. By using this idea, David is saying that the measure is not long. It is just a span of time.

"How fleeting I am." I like the NASB which has, "How transient I am." David begins to express some veiled hope here because even though life on this earth is short, we are transient. There is another place to go after this life!

"A few handbreadths." In ancient times, most measurements were done by parts of the body. For example, a cubit was basically the distance from the elbow to the tip of the middle finger. David doesn't use the cubit to describe life. Instead, he uses the much shorter width of a hand. Jeremiah 52:21 speaks of the width of an object in

the temple being "four fingers," which is probably the handbreadth, meaning it was about three inches. Instead of thinking in long distances, David wanted to focus on his life as a much shorter measure.

"My lifetime is as nothing before you." David is not saying that his life was unimportant to God. Rather, he was still speaking in terms of time. Compared with an eternal God, the length of David's life was zero. If someone lives to be over 100 years of age, that is not even a blip on the radar screen when compared to the vastness of eternity.

"A mere breath." On a cold day, we might "see our breath." When we do, one of the things that stands out to us is how quickly that steam disappears from our view. David is stating that the same is true of our lives—just as a breath goes quickly, so does our life.

"As a shadow." The Hebrew word here (*tselem*) means "an empty image," so you have some interesting translations. The KJV has "vain shew." My favorite is the NASB which has "phantom." It is the same word translated as "image" in Gen. 1:26, where mankind is created in the "image" of God. No matter what one might be, David is writing that this life is just like a fleeting image. You can't even really see it when compared with eternity.

With those seven phrases behind him, David brings his main point into view. Speaking of the whole of humanity, he writes, "Surely for nothing they are in turmoil; man heaps up wealth and does not know who will gather!" These words sound like something Solomon wrote several times in the book of Ecclesiastes—that those who are rich live their whole lives accumulating stuff, only to leave it to someone else. David uses that same concept to describe the futility of spending this short life doing nothing but thinking of the earthly side of things. If all we ever do is consider the size of our 401(k) or how big a house we can buy, we are wasting this life that we know is brief.

If you want to make the most of your life, don't use the knowledge that life is short to focus on earthly wealth and piling up stuff for this life only. Instead, use that knowledge to focus on comparing your own life with eternity and the eternal God.

Confidence in God (vv. 7-11)

After stating that very important realization, David asks a powerful question in v. 7: "And now, O Lord, for what do I wait?" Eddie Cloer writes, "It became obvious to the psalmist that the purpose of life is not wealth, success, victory, freedom from persecution, or other temporary achievements. For the answer to this thorny question, one must return to the basic truth about life: Enduring hope comes from God Himself."[1] So, the powerful line comes: "My hope is in you." For the remainder of this section, David's words will reflect that one statement of confidence. Any hope that David had in this life or in the life to come rested in and upon God alone.

In fact, with that statement of confidence made, David speaks very openly to God. The key for us to notice is the faith and focus David has that (1) God is in control, and (2) David wants things to be right with the Lord. He does so in five ways in these verses.

Redemption. First, David asks God, "Deliver me from all my transgressions." Knowing that life is short, this request should also be first for us. When we realize the brevity of life, we should seek God's forgiveness. Notice, though, that David does not try to come up with his own way of salvation. His trust is in the Lord, and he asks for the deliverance of the Lord.

Reconciliation. "Do not make me the scorn of the fool" (or the foolish). Now that God has delivered David, he requests that his life be reconciled with his words. If I claim to be one thing in my words, but act in a completely different manner, even those who are foolish can notice the difference. I need to reconcile my actions with my words so that others are drawn, not to me, but to the One who redeemed me.

Recognition. Like he had done in v. 2, David states that he is not

---

1. Cloer, *Psalms 1-50*, 544.

speaking, but now it is for a different reason. As he has come to this place of forgiveness, David is speechless because he is in awe of the wonder of God's nature, especially of His forgiving nature. Spurgeon described it this way: "Here we have a nobler silence, purged of all sullenness, and sweetened with submission."[2] For some, the only response to the wonder of God's forgiveness is silent awe. Such was the case for David at this time.

Request. In v. 10, David makes a specific request for God to remove His "stroke" from him. Other translations have words like "plague" or "hostility." It is likely that this was some specific punishment or chastisement that God had brought into David's life for sin, and David is asking for it to be removed. We do not know if it was, but when we seek God's forgiveness, it is not wrong for us to request that the punishment that we have as a clear result of our sin be removed. God will not always remove it, but it is appropriate for us to make this request.

Restatement. Verse 11 is simply a restatement in summary of this entire psalm up to this point. God will punish, and it is difficult to deal with. The Lord's punishment is "like a moth," which consumes a garment and ruins it. David is stating that far too many know that punishment because they have not recognized the brevity of life and the One who holds that life in the palm of His hand.

As you read these verses again, notice the confidence David now has. He has been through some struggle in his life, but now that he is speaking to God and seeing life from God's perspective, there is clearly a confidence about him. We should have the same response when we are focused on making the most of every day to God's glory.

Coming to God (vv. 12-13)

From the point where he started, the psalmist has

---

2. Spurgeon, *Treasury of David*, 1.2.218.

traveled a great spiritual distance. In this learning process, he has become penitent, tearful, and understanding.[3]

As is so often the case, when we go through a difficult time and keep our focus on the Lord, we mature more than we ever dreamed possible. In many ways, that is what we see in these last two verses from the pen of David. The true maturity of these words is remarkable. In these two verses, David speaks of at least four things that show his maturity.

Prayer. One of the signs of true maturity is not just the ability, but the deep desire, to pray in the midst of any type of circumstances. David asks God to hear his prayer, to hear his cry. As we have said already in the psalms, and will say again, we know that God hears our prayers, but it is not wrong to request that He hear us. It demonstrates our humility in that we do not just presume that God will listen to us because we are something great, but that we desire a conversation with Him. Prayer is speaking to our Lord and shows great maturity.

Passion. David's request is "Hold not your peace at my tears!" Those who are mature are not afraid to show emotion. They are not fearful of being passionate and taking those emotions before God. Sometimes, we can act as if the spiritually mature one is the stoic one, the one who never cries or never gets angry. In fact, God created all our emotions and wants us to present them all before Him.

Perspective. At the end of v. 12, David reiterates what he has spent so much of this psalm talking about, stating that he is "a sojourner with [God]," and a "guest" on this earth. Notice, though, that David is not just speaking about the brevity of life, but now he is also claiming God owns it all, and we are just a guest in this life. Whatever experience David had had that led to writing this psalm, it led him to realize that he was not the answer; God was. Often, we come

---

3. Cloer, *Psalms 1-50*, 545-546.

to that same perspective when we are in the crucible of suffering.

Peace. It may seem strange for someone to request that God look away from him or her. We often think of people wanting God to look upon them, but David is writing about the punishment that has underlined much of this psalm already. He is stating again that he does not want that any longer. Instead, he wants to "smile again" before this life is over. In other words, David's desire is to rebuild full fellowship with the Lord because that is what truly brings a smile to his face.

Look at those four things again: prayer, passion, perspective, and peace. Those may not be what our world says are characteristics of a mature person, but we know differently. Having these things will help us continue to mature through any difficulty that may come in this life, but only those who are seeking the way of God will know to turn to these things in the midst of strife.

Conclusion

When it's time to think about how short life is, how will you consider numbering your days? Will you consider spiritual maturity and making every moment one where you are maturing into what God would have you to be? Or will you just think about filling some type of earthly bucket list?

David shows us how to make the most of our days, but it took some bad circumstances for him to come to that place of maturity. Let's learn from his mistake and begin making the most of our days now, so that we are growing closer to the Lord and His will every day of our lives.

Satisfying a Longing Soul

PSALM 42

Oh give thanks to the Lord, for He is good, for His steadfast love endures forever! ... Let them thank the Lord for His steadfast love, for His wondrous works to the children of men! For He satisfies the longing soul, and the hungry soul He fills with good things.

Psa. 107:1, 8-9

C an you imagine being near water while nearly dying of thirst, and not being able to get to that life-giving water? That scenario happened in 2006 to a man named Dave Buschow. He and eleven others were on a survival trail and were dealing with brutal temperatures. The difficulty of the trail, as well as the high heat, led him to the point of hallucinations. At one point, he was so overtaken with thirst that he mistook a tree for a fellow traveler.

Finally, after going more than ten hours without water, he collapsed and died with his face down in the dirt. The 29-year-old man was only about 100 yards from a cave with water in it. More tragically, though, was the shocking fact that his guides had emergency water packs on them, but refused to give them to the travelers. As CBS News reported: "Buschow wasn't told that, and he wasn't offered any [water]. The guides did not want him to fail the $3,175 course.

They wanted him to dig deep, push himself beyond his known limits, and make it to the cave on his own."[1]

That type of story shocks us (as well it should), but it also shows us the desperation for water that builds within us. In Psa. 42, we have a poem of desperation penned by the Sons of Korah. This psalm, along with ten others (44-49, 84-85, 87-88), carry that designation. Korah and his descendants, the Korahites, were in charge of worship at the temple, so it would seem logical that these psalms were penned specifically for usage in the temple.

Although we are not reading the words of David in this psalm, we are still reading the words of people who have hearts that run the full range of emotions. In our psalm, the writers are hurting. They are "cast down" (vv. 5, 6, 11) and taunted (v. 7), but their hope remains strong in the Lord. How can I be sure that I remain strong in the Lord? That's the emphasis of this poem.

Dependence (vv. 1-4)

Using the picture of an animal seeking what it most needs, the poet describes how seriously and strongly his desire is for God. The word translated "pants" in this passage is found only one other time in the Old Testament. In Joel 1:20, the word is used of animals that are searching after a time of famine. Verses 19-20 of that chapter say: "To you, O Lord, I call. For fire has devoured the pastures of the wilderness, and flame has burned all the trees of the field. Even the beasts of the field pant for you because the water brooks are dried up, and fire has devoured the pastures of the wilderness." That's the same word and concept as we see in Psa. 42. The writer's soul is parched without the God of heaven and is longing to find Him.

Specifically, we are told at the end of v. 2 that the writer wants to appear before God. This phrase was commonly used of those who

---

1. http://www.cbsnews.com/news/hiker-dies-of-thirst-with-water-all-around.

would present themselves at the tabernacle and, later, the temple to worship the Lord. Could it be that the poet has been through something that had led to where he could not come before God in the tabernacle? If so, this tells us a great deal about how our anticipation for worship should be! When we are not able to worship, it should cause a thirstiness in our soul that is impossible to quench without coming near to God.

In fact, the desire to worship was so intense that the writer states, "My tears have been my food day and night" (v. 3). I need to ask a very poignant question at this point. How many of us, when something else comes up, will miss worship and soothe ourselves with a TV show or our kids' ballgame? This writer wanted so deeply to worship God that tears filled his eyes constantly at the thought of missing the opportunity to come before the Lord. That needs to be the state of my heart when I must miss! If I miss an opportunity to worship and brush it off as no big deal, that says more about my heart than I want it to. Also, note that others knew the heart of the poet since they were making fun of him, shouting, "Where is your God?" If God really cared about him, couldn't (or wouldn't) He make a way for this man to return to the temple to worship? Would anyone make fun of you for how you react to missing worship?

I also want us to notice something that we have noted a few times already in the psalms, that these poets are not afraid to take anything before God's throne. Here we have an example of a poet stating specifically what his enemies are saying to him, taunting him. While God knows what is going on in our lives and what is being said to us, it is still right for us to take everything before His throne, even the specifics of what people say. It shows a dependence upon God because we are willing to take everything before Him.

As the poet rehearses these things in his mind, he writes in v. 4: "These things I remember as I pour out my soul: how I would go with the throng and lead them in procession to the house of God with glad shouts and songs of praise, a multitude keeping festival." Notice that the writer is not just saying this was a mental exercise; something on the back burner of his mind. Instead, he writes that these thoughts came to him as he poured out his soul. These were deeply emotional thoughts to him, and they revolved around worship and praising God. When that was gone, he had lost a type of lifeline.

I am reminded of so many Christians who feel this same way. Especially later in life, many have health issues that preclude them from being able to come before God in worship. When you talk with them, they will always reflect on that thought. They want to be at worship more than anything. And the reason is simple: they have come to the place where they are truly dependent upon God, and they want to be in His presence.

Do I long to be with God in that same fashion? Does my soul pant for being near Him? Do I desire to worship Him more than I desire anything else? My actions will speak louder than my words.

Desolation (vv. 5-11a)

As the writer continues, he shares the condition that all this has left him in. While he is not leaving God (that will become abundantly clear in the last lines of the psalm), he is feeling desolate. He is hurting and expresses that hurt to the Lord. His opening question, "Why are you cast down, O my soul?" truly sets the mood for where his heart is. The Hebrew word translated "cast down" also means to be in despair, humbled, or weakened. That's why the follow-up question is, "Why are you in turmoil within me?" The situation of not being near the temple is causing inner turmoil to the poet. His soul is hurting by this absence.

Thankfully, he writes that he is not leaving the Lord. He gives himself a little pep talk by saying, "Hope in God; for I shall again praise him, my salvation and my God." Look at the power of those simple words. What is motivating the poet as he is in a set of bad circumstances? It is the hope of being able to be in God's presence again for worship.

What a strong statement of faith in the Lord! Does that motivate me? I dare say that some of us go to the other end of the spectrum. When we are traveling on vacation, we make excuses not to worship because we are taking time for ourselves. How that stands in stark contrast to the heart of this poet! Although he is writing a very personal poem, we see the motivation of his soul is to worship God. It should also be our motivation at all times.

Using the picture of a "cast down" soul again, the writer turns to his memory of being near God. At the end of v. 6, he states that he will remember the Lord "from the land of Jordan and of Hermon, from Mount Mizar." The listing of these three places tells us that he was probably from the region of Dan. In New Testament times, this area would be known as Caesarea Philippi. In that region, the Jordan River begins its descent from the base of Mount Hermon. Sometimes, "Hermon" is used of a small mountain range, and sometimes it is used of the principal peak in that range. The other mountain named here, Mount Mizar, is unknown to us. The name means "little," and it was probably a small hill or minor mountain in the Hermon range, maybe one that was close to the home of the poet.

The writer is trying to make the point that, although he is away from all he knows, he will remember the Lord as if he were sitting right at home because he has known the Lord all along. What a powerful statement by one who is desolate!

Verse 7 contains an interesting phrase: "Deep calls to deep at the roar of your waterfalls." Following that up, the poet continues with the nautical language and gives us a slight explanation for his words: "All your breakers and your waves have gone over me." He is writing that the sorrow he feels is washing over him like waves in the deepest depths of the ocean. His pain is that strong and deep from this apparent separation from the Lord. However, we need to note here that the author is overstating things. He is probably doing so for poetic effect, but by saying "all" concerning what God would do, that just was not true. Only the Son of God himself could ever claim to have the fullness of the wrath of God upon Him. Still, the writer states what we feel at times. It can feel as if everything, including God Himself, is against us.

Despite these feelings, the psalmist is going to trust in the Lord. Verse 8 needs to be engrained in all our souls because it shows a tremendous amount of trust in the Lord. Using the picture of the daytime, the psalmist is writing about times when things are going well in life, when life has fewer difficulties. In context, he is probably using this to mean those times when he is able to go back to Jerusalem to worship. Let's be honest—at those times, it is quite easy to hold to our faith in God and to state our trust in all He does.

On the other end of the spectrum, the poet writes of the night, and even then the song of the Lord is with him. Because God has brought the writer through so many daytimes, the memory of those times will help him through the nighttimes in life. The song of the Lord will remain throughout all times in life. How can the poet write that? Look at the last line of v. 8: "A prayer to the God of my life." The Lord is not just the Lord of good times. He is the God of all life. No matter what we might face, God is still in control. As the songwriter put it, "The God of the good times is still God in the bad times / The God of the day is still God of the night."

Even though the poet knows this, the pain of the moment is quite real. His faith is still in God, but the writer states that it is as if the Lord has left him. The enemies of the poet are pressing in on him, and it feels as if the Lord has left him in the moment. The taunting of the enemies is so strong that it is as if they have given "a deadly wound in my bones" (v. 10). Again, the taunt is given to the writer, "Where is your God?"

If we are honest, we would each have to admit that we have felt that way at times. We have gone through a series of negative circumstances, and maybe that was coupled with others questioning our faith, and we struggled to really see God through those times. Maybe we doubted the Lord, like the poet is doing here. He hasn't left his faith, but there are serious questions in his mind, and the taunts of his enemies only added to the difficulty he faced.

As he began v. 11, he asked the same questions he had in v. 5: "Why are you cast down, O my soul, and why are you in turmoil against me?" Have you ever felt like that? Have you ever felt separated from the Lord? Have others ever taunted you because you stood for the truth and their taunts started to have a very serious and real effect on you? Have you ever, like this poet, felt desolate or separated from God?

We all have at times. And, may I remind you that even Jesus Himself went through a time where He asked His Father, "Why have you forsaken me?" We have all cried something like that to God the Father in a moment of trial. What is the answer for those times of extreme desolation? The answer has already been stated in the psalm, but the writer also ends with it.

Desire (v. 11b)

Just as the writer asks the same questions at the beginning of v. 11 as he had back in v. 5, so he also writes the same answer: "Hope in God; for I shall again praise Him, my salvation and my God."

How do we make it through a time when we feel desolate? It started back in v. 1 and concludes here in v. 11. Our soul desires to be with God and hopes that we will be near Him.

Of course, we should never wait until there is a downturn in our circumstances before we try to draw near to God. But if our desire is always to be near the Lord, we can make it through the negative times in life because we know there will be brighter days coming.

Conclusion

As we close our look at this psalm, I want to take a moment to give you a quick outline that I think shares some points of application for us. This outline from Eddie Cloer, summarizes well how this "panting" for the Lord demonstrates itself.

- *"He yearned for God deeply."* At times, the poet writes as if he would die without the Lord. Is that true of us?

- *"He yearned for God continually."* Through both daytime and nighttime, there was a continual longing for the Lord and using that as motivation for when faith was wavering.

- *"He yearned for God with resolve."* His yearning was not just to sit back and let life happen. Instead, it was to worship God again and not to let his enemies push him down any more than they already had.[2]

I need to ask myself: Do I yearn for God—panting for Him—in just the same way? Only He can bring satisfaction for my longing soul.

---

2. Cloer, *Psalms 1-50*, 594-95.

God: The Fortress

PSALM 46

At least eighty English versions exist of Martin Luther's hymn, "A Mighty Fortress is Our God." Translations can be tricky anyway, but especially when something is so vividly written. It is nearly impossible to find a word-for-word translation of this hymn based on Psa. 46.

In this hymn, Luther writes about the struggle mankind has with Satan, but the struggles can be overcome since God is our place of refuge. One version of this hymn appeared in the Pennsylvanian Lutheran Church Book of 1868 and begins:

> A mighty fortress is our God,
> A trusty Shield and Weapon;
> He helps us free from every need,
> That hath us now o'ertaken.

> Thomas Carlyle translated the opening lines this way:
> A safe stronghold our God is still,
> A trusty shield and weapon;
> He'll help us clear from all the ill
> That hath us now o'ertaken.[1]

Whatever Luther's original words were, his point was clear and represented well the powerful words of the sons of Korah in Psa.

---

1. Morgan, *Then Sings My Soul*, 15.

46. Meant to be sung, the superscription is clear, as it ends with the simple words "A song." Interestingly, part of the superscription is "According to Alamoth." That word means "damsels," and may indicate that this was a song that ladies were to sing, or that this song was at least to be sung in a higher pitch. When we sing songs a bit higher, it often sounds brighter, more confident, and more cheerful. That spirit is alive and well in Psa. 46.

God's Presence (vv. 1-3)

This psalm was likely written after Jerusalem had been miraculously rescued from the Assyrian King Sennacherib in 2 Kings 18-19. 185,000 soldiers were killed simply by the power and providence of God, and the people of Jerusalem went from famine and fear to abundance and strength.

We may never see anything quite so dramatic in our lives, but we can still know God's help when we go through times of great trial. By speaking of "trouble" (v. 1) and the accompanying pictures in vv. 2-3, the writer is acknowledging that struggle is part of life.

But where is God when all those bad things are occurring? He is "a very present help." In fact, v. 1 describes three things about God that can help us when trouble comes our way.

He is our Place to Go. God is our refuge. The song asks, "Where could I go but to the Lord?" Of course, that hymn is meant to be rhetorical because we must always press toward God no matter what might be going on around us. Whenever trouble comes, God is the place to go.

He is the Power in which we can Grow. The poet writes that God is also our strength. The Hebrew term *'az* is also one that was sometimes used to describe boldness. In times of trouble, we can find boldness in God and have our strength rebuilt when we are hurting. We can grow in Him, maturing along the way, no matter what might be going on around us.

He is a Presence to Know. God is "a very present help" when those times of trouble come. Literally, the Hebrew phrase can say that God "is found swiftly." Sometimes, we struggle to find someone to help when we are going through struggles, but we can swiftly find God because He is very present. He never leaves us (cf. Heb. 13:5), so in times of trouble, His presence needs to be where we turn.

The remainder of vv. 2-3 give great reassurance because there is nothing that can change that would take us away from God. Not anything in the earth, the mountains, or the sea can move us from the presence of the Lord. The poet is making it clear that trouble is a real part of life, and sometimes those troubles are great and strong. It can seem as if the whole world is shaking beneath our feet. Still, we will not fear in those times because God is near. He is ever-present, and nothing can change that.

God's Protection (vv. 4-7)

In vv. 4-7, the sons of Korah rehearse much the same idea as they opened the poem with, but the picture moves from the trouble without to the protection of God that surrounds His people. Each of the four verses speaks to the protecting nature of God.

Verse 4 uses Streams. Some suggest this river was one that ran through Jerusalem. While that may be the case, the poet is using this picture to put on display the protection of God. Nourishment comes from what God does for His people. Note that, in contrast with what our world tells us, those who are near God are glad.

Verse 5 uses Sunrise. In the midst of this city—the people of God—He is there and "will help her when morning dawns." If this psalm was written in the aftermath of the slaughtering of the Assyrian army, it had happened very early in the morning, and this may reference that event. Even if it doesn't, the picture is unmistakable that God will allow suffering, but the suffering will not last forever. There comes a morning, and God is there.

Verse 6 uses Speech. In vv. 1-3, the psalmist had written about all these awful circumstances as if the earth was shifting and shaking. Now, the writer comes back to the picture and states that God is more powerful than any of it. Every nation and kingdom is unstable, and when God "utters His voice, the earth melts." Anything that stands against God's people will not stand forever because God is controlling it all, and merely His voice can and will change it.

Verse 7 uses a Stronghold. Returning to the picture of God as a refuge, the psalmist makes a slightly stronger statement now by saying that God "is our fortress." No enemy can besiege or overrun this fortress, either. Considering that the fortress is God Himself, nothing can overrun it.

Considering these four verses, where would we ever want to run for protection but to the God of heaven? He is stronger than any and every nation and provides protection from them for His people. He has stated He is able and willing to help, so why would we seek protection from anyone or anything else? When we come to God for protection, we are a part of that city filled with those who are glad.

God's Power (vv. 8-9)

If those reading this psalm did not already have reason enough to trust in God, the writer takes them back to their memory. They would have already seen the work of God, and the writer makes sure they compare God to the world's armies.

In Psa. 20:7, David wrote, "Some trust in chariots and some in horses, but we trust in the name of the Lord our God." In our psalm, the sons of Korah are trying to get their readers to do just that. Instead of thinking of the fearsome armies of men, consider the proof of what God has already done through the ages in comparison.

- Of course, we could go back to the Red Sea and consider that God, in one action, brought that army completely to its knees by drowning horse and rider in that sea.

- We could think of Jericho and how the people of Israel simply walked around that well-fortified city and won a victory by faith in God.

- We could call to mind that later in the days of Joshua, God rained down hail on a battlefield, and the hail killed more than the Israelite army killed with the sword (Josh. 10:11).

- We could go to the days of Deborah and remember the amazing victory she led against seemingly impossible odds.

- We could look at Gideon's 300 men, who wiped out an entire army without really firing a shot.

- We could consider David and how he knew it was God who gave him the victory over the trained giant Goliath.

In nearly every battle scene throughout the pages of Scripture, God's people were the underdogs, if we evaluate things only from an earthly standpoint. They were nearly always outnumbered, and most of the time they were also at a major disadvantage in training and weaponry. But they were not the underdogs because they had God on their side, and that made all the difference. When His people were faithful, God brought about amazing victories that could not be explained by simple human reasoning.

If this song was penned in the aftermath of the destruction of the Assyrian army, we have another example of that. Without Israel firing a shot, 185,000 members of the army died in the night just outside the city of Jerusalem, which they planned to overtake. Instead, the few who remained just left, and the city was untouched.

Before leaving this section, notice the emphasis of v. 9. The text does not say that God's people do certain things. Instead, the sons of Korah write that God "makes wars cease," that God "breaks the bow and shatters the spear," and that God "burns the chariots with fire." The emphasis is fully upon God and His power. While warfare is not pleasant to consider, God can even use it to show His sovereignty. At times, His people have been triumphant in warfare over an evil nation. At other times, evil nations have been used by God through warfare to punish those who claimed to be God's people (think of the book of Habakkuk). But no matter how it is used, it is all focused upon God and His power, which never wanes.

God's Place (vv. 10-11)

As the poet begins the final two verses, he says something that may seem like a sharp contrast to what he has just written, but that is the point. He has just written about warfare, which is loud, powerful, and boisterous. And in the midst of that, God says to "be still" because only then will we realize that He is God. I want to camp here for just a moment to make a point of application. Notice that there are two commands here. The first is "be still," and the second is "know that I am God," but the two are clearly connected. May I suggest that one reason we have lost God in our world is that we are so rarely still? We always have to be busy and have something to occupy our minds. We are stimulated constantly by a barrage of images, words, sounds, and experiences, and it almost seems as if quietness and stillness are sins in our society.

However, God states that when we are still, we will realize that He is God. We need to find time to let our mind rest and consider the world around us. We need to take time away from the boisterous nature of our society if we want to really think about God and know that He is God, that we are not our own gods. God's place is secure whether I recognize it or not. After commanding us to "be still" and know that He is God, we read these powerful words: "I will be exalted among the nations, I will be exalted in the earth!" Note the certainty of that statement. This is not a "maybe" or "could be" statement. It is a "this will happen" statement.

The KJV states that God will be exalted among the "heathen" instead of "nations." That is a possible translation, but it may be more interpretation than translation. The Hebrew word here (*gowy*) simply means "nations." It was sometimes used by the Jews to speak of other nations, but the word itself just means nations in general.

I bring up this distinction because it is easy to look at this statement and think that this is a verse of vengeance against those who are not followers of God. However, God will be exalted among all people. Again, if this poem was written in the aftermath of the Assyrian army being destroyed by God, one of the major effects of that victory was that the people in Jerusalem—God's people—saw His power and exalted Him. God will be exalted among all nations, and sometimes even His own people need a wakeup call to exalt Him.

God's place is on high, but His place is also near. Verse 11 contains a simple but beautiful phrase: "The Lord of hosts is with us." The description "the Lord of hosts" is perfect for this psalm. *Jehovah-tsaba* literally means, "the Almighty over that which goes out." *Tsaba* was often used for an army that was sent out to warfare. The writer is saying that all these wars he has been writing about are under the control of the mighty hand of God. He is the Lord of everyone who goes out. However, God doesn't leave when the army does. Though the army may go out, God "is with us." Somehow, the omnipresent God is able to be over the armies as they march out to war and still be at home with those who are there. He is with His people wherever they may happen to be.

To tie it all together, the writer ends by building upon how he started the psalm. In v. 1, he said, "God is our refuge and strength," and now, as he ends, he states, "The God of Jacob is our fortress."

God's place is exalted, but also near. It is a place where we can go. Since God is near, we don't have to go far when wars erupt in our lives. We simply go to the One who is near, and He is our fortress. He is our place of protection through any struggle we might face.

Conclusion

Jesus said it as clearly as it can be said: "In the world you will have tribulation" (John 16:33). Some may say, "But Jesus was speaking to the apostles." That's true, but the message continued through the apostles. Peter told his readers, "Beloved, do not be surprised at the fiery trial when it comes upon you to test you, as though something strange were happening to you" (1 Pet. 4:12). Paul wrote, "Indeed, all who desire to live a godly life in Christ Jesus will be persecuted" (2 Tim. 3:12). Life for the follower of Christ is not always going to be easy. It's a life of joy, but there will be times of warfare throughout our life. Where can we go? "Be still and know that I am God." God states that we need to just slow down and realize that He is in control and that nothing surprises Him.

Martin Luther didn't just write one verse to his hymn based on Psa. 46. He understood the power that was behind not just the psalm, but the God who is praised in this psalm. So in a later verse, Luther penned:

> And though this world with devils filled,
> Should threaten to undo us,
> We will not fear, for God hath willed,
> His truth to triumph through us.

I love those lines because they reflect the later part of Psalm 46. When everything is in turmoil, let your mind reflect on the fact that God has already promised that He will be victorious. The only real question will be, "Am I on His side?"

Godly Sorrow Produces Repentance

PSALM 51

> Now in the eighteenth year of King Jeroboam the son of Nebat, Abijam began to reign over Judah. He reigned for three years in Jerusalem. His mother's name was Maacah the daughter of Abishalom. And he walked in all the sins that his father did before him, and his heart was not wholly true to the Lord his God, as the heart of David his father. Nevertheless, for David's sake the Lord his God gave him a lamp in Jerusalem, setting up his son after him, and establishing Jerusalem, because David did what was right in the eyes of the Lord and did not turn aside from anything that He commanded him all the days of his life.
>
> 1 Kings 15:1-5

O h, how I wish that were the end of that sentence, but the inspired writer of 1 Kings added these sobering words: "except in the matter of Uriah the Hittite" (v. 5). David's life is one that is filled with glorious moments, and he is a true biblical hero. However, when we say that, there is always a "but" we must add to the sentence because the Bible does not give us a sugar-coated picture of its heroes. Even the great King David, the most beloved of all the kings of Israel, had that moment when he lusted after Bathsheba and tried to cover it up by having her husband killed. It is nothing short of a vile and sordid account in the biblical record, one that we wish were not there. But it is a powerful reminder of the allure of temptation and the insanity of trying to cover up our evil ways.

In His providence, God sent Nathan to confront the king with this sin, and David's heart was broken. In his sorrow, he wrote the words of Psa. 51 in which we see something both powerful and important. Read the psalm carefully, and you will not see David sorrowful because he got caught. You will see the New Testament truism come to life: "Godly sorrow produces repentance" (2 Cor. 7:10 NKJV).

In David's sorrow, we see a poem that puts on full display what repentance really looks like. In this chapter, we are going to examine Psa. 51 and see that repentance. But before we look at David's words, we need to ask ourselves this question: When I am confronted with my own sin, will my heart be like David's? Will I be sorry I got caught, or will my heart break because I have sinned against the God of heaven? If I am to show true repentance, my heart needs to be like David's in this very penitent psalm.

A Penitent Appeal (vv. 1-2)

While you will see first person pronouns (like "I" and "me") throughout the psalm, it is obvious that David realizes God is really in control. He comes right out at the beginning, asking God to grant forgiveness. We must note that this is an appeal, not a demand. David's request is based upon God's character. Specifically, David appeals to two very important parts of God's character.

"Steadfast love" translates the Hebrew word *chesed*. This word, which simply means "full goodness," is so much a trait of God that David himself elsewhere wrote, "[God] is my steadfast love" (Psa. 144:2). This same word is translated as "mercy" in the KJV some 149 times and has to do with the idea of patient goodness.

"Abundant mercy" ("tender mercies," KJV) comes from the Hebrew word *racham*, which also could be used to describe the womb of a mother. It was a very intimate word that shows someone holding another person near and not letting that person go. Based on these two traits of God, David makes four requests:

"Have mercy" (v. 1). This phrase could literally be translated "show pity on me." David is penitent, begging for God to look down upon him and show him pity.

"Blot out my transgressions" (v. 1). Some translations have the singular (transgression) here, but the Hebrew word is plural. David is using a very strong word when he says "blot out." In fact, the same Hebrew word is found in Gen. 6:7 where God saw the evil of Noah's day and said, "I will destroy man whom I have created from the face of the earth" (KJV, ASV). The word literally means "obliterate." David is not just seeking for his sin to be pushed to the back burner. He is asking God to remove it completely from His record.

"Wash me thoroughly from my iniquity" (v. 2). The word for iniquity is *avon*, which means "perversity." I want us to get this: David did not downplay his sin as just some small thing. When he realized what he had done, he described it as perversion. That is what sin is. It is taking what God has given us and perverting it, and we need to call every sin a perversion, not just some sins we consider to be more out of bounds. David's request was that these perversions be made clean by the soap of a fuller.

"Cleanse me from my sin" (v. 2). This request may seem almost like a summary statement, but David is asking God to make him clean of the things that have made him filthy. When we sin, we need to realize that we are unclean before the holiness of God, and only that perfectly holy God can make us clean again.

When I realize my sin, I need to ask myself if I have the same viewpoint as David did. This was not just some small matter that needed to be attended to. It is an appeal made to God for total cleansing that only God could provide.

A Personal Admission (vv. 3-6)

Verses 3-6 of Psa. 51 contain the most controversial verse in the poem (v. 5), but too often we get so caught up in the controversy that we miss the simple fact that David is pouring out his soul in a very personal way before the throne of God.

David begins by making a straightforward statement: "I know my transgressions." Those words may seem simple, but look at what David is admitting in that short statement.

- There is such a thing as a standard, and that standard can be violated. It is impossible to transgress a law or standard that does not exist in the first place.

- David has violated that standard. How often do we try to act as if there is a standard, but we have not violated it? Paul would make it plain: "All have sinned, and fall short of the glory of God" (Rom. 3:23). Am I willing to really admit that?

- Sin is personal. David did not write, "I know there is sin in the world." Instead, he wrote, "I know my sin." Yes, I need to be concerned about sin in the lives of others, and I need to do all I can to help them come to the light. But I also need to avoid the "log that is in [my] own eye" (Matt. 7:3). When I have sin, I need to realize it for what it is: *mine*.

The line in this psalm that I think we need to impress in our minds when we consider repentance is this one: "My sin is ever before me." David is not just feeling guilt (although he certainly is); he is haunted by what sin is. "His contrition for his sin was not a slight sudden passion, but an abiding grief."[1]

Verse 4 shows how "godly sorrow produces repentance," in that David describes this myriad of sins as being against God, and God

---

1. Henry, *Commentary*, 430.

alone. Various lists could be given to show all those whom David had sinned against (Bathsheba, the nation, Uriah, the army, etc.), but David realizes that sin is a very personal thing with the Lord. In the end, every sin—whether public or private, big or small—is a sin against God in a personal way.

This realization also led David to a deeper understanding of God, and David says God will be justified when He speaks and blameless when He judges. Whatever punishment or retribution is given to David because of this sin will be merited because God is holy and righteous. And notice that this punishment would be justified, even though David is repenting of the sin. There are still consequences for sin, and David knows that God is just and right in meting out punishment when such is necessary.

The personal nature of this admission of David comes to its climax in the most controversial verse in the psalm, as David writes, "Behold, I was brought forth in iniquity, and in sin did my mother conceive me" (v. 5). To borrow an old expression, this is a "sugar stick" passage for those who hold to Calvinism and want to teach that we are born sinners. This doctrine is called "total (or hereditary) depravity," and it means that we inherit sin from our parents just like we inherit eye color or our basic frame.

That is not what David was intending in these words. For one thing, David is writing a poem filled with symbolic language. Did he really expect God to use "hyssop" in the cleansing process (v. 7)? Did God really break David's bones (v. 8)? Of course not. David was stating that his sin was so great that it was as if everything around him, even since the beginning of his life, had been sinful. We still talk that way and use hyperbole. "Everything has gone wrong today," we might state. Well, it may have been a terrible day, but not every single thing has gone wrong.

When we get caught up on the controversy, we miss David's heart that was yearning for some good to come into his life. This sin is that personal to him, and he is a man pleading for forgiveness in the midst of hurting from guilt and realization.

David also states that the personal nature of sin does not start with the action. God desires "truth in the inward being," and so David asks God to make sure he has the Lord's wisdom in his "secret heart." Some of us need to get this point in our lives. Sin does not start with an action; it starts in the heart. Jesus would make this abundantly clear in the Sermon on the Mount, where He would speak of murder and how it actually begins with hatred (Matt. 5:21-22), as well as adultery and how that starts with lust (5:27-28).

We cannot harbor secret sins and still be considered holy before God. Additionally, if we want to act right before the Lord, it starts by getting our heart right with the Lord. I need to fill my heart with holiness, goodness, and love. If I do, those are the things that will flow forth in my actions.

We must make sure, as David did in these verses (and throughout the psalm) that we realize the personal nature of sin. This is between me and God, and my sin will ruin my relationship with Him and my soul for eternity, so I need to get my heart right with Him.

A Powerful Application (vv. 7-12)

After making his admission of sin, David then again asks for forgiveness from the Lord. In this section, David opens with a bit more poetic language than he had used in vv. 1-2. He makes it clear once again that it is only God who can provide the forgiveness David desires, but he speaks in a very interesting way. For that forgiveness to occur, David asks God in two symbolic ways to remove the sin.

The first is to be purged with hyssop. The hyssop plant was an herb, but it was most commonly used as something which applied other things. The hyssop plant was dipped in something and then used to either sprinkle or brush that against what needed to be ceremonially cleansed. In one example in Lev. 14, hyssop was to be used as part of the ceremony to show that a leper was cleansed (vv. 1-32). David was using that imagery to show that he desired God to cleanse him just like others were shown to be clean. In fact, the word translated "purge" (or "purify") meant that one was pronounced completely clean.

The second image is that of washing and becoming whiter than snow. Again, David is using images from ceremonial cleansing. For someone to be pronounced clean under the law, they not only had to repent, but they often had to wash their clothes so that nothing defiling was associated with them any longer. David is not taking that upon himself, however. He is asking God to do the washing because only then can he be truly clean.

If God would do that for David, he knows what awaits him: "Let me hear joy and gladness." When we are living in sin and guilt is part of our lives, it is hard—if not impossible—to have true joy. David's imagery speaks to how God has broken his bones. David is basically saying that his whole being is affected by this sin and its guilt. There is always a nagging at our conscience when we are involved in sin. If we are forgiven, though, our conscience is free to find great joy in what God has provided.

From vv. 9-12, David piles line upon line of what forgiveness would mean to him and what he desires the Lord to do. In these verses, there are at least eight statements. Note these dos and don'ts that David is begging of God.

1. **Do Rebuild.** David asks God to hide His face from the sins David has committed. Sin separates us from God (Isa. 59:2), but God can rebuild that relationship through forgiveness.

2. **Do Remove.** We have already seen this imagery (v. 1) where David asks God to completely remove the sins by obliterating them from the record book.

3. **Do Refashion.** David's heart had not been clean, but now he asks God to refashion his heart into one that is. God is the only one who can do this type of creating, as this is the same Hebrew word (*bara*) that is found in Gen. 1:1: "In the beginning God created the heavens and the earth." The same power that created everything with just His word can recreate a heart that is clean and pure from one that had been impure.

4. **Do Renew.** David asks God to "renew a right (or steadfast) spirit within" him. David is not one who was outside the realm of God's people. He was one of God's children, but he fell into serious sin. His heart had been right, but it had also been overtaken by sin. He wants God to renew that good heart—that good spirit—he had before.

5. **Do Restore.** I love the first line of v. 12; not only does it talk about joy, but it shows that salvation belongs to the Lord and in that is joy. Salvation is God's alone to give, but when He grants it and we are forgiven, joy should fill our lives!

6. **Do Reenergize.** Having been restored, then, David asks God to "uphold" (or "sustain") him with a willing spirit. There will be a new energy to David as he is now walking closely with the Lord and has his spirit within him.

In looking at the dos, we skipped v. 11, where the don'ts are found. Note them:

1. **Do Not Desert Me.** In an earlier psalm, David had written that only "the upright shall behold [God's] face" (11:7). That presence meant so much to David, but now in his sin, he felt separated from the presence of God. He pleads with God to remain near, so that he could know that fellowship with God now and behold God's face later.

2. **Do Not Discard Me.** We do not know how much those

in the Old Testament knew about the Holy Spirit, but we do know that David had seen God's Spirit removed from the life of King Saul (1 Sam. 16:13-14), and now he feels the same could happen to him on a permanent basis if this sin is not forgiven. Such was too much for David to contemplate.

Though David had sinned, I think we see in these words a heart that was longing for God. He wants God's full application of forgiveness; David realizes what he has done and what that sin has done to his relationship with the Lord.

A Proving Action (vv. 13-17)

About 1,000 years after this poem was written, another inspired man, John the Baptist, would say to those around him, "Bear fruit in keeping with repentance" (Matt. 3:8). To be pure, repentance must be accompanied by actions that prove our lives are different. David spends the rest of this psalm showing that he realizes just that, both personally and nationally. In vv. 13-17, he writes of it personally. In at least three ways, David writes about what he is going to do.

Words of Teaching. Notice that v. 13 starts with the word "then." David trusts that God will grant this forgiveness because David knows the nature of the Lord. However, when the Lord forgives, David is not going to sit back and do nothing. He is going to "teach transgressors" the ways of God. Just as David had transgression in his life (v. 1), so do others, and David wants to teach what God has done for him. Do we?

Words of Turning. "Sinners will return to you." David had sin (v. 2), but he was turning back to God. Now, he wanted to tell others how to do the same. David wanted to be so clear in what he taught that he promised others would turn to the Lord from the error of their ways. When God forgives me, do I use that as motivation to teach anyone else how to turn to Him?

Words of Tribute. In v. 14, David says he "will sing aloud" about the righteousness of God, and in v. 15, he says his "mouth will declare" the praise of the Lord. But that is true only because David realizes God will have forgiven him of an awful sin, one David calls "blood guiltiness." He had one of his best men killed, but God will forgive that if one's heart is right. We may look at that and think, "Well, I never did anything that bad." But sin is sin. My sin was an affront to a perfectly holy God, and I deserve great punishment for my sins. When I realize that God has forgiven me, how can I help but sing His praise and declare how wonderful the Lord is!

To summarize this thought, David writes words that should echo in our minds when we think of what God desires. Does the Lord want us to do the right things? Of course He does, or He would not have commands for us in Scripture from beginning to end. But the Lord looks at our heart and wants us to live as He would require. Spurgeon summarized vv. 16-17 with these beautiful words:

> A heart crushed is a fragrant heart. Men condemn those who are contemptible in their own eyes, but the Lord seeth not as man seeth. He despises what men esteem, and values that which they despise. Never yet has God spurned a lowly, weeping penitent, and never will He while God is love, and while Jesus is called the man who receiveth sinners. Bullocks and rams He desires not, but contrite hearts He seeks after.[2]

I think some of the most powerful words we ever sing are, "Is thy heart right with God?" It must start with my heart and attitude, or I am not being pleasing to the Lord. David clearly shows us that, for true repentance to occur, it must be accompanied by actions that

---

2. Spurgeon, *Treasury of David*, 1.2.407.

are fruits of repentance.

A Prominent Assertion (vv. 18-19)

To close out the poem, David turns from the personal to the national. It is clear David is still writing about forgiveness, but he turns finally to what this could mean for Jerusalem and Israel. David was the king of a nation, and with this awakening in his spirit, he wants to use that position to pray for his nation and for what it would mean if God again showed His favor to Israel.

Some have suggested that these final two verses were added later, since they speak of the walls of Jerusalem being built, and there is no indication that the walls around the city were in any way compromised during the rule of David. That is possible, but it is also possible that David was just using that imagery (remember we are dealing with poetry) of security, which walls provided. God had been hard on the nation of Israel due to David's sin, so their security was hurting. David is asking God to return that security as He forgives a penitent king.

We are calling these last two verses "a prominent assertion" because of the words David uses to end this psalm. If God will shine His face upon the nation again, David makes the bold assertion that worship will be restored.

Conclusion

And with that thought, we also want to end, but notice the journey this psalm has led us on and what it means for our lives. This psalm began with David begging for God's forgiveness from a broken heart. Where does it end? Worship. That is a journey we do not need to take lightly. When we are forgiven of our sin by the holy God of heaven, it should lead us to pure, joy-filled, and unceasing worship.

We do not deserve either the forgiveness of God or the opportunity to honor Him through worship. However, in His grace and mercy, He grants both to us, and one should naturally lead to deepening the meaning of the other.

Deliverance from Every Trouble

PSALM 54

Mentioned along with the cities of Maon, Carmel, and Jutah in Josh. 15:55, the city of Ziph was a town in the hill country of Judah. We don't know a lot about it, but it seems to have been a fairly important part of the kingdom of Saul, the first king of Israel. One way we know that is that twice the people of Ziph tried to hand David over to Saul (1 Sam 23, 26). We are not told which of these two times serves as the background for Psa. 54, but it seems as though the first fits slightly better. In the superscription of the psalm, we are told these words were written "When the Ziphites went and told Saul, 'Is not David hiding among us?'" That question is asked by these people in 1 Sam. 23:19, and they assured Saul that they would make David surrender to the king. Saul blessed them and told them to go.

In the remainder of 1 Sam. 23-24, David gained the advantage to the point that he actually spared the life of King Saul out of respect for him being God's anointed king. Though David was in the right in this account, the simple fact that he was on the run shows us where he was in life. He was a fugitive from the king, but through all the running and hiding, David kept his eyes firmly fixed on God. That is not to say that David was always strong. Of course, he was frightened at times. But his faith remained in God, so he could pen words like the ones found in this brief psalm.

Throughout the years, some in the Christian world have taken the words of Psa. 54 and applied them to various writings and sermons about the events in the final week leading up to Jesus' crucifixion. Since some of the themes of this psalm clearly play out in the trial and death of Jesus, that is a possible use of these Old Testament words. However, I think to do that robs the psalm's personal message. This was not a Messianic psalm; David was not trying to write about the future. Instead, he was writing something very personal about his own life and how God had been with him throughout.

We need words like this when enemies surround us. It may not be an army trying to turn us in, but God's people have enemies who wish to see us fail. They certainly wish to see us "turned over" to the dark ways of Satan, and we need words like these to help us keep our eyes firmly fixed on God. As we walk through this psalm, never let your mind wander from how David's trust in the Lord is clear and strong.

Supplication (vv. 1-2)

As so many of the psalms do, this one opens with a prayer. In fact, the entire psalm is a prayer meant to be sung. The opening words make it clear that this prayer was one that came from the depth of David's soul. David prays for three things:

Salvation. Calling on God, David prays that God will save him by His name. The word David chose for "save" was one often used in battle. It was a word that meant "to liberate." David is speaking of a literal battle, but he knows that, even in physical warfare, it is only God who is ultimately in control and can bring about liberation.

Vindication. Several translations (e.g., KJV) use the word "judge" here instead of "vindicate." That is probably a better translation, as David simply chose a common word for judging. The implication is clear in that David wants God to realize his innocence in spite of what enemies around him are saying. That is why the ESV and other translations have "vindicate." The idea here is more of "justice" than of judging, at least as far as David's intention is concerned.

Attention. In two ways, David asks God to grant him attention. "Hear my prayer" is the first, and "give ear to the words of my mouth" is the second. Speaking of prayer, Spurgeon said, "This has ever been the defense of saints."[1] David uses parallelism here to show the fervent nature of his desire. It was common for Hebrew writers to say the same thing in two different ways to indicate emphasis. David, to use our modern terminology, is pleading with God to hear what he has to say in this poem.

In Phil. 4, Paul would tell New Testament Christians that their prayers also needed to be "supplications." That Greek word (*deesis*) means to "entreat," and Thayer suggests that it means we ask God about a particular matter.[2] That is exactly what we see David showing us as he opens Psa. 54. He is entreating God—giving a supplication—over a particular matter. In the next verse, we learn what that matter is.

Struggle (v. 3)

David's problem is with "strangers." The Hebrew word here was one that came from an Arabic term that meant "to turn from the way" and then to lodge at someone's house. That is important in this discussion because David is not writing about some random stranger; he is writing about people who have turned from the way of God. They are not just strangers to David—in other words, these are not just people unknown to David's contact list. These people are strangers to God; they are against the Lord. The Ziphites were not strangers in the sense that they should not have been in the land.

---

1. Spurgeon, *Treasury of David*, 1.2.440.

2. John Henry Thayer, *A Greek-English Lexicon of the New Testament* (Grand Rapids: Baker, 1977), 126.

They were part of the nation, but they were strangers in how they acted. For no good reason, they had decided to remain faithful to Saul despite his sin, instead of accepting God's plan and following David's ascension to the throne. David writes that these are the types of people who "have risen against" him and "seek [his] life." Matthew Henry summarizes well these enemies:

> They were very formidable and threatening; they not only hated [David] and wished him ill, but they rose up against him in a body, joining their power to do him a mischief. They were very spiteful and malicious. ... They hunt for the precious life; no less will satisfy them.[3]

You may not have people literally seeking your life, but if you were to look at this description poetically, does it not sound like what we sometimes face as the people of God? There are people who seek us and would like nothing more than to end our ways.

David points out the root of it all as he ends v. 3: "They do not set God before themselves." When we boil it down, that is the basis for evil that runs this far, just as it had with those seeking David. Why would they not want to save alive the one who would one day ascend the throne? Because David was God's anointed, and these people did not have God before them.

When we do not put God before us, we will find ourselves doing the same things. We may not literally seek someone's life, but we may seek to defame someone's character, or we may want to exact a brutal retaliation on someone. We need God before us to restrain us from what we would do if we were to have our own way all the time. And what is true individually is true in any context—"Righteousness exalts a nation" wrote Solomon (Prov. 14:34). We can safely deduce then, that a nation that forgets God will run into awful practices that

---

3. Henry, *Commentary*, 440.

are not worthy of exaltation. The same is true of a business or even a congregation. But at this point, David is thinking of himself because his struggle is against a godless enemy who wanted only to kill him.

Sustaining (vv. 4-5)

After a pause (*selah*), David begins to write great words of trust, which will be his focus for the remaining verses of this poem. In vv. 4-5, David writes about the sustaining nature of God by talking about who God is, then what God does.

Who God is (v. 4). If you ever need fresh ways to express the wonderful nature of God, take the time to read Psalms. These poets write so many beautiful descriptions of God and His nature. This verse is no different. In it, David shares two simple but beautiful descriptions of the Lord.

1. ***Helper.*** Here David is facing enemies who want nothing more than to destroy him. Where could he turn? He goes to where there is help—to God. The Hebrew word here is a generic one for "help" or "support," but some suggest that the word was sometimes used of a girder, which helped to hold up a building. If that's the case, then you have a very natural connection to the other description of God in this verse.

2. ***Upholder.*** The word here was one that carried with it the idea of laying something on something else for support. You can see now why I pointed out the idea of a girder in the other phrase. The KJV and other translations put the emphasis of this phrase on other people ("The Lord is with them that uphold my soul"), but that is not necessary from the original language. God is the one who, whether by Himself or through others, upholds our life. In the midst of this great struggle, David needed to remind himself of that and rest on that great character trait of the Lord.

What God does (v. 5). God does countless things, but David's focus here is on how the Lord deals with those who oppose the righteous. David writes with a great deal of certainty: "He will return the evil to my enemies." The word "enemies" is very interesting. It came from a word that was originally used to picture putting multiple strings together to make a rope. As it takes more and more tension and work, the rope gets harder and stronger. The idea, then, is that these people are harder and harder to deal with. Thus, they are enemies.

God knows that, and He is in control of the whole situation. God sees the evil that has been done, and David writes that the Lord will return that evil upon these people. Specifically, David even asks God to "put an end" to these evildoers. Cloer summarizes v. 5 very well: "In God's regard for what is right—His 'faithfulness'—He will not allow such conduct to pass by without justice being served. God has promised His people protection, and David believes that He will keep that promise. God cannot, he believes, be false to His word."[4] When we reflect on the nature of God and how the Lord is ultimately in control, I just wonder if our heart is calm and staid as David's. It was not just true literally, but also in a calming sense, that the Lord sustained the life of David. That needs to be true of us as well.

Sacrifice (v. 6)

Such a realization should always lead God's people to praise the Lord, and David states just that in v. 6. This is not one of the required offerings of the Law, but David writes that he will bring an offering willingly. Maybe the most famous example of one of these offerings is back in Exod. 35-36, where the tabernacle was about to be built. Moses told the people to bring what they desired to help with the building of the tabernacle. Exodus 35:29 states, "All the men and women, the people of Israel, whose heart moved them to bring

---

4. Cloer, *Psalms 51-100*, 61.

anything for the work that the Lord had commanded by Moses to be done brought it as a freewill offering to the Lord." Exodus 36:3 tells us that the people kept bringing these offerings freely every morning.

That is the type of heart that David is displaying in our psalm. It is spontaneous and comes from a time of great joy in praise to the Lord. But what is David going to do? He is going to bring this sacrifice "to give thanks to [the] name" of the Lord, "for it is good." There really is nothing deep or difficult to understand about David's words here, but there is a deep point of application we need to make for ourselves.

Am I ever moved so much by the goodness and nature of God that I am motivated to worship Him "just because"? David didn't wait for one of the annual feasts, nor was this offering one of the required ones. We often think we have to wait until Sunday to bring our praise to the Lord. That should not be the way our mind works. God's name is always good, and we see His handiwork around us at all times. When we do, it should inspire us to bring Him an offering of worship wherever we may find ourselves.

Salvation (v. 7)

As is so often the case in the Psalms, the poem builds to the major reason for praise. David's words in v. 7 are words of deliverance, of salvation. But I love that David steps back just a bit from the historical setting and writes, "For He has delivered me from every trouble." God did not just deliver David from the Ziphites. God had delivered David time and again, and it is powerful that David recognized that in his life.

Throughout his life, David had seen God deliver him from enemies. Of course, we could think most famously of his battle with the giant Goliath, but there are many others. As David reflects on that, he states "my eye has looked in triumph on my enemies." We might word it this way: "I've seen this play out before, and God has always helped me win." So why wouldn't David trust and praise God in his current circumstances?

It may not be a literal army we face, but any triumph we have is due to the power and deliverance of God. We need to look back over our lives and see where He has guided and delivered us, and let that be a strong motivation for our lives each time we face another enemy and struggle.

Conclusion

If we are correct about the historical context of this psalm, David is quite alone (especially compared to the many who would be his helpers and aides as king). He is facing a formidable foe who is out to get him. He is a fugitive. Everything, it would seem, was against him. However, his trust in God is strong and provides us with a powerful reminder of how we can have our faith in the Lord no matter who or what might stand against us. As he closed his writings on this psalm, Spurgeon wrote these beautiful words: "In closing, let us trust that if we are friendless as this man of God, we may resort to prayer as he did, exercise the like faith, and find ourselves ere long singing the same joyous hymn of praise."[5]

When trouble comes, even when it seems as if enemies surround you, let your mind reflect on God, your helper and upholder. Lean on His mighty arm. Praise Him and trust Him. He has delivered you in the past, and He will do so again.

---

5. Spurgeon, *Treasury of David*, 1.2.442.

The King's Prayer

C an you imagine being the king of an entire nation? While many monarchs throughout the years have been quite evil, just imagine for a moment the tremendous pressure brought on by being the leader of a nation. Even if you do not care all that much for your subjects, you still must have the understanding that everything you do and every decision you make reflects the reputation and future of the nation.

While not a king, the same is true for leaders of other nations, such as our own presidents. Whether you agree with a particular president's views or decisions, the office is worthy of admiration. If for no other reason, this is true because of the tremendous pressure of holding that office and of how decisions made today will affect the entire nation for any number of years.

Understanding that pressure, Abraham Lincoln once said this: "I have been driven many times upon my knees by the overwhelming conviction that I had nowhere else to go. My own wisdom and that of all about me seemed insufficient for that day." You and I may not know the same type of pressure that Lincoln, another president, or any monarch may feel, but we can all relate to the emotion behind his words.

David surely knew that same pressure. While we know a lot about David from the biblical record, there is no way for the Bible to convey to us the day-to-day tension and pressure that David (or any other king, for that matter) must have felt just from the responsibility of sitting in such a position of power.

However, we do get an idea, especially from some of the Psalms, of David's heart in handling this pressure. As just one example, I think that comes across in Psa. 61. Of course, David made plenty of mistakes as king, but his heart regularly returned to God and longed to be right in the sight of the Lord. That heart comes across clearly in this psalm. While brief, David prays words that show a longing for the Lord to look after his life and his reign.

You and I may not be kings or queens of a nation, but we all feel great responsibilities in our life, and we know the constant pressure that comes from that. Maybe these words can be adapted into our own lives, and we can know better how to pray when we are struggling with handling our responsibilities.

A Prayer of Pain (vv. 1-2a)

David begins by describing the pressure he is under, as he asks God to hear his "cry." The word here was one that was filled with great emotion. It was a word that could be used of one who was crying out in extreme pain or of one who was shouting with joy. That is the way David describes what he wants to take before God's throne, but it is also described as a simple "prayer." Please notice: it is not wrong to be emotional—even extremely so—in prayer.

David's situation is bad enough that he describes it as being at the "ends of the earth." We are not told in the psalm when this poem was written, but it is possible that David penned these words after Absalom had rebelled, and David fled to the place called Mehanaim. If that is the case, he was not a huge distance away from Jerusalem, but for David it was far enough! Just to be away from what he knew was like being banished to the ends of the earth.

It is also possible that David was simply writing this phrase as one that expressed his feelings. Emotionally, something had occurred that made David feel as if he was at the end of the earth and desperate for the protection of the Lord.

Whatever the situation, David writes that his "heart is faint." I believe the KJV does a better job here in using the word "overwhelmed." The Hebrew word *ataph* does mean "faint" or "weary," but it also means "to envelop" or "cover." David is saying that it is as if some situation is enveloping him, and he is fainting under the pressure of it all.

A Prayer of Protection (vv. 2b-4)

With that as the background, David makes his requests for God to protect him. The first, at the end of v. 2, reads, "Lead me to the rock that is higher than I." That one phrase has been used over and again throughout the years in hymns, poems, and even funeral addresses to provide words of comfort. But what was David actually requesting? The phrase could also be translated "a rock that is too high for me" (Amplified Bible). While perhaps not as poetically beautiful, we might be able to grasp that a little better.

Whatever David's situation, he realizes that the protection he needs is more than he could ever do on his own. This may seem obvious, but I think it needs to be said: If a king, with all the resources available to him, realized that he could not protect himself without the help of God, how much more do I need to pray this prayer!

Erastus Johnson was not a king, but he knew he needed to have the same feelings as David. So in 1873, he penned these words:

> O sometimes the shadows are deep,
> And rough seems the path to the goal;
> And sorrows, how often they sweep
> Like tempests down over the soul.

O then to the Rock let me fly,
To the Rock that is higher than I;
O then to the Rock let me fly,
To the Rock that is higher than I.

David's prayer is not one of blind faith. In v. 4, David states that God has provided for him in the past. God has been a refuge and a tower to David; two descriptions that are very common in the Psalms.

Way back in Exodus 14, as the people of Israel were preparing to cross the Red Sea, God instructed them every step of the way. In Exod. 14:2, God said to Moses, "Tell the people of Israel to turn back and encamp in front of Pi-hahiroth, between Migdol and the sea, in front of Baal-Zephon; you shall encamp facing it." Why there? God said in v. 3 that Pharaoh would think that the people were trapped in the wilderness. Of course, the Red Sea itself would be a major part of that, but so would these places. One of them named there is Migdol, which is a word that was used of a well-fortified city or castle that had towers. Guess what word is used in Psa. 61:4? God is a strong *migdol* against the enemy! He is well-fortified, and the idea of a tower means He is able to see enemies and provide perfect protection. It is no wonder, then, that David continues with more pictures of God's protection and writes of his desire to be under the protection of God forever. Verse 4 contains two pictures of God's protection that David is seeking.

The first is of a tent. Some have suggested David had the tabernacle specifically in mind. That is certainly possible, but it is not a necessary conclusion to draw from his words. He simply wants to be where God is, and David pictures that as a dwelling place so that he can know where it is and go there. If David is literally enduring a period of wandering, this image would be more significant since he would desire a level of welcome and not just a place to be. He is seeking the welcome and hospitality of God during a time of great strain.

The other picture of protection is that of wings. Of course, David is picturing here the hen protecting her chicks under her wings. Hens don't have to think about doing that protective act; they do it by natural instinct. So it is with God protecting His people. It is part of who He is. Jesus would use this same image as the desire of His heart for Jerusalem when He wept over that city (Matt. 23:37).

Putting the images of a tent and wings together, Matthew Henry writes, "Those that have found God a shelter to them ought still to have recourse to Him in all their straits. This advantage those have that abide in God's tabernacle, that in the time of trouble He shall hide them there."[1] When the pressures of this life seem to be too much for you, remember these words of David. Remember how God has protected you in the past and go to Him, seeking His wonderful protection again.

A Prayer of Perspective (v. 5)

After pausing to reflect (*selah*), David returns to his memory (as he had in v. 3). In v. 5, David again writes about how God has been his helper in the past, and this memory serves as a type of anchor for David in this time of struggle. The words of v. 5 also serve as the transition point in the psalm, as David will use what he writes here to transition from writing for himself to writing about himself. All of that is built on the perspective of memory that David uses here. David uses two memories to provide his perspective.

Hearing. David says to God, "You have heard my vows." The Hebrew word translated "heard" (*shama*) is actually stronger than just taking something in through the ears. In fact, every parent will understand this because the word can also mean "respond to." How often have you asked your children, "Did you hear me?" when you knew they took in the words you had said. But had they really heard you? There is no way to tell unless there was a response. David is saying

------

1. Henry, *Commentary*, 463.

that about God. In some way, David knows that God has heard vows David had made in the past because God responded to them. We do not know what specific vows or what specific responses David had in mind here, but that does not detract from the emphasis David is drawing. It had been clear in the past that God had heard his words, and the king is drawing on that in a statement of confidence that God will also hear the words of this poem.

Heritage. The remainder of v. 5 is a powerful statement of trust, especially considering that David is going through a time of struggle. "You have given me the heritage of those who fear your name." Instead of "heritage," you could put the word "inheritance." David knew the blessing of being part of the people of God, and part of that blessing—a major part—was the ability to draw near to the Lord, no matter what might be going on around him. While even those who refused the way of God inherited Canaan, those who trusted and followed God knew this great inheritance that David is writing about in a special and full way.

Sometimes, it takes a struggle to give us perspective like David shares in these words. We may not be evicted from our home as he was, but we may experience a time when our heart is breaking or our emotions are completely on edge. It could be a time of tremendous stress. Whatever it is, these times can be used by the Lord to remind us of what He has done for us and can help us build our perspective of faith.

A Prayer of Preservation (vv. 6-7)

Using the perspective he just wrote about, David begins to write in the third person as if he were a citizen in the kingdom. The words of vv. 6-7 may have been things the citizens were saying, or they may just be the desired result David himself was seeking, whether anyone else was or not. The words of these two verses are very powerful, as David prays for preservation. But notice the lack of selfishness. David writes about two kinds of preservation in these verses.

First, David seeks self-preservation. While at first glance the entire section may look as if David were writing only about his own life, that is only part of what he is seeking. It is not wrong for David to ask for God to preserve his life, especially considering the terrible difficulty David is in. The word "prolong" can literally be translated "days upon days," and this was something David had prayed for and received. In Psa. 21:4, David wrote, "He asked life of you; you gave it to him, length of days forever and ever." So David is reiterating that same concept in these words, but there is more on his mind.

David also seeks sovereign preservation. "May his years endure to all generations" begins this part of the request, which really runs through v. 7 as well. There is no way David could fulfill this request personally, but he could seek for his throne to continue and to do so in faithfulness to the Lord. It would be difficult to imagine a monarch not wanting to either have a natural heir or being able to choose his/her heir to the throne. That is what David is seeking here, but notice that David is not just seeking that for some type of selfish reason. Look at the end of verse 7: "Appoint steadfast love and faithfulness to watch over him!" David seeks that in his own life, but he is also asking it for the future. Whoever sits on the throne after David, the desire of this king's heart is that God continues to watch over and show faithfulness to him.

I want you to think about the balance of this part of the prayer and how it could have a dramatic impact on your life when you go through a season of struggle. Is it wrong to pray for yourself and to ask God to help you through some time of difficulty? Of course not! But one of the best ways to make it through a time of struggle is to do your best to think of others. It may not be your children (or it may be), but consider how God can help, not only you, but others who struggle in ways similar to you. Pray prayers of preservation for others who are struggling (or will struggle) with what you are going through.

A Prayer of Praise (v. 8)

It doesn't surprise us in the least that David ends this poem with words of praise. Though David is going through a time of great struggle, his perspective is right, and that always brings us to words of praise. These final words in v. 8 are words of both joy and trust, which seem to naturally go together. Take them in reverse order.

David ends by saying that he is going to vow daily to the Lord. We are not told exactly what David has in mind as far as the specifics of these vows, but the words of this psalm have to give us some indication that they are going to be vows of trust. He is going to promise daily to stay near the Lord and, likely, to lead others to do the same. The New Testament does not tell us that we have to make some type of formal vow, but we are told to be a "living sacrifice" to the Lord (Rom. 12:2), so we should constantly be making sincere vows to the Lord of how we are going to live.

Along with those vows, David is going to "sing praises" to the name of the Lord. When we follow the Lord wholeheartedly, we are filled with joy. While we may not audibly sing praises, our mind is filled with praise for the One who has helped us over and over. Writing about this verse as a whole, Eddie Cloer does a great job in summarizing the intent of David:

> Out of gratitude for what God had done for him and for His people, David wants to thank Him joyfully. He considers the exalting of God in praise as part of his daily walk with Him. He wants the exaltation of God to be a dominate part of his personality in this life as he looks with anticipation toward the next.[2]

---

2. Cloer, *Psalms 51-100,* 183.

Conclusion

When you have come to the end of yourself, where will you turn? Lincoln stated that he realized he needed to go to his knees in prayer because there was nowhere else to turn. Too often, we are driven away from God by the pressures of life, instead of taking a moment to remember what God has already done for us. Take a few moments to seek the rock, the refuge, the tower, the tent, and the sheltering wings of God. Chances are, you have known His protection before in your life if you will just remember it.

Why not seek God and return there again?

The Great Commission in Psalms

PSALM 67

Four consecutive psalms (65-68) carry the superscription note, "A song." The first three are all words of praise, virtually from beginning to end. And why not! God is certainly worthy of all the praise and adoration we could ever give to Him and more. What sets Psa. 67 apart is an emphasis not often seen in the literature of the Old Testament. The story of the Old Testament is clearly one that is focused on the chosen people of God, the Jews, under the Law of Moses. From the call of Abram in Gen. 12, the scope of the Bible narrows to Israel because it is that nation that would prepare the way for the coming Messiah.

However, for brief glimpses we are reminded that God was still sovereign over all nations, and He was also calling them to repent of sin and praise Him. Maybe the clearest example of this is the book of Jonah where there is no real indication of anything "Jewish." The prophet is sent to Nineveh and preaches a strong message of repentance to that city, leading to just that result. There are nearly countless lessons from that book, but one message we must never fail to see is that God was calling people other than the Jews to Him.

Often in the Psalms, we see the term "nations," and it is used in a way that is almost "anti-God." It is often used as a term to speak of those who are against the ways of God, as opposed to those who were living righteously under the Old Testament Law. However, that was not always the case, and Psa. 67 is one of the clearest examples of that in this entire book of poetry. Some seven times in this seven-verse poem, various terms (including "nations") are used to describe those who are not Israelites.

But this is not a poem of condemnation. In this psalm, the poet is calling for everyone on the earth to praise the Lord. While that result may not occur, should that not be our desire as well? Too often, it is easy for us to get caught up in our own culture (or even our own congregation) and fail to look around the world at nations and peoples who need the Lord.

Jesus, however, had a worldwide vision for His people. Before ascending into heaven, He told His followers, "Go therefore and make disciples of all nations" (Matt. 28:19). Did you see it? *All* nations. Through that prism, we need to look at the world. Every person, no matter his nationality, is in need of the saving message of Christ. But we can continue to press forward with that message, and we must. Summarizing the emphasis of this psalm, Eddie Cloer wrote,

> ...One truth that this psalm advocates is that God's love in Old Testament times was not confined to Israel alone. People who have been knitted together in communities by whatever bond are all within the writer's prayer. He sees all people as being under God's kingship. He declares that the world beyond Israel had not been left orphaned. God loves all nations and seeks their conversion to Himself. Israel, the people who knew God, were to make Him known to every nation.[1]

With that mindset, consider this Old Testament version of the Great Commission.

---

1. Cloer, *Psalms 51-100*, 276.

Radiance (v. 1)

In many ways, the first verse is the "what," and the remainder of the psalm is the "so what." The "what" of Psa. 67 is the glory of God, while the rest of the psalm will share what comes when we recognize God's majesty.

One of the most well-known passages in the book of Numbers was a blessing given by Aaron. The first high priest said, "The Lord bless you and keep you; the Lord make His face to shine upon you and be gracious to you; the Lord lift up His countenance upon you and give you peace" (6:24-26). David, it seems, is drawing from that beautiful blessing to speak of how wonderful God is. In doing so, David makes three requests:

Be gracious to us. Anyone who thinks the Old Testament is nothing but law, and that grace is reserved for the New Testament, has failed to spend serious time in the Old Testament. While we may see grace mentioned more in the New Testament, and while the ultimate example of it is in Christ, grace was often expressed under the Law of Moses. David is seeking from God a gift that is undeserved and that only God can give. As a lover of the Lord, David knew God would answer this request because God is always gracious, giving to His people what we do not deserve.

Bless us. While speaking of grace, the poet probably also has in mind the provision God gives. We know "every good gift and every perfect gift is from above, coming down from the Father of lights" (Jas. 1:17), but it is not sinful or foolish to pray continually for those good blessings. Some blessings may be physical, but we know that many are spiritual or, at the very least, subtle.

Make His face to shine upon us. In the original Hebrew, the word "shine" is not found, so the phrase is basically "Let light from your face be with us." The emphasis is on the grace and blessings of God to remain with His people continually. "The sunshine of His face would be daily encouragement and comfort for the people."[2]

It is only fitting that this is one place where the poet states we should pause (*selah*). When we consider the grace and provision of God, and that He gives these continually, how can we help but pause and stand in awe of Him? The words of v. 1 need to fill our minds because they reflect the majesty of God, but they also show our complete dependence on Him for anything good in our lives.

Reason (vv. 2-5)

With the knowledge of the radiance and majesty of God in mind, the poet spends the middle verses of this psalm sharing some reasons why people should praise the Lord and come to know His glory.

This section of the poem (vv. 2-5) is interesting in that one verse is repeated, word-for-word, twice. Verse 3 and 5 are exactly the same, calling for the praise of God. However, when we consider these reasons that point us to God and His glory, the call to praise should not be overly surprising. At least five qualities of God are shown in these verses that should give us the desire to lift Him up in praise.

Leadership. The poet writes, "That Your way may be known on earth" (v. 2). We might think of this phrase this way: the psalmist wants people to walk the same path as the Lord. Of course, David had written that this path is not always easy or even well-lit (cf. Psa. 23:4), but the way of God is always right. God leads where we need to go, and our prayer should be that of this psalmist—that all the earth would know and walk that way.

Saving power. The KJV translates this phrase as "saving health" (v. 2) because the idea here is that of all the delivering acts of God. The poet does not just have spiritual or eternal salvation in mind. Instead, the psalmist wants people to understand that God is able to deliver from any and all trouble for His people. Why, then, would

---

2. Ibid., 277.

we not want people around the world to come to the knowledge of God? After all, only He could alleviate all our struggles if we would just trust and obey.

Joy. One of the common themes of Psalms is that of joy in the Lord. But here, the psalmist is calling for "the nations" to know that gladness and joy (v. 4). This is not just a personal joy being expressed; rather, it is a call for all people to know the joy that only comes from following God. By the way, if we would follow the way of God (v. 2) along with all people, there would always be joy!

Justice. One of the great qualities of the Lord is His justice, which the psalmist here calls "equity" (v. 4). We will study psalms later in this book that deal more directly with God's justice, but we should understand at this point that God's judgment is worthy of our praise because it is the only justice that is true justice. It is perfect, and the Lord never misses evidence or changes the standard.

Guidance. Circling back to the idea of leadership, the poet writes that God would "guide (govern, KJV) the nations upon the earth" (v. 4). We listed this as a fifth trait of God, but of course it continues the picture of leadership found in v. 2. God's leadership is perfect guidance. Tied to the idea of justice found earlier in the verse, Cloer writes,

> These nations would be happy to have God as their Judge. He would not be the One who condemns them; but He would be their Leader, Guide, Sovereign, and Sustainer. They believed that He would rule with a just and faithful government. He is the only One who could save, rule, and sustain them; therefore, He alone could bring them happiness.[3]

When we put those five qualities together, we can see why the poet calls twice for the people to praise the Lord. Any one of these traits of our Lord would be enough to cause us to want to praise

---

3. Ibid., 279.

Him, but taken together, they should make us be filled with wonder at His majesty. Again, notice the emphasis on these things being done by all peoples and nations. The Lord is not just the leader of a small and select group. Our goal should be to have all people around the world to know and love these perfect qualities that are only found in the Lord our God!

Respect (vv. 6-7)

To close out this great psalm of praise, the poet speaks to what God has done and how that should lead people around the world to respect the Lord. The example given by the psalmist is that of the "increase" that "the earth has yielded." Since the poet says that God "*shall* bless us" (notice the future tense), he is pointing out the consistent goodness of the Lord. Year after year, the people had eaten of the harvest provided by the ground. When in a proper mindset, they knew that this harvest came about because God is faithful and good.

Others must have seen that as well, so the cry goes out, "Let all the ends of the earth fear Him!" The idea is that the entire world should come to know the goodness of the Lord and respect Him because He is faithful. No one is left out of this call. God is worthy of the respect of all peoples in all lands.

Conclusion

God has certainly been good to His people, but do we have the same heart and mindset as this psalmist? We are commanded to "preach the Gospel" around the world, doing so in all nations (Matt. 28:19-20; Mark 16:15-16). I find it sad, not just that we often fail to obey that command, but that we even need such a command! God has been faithful and loving to us. He has shown us Himself through the matchless life and sacrifice of Jesus Christ. We know the salvation that only comes through what Jesus did for us on the cross. How could we help but share that message? Why would we ever withhold that great love and sacrifice from anyone?

The same radiance God had in the Old Testament accompanies Him today. The same attributes the psalmist wrote of are part of the eternal nature of God. The nations need to hear, but for that to happen, we must be willing to tell.

Finding Peace in God's Judgment

A braham asked one of the greatest questions in the Bible. As he was bargaining with God over the city of Sodom, he asked, "Shall not the Judge of all the earth do what is just?" (Gen. 18:25). I'm certain Abraham was asking that question in all sincerity since he did not know how this situation was going to turn out. When you and I read those words, knowing the fullness of Scripture (coupled with personal experience), we read it in a rhetorical way. We think, "Of course, God will do what is right. His judgments are always perfect."

But when we really stop to consider God's judgment, it can cause us a bit of struggle. We don't like to think of what the judgment of God can imply. We like to think of God giving rewards and blessing those who have done what is right. But we know that implies that there are those who have not done what is right, and it brings to our mind the very important reminder that there will be punishment for those opposed to God. When we really stop to think of that, it can be difficult to consider.

Psalm 75 is one of the many poems in this book of which we are uncertain when it was written. In other words, we don't know the specific Bible story that provides the context for these words. However, it is of interest that we know something of how this poem was meant to be sung. In the superscription, we are told that this psalm was one to the choirmaster, and then we have the note "According to do not destroy." Three other psalms (57, 58, 59) also contain that notation, but the words "according to" have been added by the translators. What it seems is that "Do not destroy" (or, literally, "Destroy not") was a tune at that time to which these words could be sung.

Whatever Asaph (the poet here) had in mind, so far as the circumstances of writing, this poem clearly concerns the judgment of God. This poem is different from others in that it seems to be written from different perspectives, all speaking about the same thing. There are some words of the people, some words of God, and some words by the poet. We will use those three divisions to provide our outline for Psa. 75 as we consider how we can find peace in the judgment of God.

The Shouting of Grateful People (v. 1)

Some suggest that v. 1 implies that the people of God had not been able to praise God for some time as they would like. Twice in this one verse they state, "We give thanks," which is a Hebrew word that can also be translated, "We confess." This idea is given more clearly when the people state, "For your name is near." While we do not know the historical setting for these words, just this simple reminder in v. 1 should impress on us the importance of gratitude. There are times when it can seem as though God's name is far from us, not necessarily because of our own sin, but just because of other circumstances. However, when we are reminded again of the greatness of the name of God, it should lead us to deep-seated praise.

The final line of v. 1 is likely mistranslated in the ESV. There is a footnote that accurately tells us that it should read, "They recount your wondrous deeds." Some other translations have "Men recount (or declare)." The idea here is one of praise because God has shown Himself in power to people who were not His people.

There are times when those who are against God cannot deny His power and presence. They turn and speak the deeds of God, even if they do not give Him full credit for what has been done.

The knowledge that others are now considering the acts of God and bringing to mind the name of God should always make us a grateful people. God is always near, whether we recognize it or not. But when we do recognize it, we should always be grateful to Him and express it as we see here. With that singular verse behind us, the speaker in the psalm changes to the Lord Himself.

The Sovereignty of God's Power (vv. 2-5)

In vv. 2-3, God Himself sets forth words of great power. In some ways, these words are the Lord giving us a short version of His résumé, proving Himself to be the One who is able to judge. In these verses, notice the emphasis on how the Lord is always the One in control. You see that in at least three ways.

First, God speaks of His perfect timing. "At the set time that I appoint, I will judge." One of the most difficult things for us to grasp about God is His timing. Most of the time, He operates on a much slower timetable than we do. We are rushed for the simple reason that we are bound by time. We know we only have a short time here, and each part of our life seems even shorter, so we struggle to trust the Lord when He delays (as we see it). But God claims that He will set an appointed time to judge. In context, He is saying this about judging a nation or a people, not just the final judgment. While it may seem late to us, it is just right for the overall plans of God.

Second, God speaks of His fairness. He will judge "with equity." This ties back into the question that we opened with, when Abraham asked God, "Shall not the Judge of all the earth do what is right?" Here's the problem: what we consider to be right or fair is often not. God, however, is perfect. He is the only One who is capable of making perfectly informed and perfectly fair judgments. While we may look upon a nation or people and think that God isn't acting as we would, God sees the full picture; He judges fairly and rightly at all times.

Third, God speaks of His steadiness. When something happens in this world to a nation or people, it is as if the world is shaking and tottering. Everything seems to be changing in such a way that the world itself is not going to make it. But the Lord wants us to remember that He alone holds up the pillars of the world. When the balance of power seems to be unbalanced, the Lord knows exactly what is going on. So He is not just the Judge; He is the One who is judging to hold everything together for His ultimate plans. That's true power!

With that as a powerful background, then, the Lord gives some warnings in vv. 4-5. Clearly for the sake of emphasis, the Lord speaks over and again in these two verses about arrogance. Using very straightforward language ("Do not boast") and very poetic language ("Do not lift up your horn on high"), God is making it clear that the one thing He will not tolerate in any form is pride.

The picture of a horn is very interesting. The Hebrew word seems to have come, at least in part, from a Sanscrit word for "head."[1] The meaning, then, was something that came out of the head, or extended the head. So, when you have the picture here of a horn, you have the idea of someone whose head has gotten too big! They are growing horns, figuratively speaking, and are developing an inflated sense of themselves. Just like a bull or other animal would show its horns as a sign of strength, too many people think they have all the strength they need in their own heads.

Using one final picture, the Lord says that those who are this way speak "with haughty neck." Often in Scripture, we see people described as "stiff-necked," and this is the same picture. The basic idea behind this picture is that these people are so caught up in

---

1. Carl Friedrich Keil and Franz Delitzsch, *Commentary on the Old Testament*, vol. 5 (Peabody, MA: Hendrickson, 1996), 505.

pride that it is as if they are physically unable to bow their neck. They cannot lower their head in humility, even before God. If there is anything the Lord cannot stand for, it is pride run amok, and that is what He is promising to judge in this part of the psalm. With that in mind, let's make two points of application before going to the final section of the poem.

First, we need to make application to others. It is easy for us to look at nations and peoples who blaspheme the name of God and are completely unholy and wonder where God is. Some have been against Him for many, many years and are even harming those who wear the name of Christ. Many accounts in Scripture, as well as reminders like the one here, help us put this in perspective. God knows and sees. He hasn't missed anything, and He will judge. But He will do it not only in His perfect time, but at the right time and in the right way. Follow the course of history, and you see that perfectly.

But we also need to make application for our own lives and our own nation. If these words are true, then we are reminded once again of what will happen to a group of people who refuse to bow their head before the Lord. When pride comes, destruction follows (Prov. 16:18). While God is longsuffering and merciful, He will not stand for arrogance against Him forever. And it is easy to say that this is society's problem, but I must look at my own life and ask if I am lowering my head in humility before the Lord at all times and in every decision I must make.

The Summary of a Godly Poet (vv. 6-10)

Having written some words of gratitude that were being said by the people, and having written words as if they were from a perfectly just God, Asaph (the poet) begins to write his own reflections.

This is what I love about this psalm: the poet does not change the subject. He continues to write about the Lord's judgment, and now he wants to share his thoughts on this great subject. In the final verses of the psalm, he describes the judgment of God in three ways.

The Direction. In vv. 6-7, Asaph writes of the place from which judgment comes. It is not from "the east or from the west," and it is also not from the "wilderness." From those places, Asaph writes, the people of God cannot be lifted up ("exaltation," NASB). What the writer is saying is that any positive reinforcement the people might get will not come from other people. While other nations may give a group of people a pat on the back at times, the only true exaltation comes from the Lord. It is worth noting that the word "lifting up" or "exaltation" is actually a plural word in the Hebrew. The indication is that any and every time a nation finds true lifting up, it is from God. That would be especially true for the Israelites, as His chosen people. Verse 7 points out that this goes both ways, as God does not just lift up but also puts down. If we want to find true reward as a nation, the only place from which that will come is from the God of heaven. And that is true of more than just a nation—any exaltation we might receive individually, as a congregation, or as a family is ultimately from the Lord and should be treated as such.

The Draining. Verse 8 may well be the most picturesque verse in this psalm, as Asaph uses the imagery of God holding a cup of well-mixed wine in His hand and draining it down. The only problem with this image is that it is one that we don't use much any longer, and we can miss just how powerful a picture this is. As I see it, there are three parts to this picture.

First, is the picture of the cup in the hand of God. The cup is meant to picture the wrath of God's judgment, and that picture is used many times in Scripture. Probably the most well-known is when Jesus Himself used the image in the Garden of Gethsemane. In His prayer, He cried to the Lord, "Let this cup pass from me" (Matt. 26:39). His prayer was worded in that way because Christ knew He was going to bear the wrath of God for the sins of the world. Back in our psalm,

Asaph uses that imagery to show that God's wrath is in His own hand.

Second, the picture is of mixing wine. It is well mixed, meaning God knows exactly the judgment that needs to be executed. Spurgeon describes the mixture this way: "Spices of anger, justice, and incensed mercy are there."[2] It is not just wrath, but it is the exact right "mixture" that only God can make and that is exactly right for each and every situation.

Finally, the picture is of a pouring out upon the wicked. Note that Asaph says it will come to "all the wicked of the earth." No one who does what is sinful and blasphemous will miss the punitive wrath of God. In fact, to close out this part of the picture, the poet writes that it "shall drain down to the dregs." Borrowing the picture of a drink, when God pours out His wrath, those who feel that wrath will drink it to the last drop. That is a powerful and frightening image for anyone who would dare stand against the ways of the Lord Almighty.

The Declaration. As Asaph closes out the poem, he does so with a strong declaration. He even states in v. 9, "I will declare it forever" and "will sing praises to the God of Jacob." Notice the sharp contrast. As opposed to the wicked, who will feel God's wrath and drink it down to the last drop, the righteous will declare the goodness of the Lord.

In fact, Asaph writes that he will try to be more like God. Back in vv. 4-5, the Lord had said He would not allow people to be arrogant, and He used the picture of the horns. Notice how Asaph ends the psalm: "All the horns of the wicked I will cut off, but the horns of the righteous shall be lifted up." Is this saying that the righteous have reason to be arrogant? Of course not! What we are reading here concerns the sovereign nature of God. In the end, the righteous will be exalted, not because of who they are, but because they are exalting God. He will always be victorious, and oftentimes He will demonstrate that by exalting His people. What looks strong—the wicked—will not only be brought low. It will be destroyed. God never comes up in sec-

2. Spurgeon, *Treasury of David*, 2.1.295.

ond place. He and His people are victorious because He is perfect in His justice and in His power, and those two work in perfect tandem.

Conclusion

So what are we to learn from this psalm? The judgment of God is not a subject we consider often. When we do, it is usually one that can be somewhat frightening to us. That's actually not a bad thing because it reminds us that God is greater and stronger than we are.

This psalm is clearly one about finding peace in the judgment of the Lord. How can we do that? We find peace by making certain we are on the side of the righteous and not being arrogant about it. Why? Because God will reward the righteous and bring low the sinful, and He will not miss any of it at all. We can find peace in knowing that no other person, who is frail and forgetful, will be our judge, but the Lord will. We can find peace in knowing that those who are with the Lord, no matter what the circumstances may look like now, will be victorious in the end.

In many ways, Psa. 75 is a precursor to the book of Revelation. "How long?" was the cry of the faithful, and the answer found in the remainder of the book is that God will judge in His time and on His terms, but it will be clear, full, and righteous. In the end, God's people are victorious, and there is peace in that.

God: The Perfect Judge

PSALM 82

The contrast between man and God is quite large. Too often, we try to bring God down to our level and make Him more like us. There are, of course, certain traits God has that we also have. However, even those traits show us a contrast because God always possesses those traits in every perfect way, while we often struggle. There can also be great danger in trying to make God so much like ourselves. If we are not careful, we bring God so far down to our level that we virtually create our own god. We can focus so strongly on one attribute that we forget another, and in doing so, we are not really seeking or knowing the God of the Bible.

In Psa. 82, we have an example of this contrast, and it is over an attribute of God that can be easily overlooked: His justice. While we know God is just, we live in a world where justice is never exactly fair, where mistakes are going to be made. We struggle to understand how anyone—even God—could be perfectly just. But in this psalm, Asaph draws that contrast for us in a very clear way. Consider this paragraph from Eddie Cloer as he writes about the purpose of this psalm:

> As a psalm that grew up within the context of misguided leadership, it carries with it rebukes that sting like the words of a prophet. The high offices of public service had been occupied by unscrupulous men

who had bent or ignored justice for the benefit of the wicked and had taken advantage of the poor and the weak. The civil magistrates and judges, and perhaps even the king, had misused judicial offices for unholy purposes. This abuse of power had to be condemned and judged. The psalmist cries out for God, the true Judge, to bring officials who have flaunted God's compassion and righteousness into judgment.[1]

While it would be easy to turn this psalm into one that condemns our nation, especially the legal system, for overstepping its bounds, I don't want to make that the primary application of this poem. Instead, using the idea of a justice system as the background, I want us to see how this psalm paints for us a clear contrast between the perfection of God and our own imperfections. If God is above even those we entrust with the law, then He is truly greater than all. In this chapter, we will divide this psalm into three parts to notice this contrast between man's imperfect justice and God's perfect justice.

God's Place (v. 1)

The psalm will begin and end with God, and the middle verses will be about man. In the opening verse, Asaph talks about the place of God among other judges. However, the way in which this is worded seems to be quite strange. The ESV translates the verse this way: "God has taken His place in the divine council; in the midst of the gods He holds judgment." At first glance, it can seem to be saying that Asaph is writing that there is a multiplicity of gods and that Jehovah is just one among many other divine beings.

However, we need to dig a little deeper. The NASB translates the verse this way: "God takes His stand in His own congregation; He judges in the midst of the rulers." The word translated "gods" or "rul-

---

1. Cloer, *Psalms 51-100*, 569.

ers" is the word *elohim*, which is the plural form of the word for God. The same word is used down in v. 6, "I said, You are gods.'" While the word obviously can mean deity, the word is also used in Scripture in other ways. For example, in Job 1:6 the word is translated "sons of God" and probably means angels. In Psa. 29:1, the same word is translated as "heavenly beings" and could be speaking either of men or of people of very high rank. So what is Asaph saying about God? Likely, "rulers" is a better translation than "gods," and the picture here is that God will be among those who make judgment.

Notice that Asaph says God will be "in the midst" of these others. The word is one that means "in the middle of." In fact, not to be too graphic, but it was a word that could be used to describe the entrails of an animal because they are in the middle. God will not be on the periphery; He must be in the middle. He will be in the center because He is the only wise One. With that strong lesson in view, the poet spends the majority of the psalm writing about man and drawing our contrast for us.

Man's Partiality (vv. 2-7)

While God's place is in the center, man also has power to judge. In these verses, Asaph talks about the struggle men and women have to judge rightly. He does so in four parts.

The Oppression (v. 2). The cry of v. 2 is one from obvious pain. Opening with the words "how long" shows that this partiality is something that has been going on for some time. But notice that it is not just that mistakes are being made. Even the best human judge is going to make mistakes at times. A human judge simply cannot know every fact and at times will misread a person's words or intent. When we judge others, we will often miss certain things that would have made our judgment more fair and right.

What Asaph is crying out against is far deeper than honest

mistakes made by fallible people. He says that these judges are showing "partiality to the wicked." They are tipping the scales of justice to those who are being unjust. And this way of doing things is embedded in the society. Again, notice how the verse opens with the words "How long?" Asaph is making an impassioned plea for these unjust leaders to recognize and repent. By the way, that's why you see a pause (*selah*) after this verse. It is almost as if the writer is giving the leaders time to pause and consider what they have been doing. Oppression is false justice, and God will not stand for it.

The Objectives (vv. 3-4). Obviously, the intent of the poem going forward shows that the leaders would take this pause, but they would not change. So Asaph turns next to the objectives, which is more than just getting decisions right. He calls for two objectives.

First, he wants the leaders to be right. Note that Asaph's words are clearly intended to be for those who are most easily oppressed by cruel leaders. He talks about those who are "weak" and "fatherless" and "afflicted" and "destitute." When you have people with no real human connection and little money, you have people who are ripe for oppression. Asaph appeals to these leaders to do what is right by those who have no voice of their own. After all, isn't that what God does for all of us? And more than that, doesn't God continually show a compassionate heart for just these types of people? If we are going to be most like God, we must have a heart for those who struggle to have a voice of their own, and we must do what is right for them.

Second, he wants them to be a rescuer. More than just making some legal decisions, Asaph uses the picture in v. 4 of a rescuer. He is not just calling for the judges to make right decisions because they need to be following the letter of the law. It is because the wicked are preying on those who are hurting, and the hurting need an advocate. They need a rescuer. These leaders have been put in this place for a purpose, and they are missing their purpose. In writing on this verse, Spurgeon put it beautifully: "It is a brave thing when a judge can liberate a victim like a fly from the spider's web, and a horrible case when magistrate and plunderer are in league. Law has too often been an instrument for vengeance in the hand of unscrupulous men, an instrument as deadly as poison or the dagger."[2]

If you are in any position of leadership where you make judgments (and nearly every person is), remember that God has put you there for a bigger purpose than just covering your own hide. He has put you there to help those who have little or no voice on their own. Do what is right and be a rescuer.

The Obstacle (v. 5). The reason is because those who are in these positions have a great obstacle to overcome: "They have neither knowledge nor understanding, they walk about in darkness; all the foundations of the earth are shaken." Look at how strong this description is. God is saying in the first line that these judges, as smart as they might be, really know nothing. They have forgotten why they were put in places of leadership (like we just spoke of), but they are also ignorant of anything when compared to an all-wise God. They are just not as smart as we might think them to be. And before we get all high and mighty about judges or other leaders in our nation, remember that we are all leaders at times and that we must make judgments, too.

By saying they walk around in darkness, Asaph reveals the major problem. I don't think "darkness" is used here only of evil, although sin and evil play a part in it. I believe Asaph is saying that these leaders are intentionally blind to what is going on around them. Of course, part of that comes from sin, but it is sin that is so hardened that these leaders have just stopped seeing the struggles of those who most need justice. Remember the pause after v. 2? Why do you think Asaph just went on writing? These leaders wouldn't recognize what was going on, no matter how long you paused to let them think! They are in darkness.

---

2. Spurgeon, *Treasury of David*, 2.1.412.

The final line of v. 5 is a powerful image. These leaders have been ignorant and walking in darkness for so long that the "foundations of the earth" are shaking all around them, and they don't even recognize it. Justice has been completely done away with. The structure of order, justice, law, and righteousness is being destroyed, but these leaders either don't know or don't care. When we fail to do things the way God wants them done, the foundations will shake. Eventually, they will crumble and fall. We have seen it over and again throughout history. What is most tragic, however, is that often those who are doing the things that are causing the foundations to shake just don't see or care because they have so taken their eyes off of God that they would never see Him or His ways as the solution.

The Outcome (vv. 6-7). In vv. 6-7, Asaph writes as if God were speaking, and the Lord gives the inevitable outcome of avoiding His ways of justice and right. First, the Lord states that these are actual leaders. This is not a made-up situation. Again, as in v. 1, "gods" probably carries with this the idea of high rulers. By saying that they were "sons of the Most High," the Lord is reminding us of a very important principle of leadership. There is no authority other than that which comes from God. Jesus said to Pilate, "You would have no authority over me at all unless it had been given you from above" (John 19:11). Paul wrote to the Romans, "There is no authority except from God, and those that exist have been instituted by God" (Rom. 13:1).

Leadership and authority ultimately stem from the authority of God. Governmental leaders are not just answerable to the Constitution or to the people or to a monarchial line. They are answerable to the Lord. The same is true of parents, who lead a home and only have authority because God gave it to them. The same is true of elders, who will answer for their leadership in a congregation. The same is true of business leaders, teachers, coaches, and any other leader, all of whom will answer for how they used or abused their authority. The reason is because all authority ultimately flows from God.

These leaders to which Asaph is writing are told by the Lord, "Like men you shall die, and fall like any prince." What a sobering reminder. We may rise to the highest levels of leadership that a nation or organization has, but in the end, we are still going to leave this life. We will answer for how we have handled that leadership. No title, no office, no leadership level, no rank is going to save us in the end. As Spurgeon said of the leader, "He must leave the bench to stand at the bar."[3] You may be a fantastic leader, and you may move up the ranks. With that comes the great temptation to think that you are above the law, or that you can use those powers for your own interest. But you will never escape the decisions you have made. You will still pass from this life, and you will answer for how you have led.

Asaph's Prayer (v. 8)

After reflecting on the partiality of human leaders and how they are frail and will ultimately die, Asaph ends with a strong prayer. But it is a prayer I'm not sure we pray very often: "Arise, O God, judge the earth; for you shall inherit all the nations!"

We often pray that God will bless America, or that God will forgive and heal America. Those may be great prayers, and I have no doubt we mean them deeply. But I wonder if we would ever pray, "God, judge America." That's an unsettling thought.

However, it is just as sobering to contemplate asking God to judge me as a leader in different areas of my life. Instead of just thinking about this nationally, would I ask God to judge me as a parent, an elder, a teacher, a preacher, an employer, a department head, a team leader, a coach, or any other area of leadership?

After all, God rules over all anyway. While human leaders fall (v. 7), God rises (v. 8) because He is the One from whom all authority flows. Our prayer needs to be that the Lord's will would govern our

---

3. Ibid.

leaders in every area and that we would lead as He would.

Conclusion

I'm not a government leader; I'm not a judge like Asaph was writing about. So what can this psalm possibly mean to me today? As we have studied this short poem together, I hope you have seen that these words have a lot of meaning for each of us.

God will not stand for those who abuse power, and He will not stand for those who do not use power to help those who cannot help themselves. Each of us has some area of our life where we are leading those who need us on their side.

- It's the homemaker who is raising children in such a way that those children are growing closer to the Lord and learning that He is ultimately in control of their lives. She is living out proper leadership.

- It's the businessman who uses the money he makes to help others, instead of just hoarding it all for himself. By cultivating that heart of compassion, he will have money for himself and will show compassion for others.

- It's the eldership who goes through a difficult time but refuses to become a board of directors. Instead, they focus on redoubling their efforts to shepherd the congregation to the best of their ability.

- It's the dad who disciplines his children, but who also admits when he has made a mistake and seeks their forgiveness.

You don't have to be the President or sit on the Supreme Court for this psalm to make a difference in your life. What you must do is understand how high, holy, and perfectly just the Lord is and seek daily to be like Him in every decision you make.

God: Our Shelter

PSALM 91

It is one of the most iconic lines in the history of cinema, but of course, it was first written in a book. Frank L. Baum wrote the long story that eventually was adapted into one of the first marvels of Technicolor. The shoes were changed from silver to ruby red, and the story was pared down to just one part of Baum's original book. But, the iconic line that has become part of our cultural landscape is where Dorothy clicks her heels together three times and says, "There's no place like home." For some, the word "home" can conjure up images of things that are anything but pleasant. But for most of us, the image of home is one of the more beloved and relaxing ideas we can bring to mind. While not everything is perfect, we equate home with a feeling of safety and protection.

We do not know who wrote Psa. 91, though Jewish leaders often make the assumption that if a psalm is unaccounted for, it should be attributed to the writer of the previous psalm. If that is the case, then Moses would be the author since we know he wrote Psa. 90. No matter who the human poet was, though, the words of the 91st Psalm are powerful in that they remind God's followers that He is the place of safety and protection.

At various times in our life, we feel as if there is nowhere we can run to feel completely safe and protected. The words of Psa.

91 serve as a clear reminder that the one who runs to the Lord is always running to the right place of safety. God is our shelter.

As we consider this psalm, we want to divide this poem into four parts and show how the entirety of the psalm should help us place our trust in the God who alone can bring us shelter from everything this world might throw our way.

Dwelling (vv. 1-2, 9-10)

From the very first line of the psalm, we see the intention of the writer. By stating that this is about the one "who dwells in the shelter of the Most High," the poet is making a clear distinction. All the positive attributes we will read about in this psalm are reserved for those who are near to the Lord and dwell with Him. In other words, this poem is not for everyone. That is further emphasized by saying that those who are with God "abide in [His] shadow." Look at those words: "dwells" and "abides," and you already see the calm that is found where God is. The one who is dwelling and abiding in God can utter the words of v. 2: "My refuge and my fortress, my God, in whom I trust." We have studied the picture of a refuge and a fortress already in this book, but I want to key in on that last phrase, "in whom I trust."

We live in a world that says you cannot really trust God because a lot of bad things happen in this world. The psalmist makes it clear, though, that the one who is willing to stay with God can place his or her trust in the Lord. God is trustworthy, no matter what might be going on in the world around us. However, we will not feel that way about the Lord—we will not know that He is fully trustworthy—if we are not "abiding" in Him. If we are just jumping in and out of faithfulness, we will never trust the Lord through truly dark and difficult times and see how faithful He is to His children.

Later in the psalm (vv. 9-10), the poet comes back to this concept of dwelling in the Lord. Verse 10 may seem almost controversial because the poet writes that when one takes refuge in the Lord, "No evil shall be allowed to befall you, no plague come near your tent." Is he saying that nothing bad ever happens to the one who is following the Lord? If so, does that mean that if I get sick or lose a job. That I haven't been faithful?

We know that's not the case, both from various men and women in the Bible who were faithful yet suffered (think of Paul), as well as from our own personal experience. However, to the one who is faithful to the Lord, this world simply cannot attack his or her attitude. If we remain here, even though bad things may happen, those things are bringing the faithful one ever closer to the Lord. Even should those bad things bring about the end of our life, they have only served to bring us into the presence of our Lord more quickly.

While the poet may have been saying in a metaphorical sense that nothing bad happens to the one who is faithful to the Lord, we can interpret these words in a way that is perfectly consistent with the rest of Scripture by reminding ourselves that, when bad things come, they draw the one who is faithful even closer to God, so those things are not really that bad when compared with the glory of eternity.

However, we must notice that this mindset is only true of the one who is dwelling in God. If you are trying to straddle the fence and do not stay near to the Lord, you will not know what this mindset means. You will feel harmed in very deep and real ways when negative circumstances come and will not move closer to the Lord through those darker times. It is far better for us to be people who are dwelling in God and finding our constant place of refuge in Him.

Deliverance (vv. 3-8)

In case you need encouragement to find your shelter in the Lord, the poet uses vv. 3-8 to write various reasons why one would want to be dwelling in the Lord. While there are many things listed in these verses, each one of them has to do with God's protection. God is our shelter. In these verses that speak to the protection and deliverance of the Lord, we read of several ways in which God pictures His protection.

In v. 3, the picture is of things that are seen in nature. A fowler was one who laid a trap and tried to ensnare an animal (a bird). In a spiritual way, of course, Satan is the one who tries to ensnare the people of God and often lays traps for us. However, Scripture reminds us clearly that "we are not ignorant of [Satan's] designs" (2 Cor. 2:11). From personal experience, as well as through Scripture, we know how Satan operates. He may be very good at what he does, but we know what he does and can stand on ready. But we are told in our psalm that God delivers us from that. He will provide a way out, much like 1 Cor. 10:13 reminds us.

The further picture of nature in v. 3 is that of pestilence. We might consider here those things that would harm or rot our thinking. Pestilence eats away at what is good, and there are many things in this world that strive to do just that, spiritually speaking. But we can remain strong through faith in our trustworthy God. If our mind will stay true and dedicated to Him, we can keep our thinking and remain fully aware and ready to walk through anything this world might throw our way.

Verse 4 is a beautiful verse because, on the heels of such frightening things, we might think that the way to be delivered is to run. But we are reminded that God doesn't tell us to run; instead, He brings us near. In other words, when trouble comes, God is right there with us, walking through them with His protective wings overshadowing us. The faithfulness of God, the poet writes, "Is a shield and buckler." It is our complete protection, providing a shield and, essentially, a coat of mail.

How strong is the protection of God? No weapon and no time of day can penetrate it. That is the message of vv. 5-6. Notice the times (night, day, darkness, noonday). It doesn't matter what might frighten you or when you might be more fearful; God's faithfulness is always present to help you. But we must say it again: you must be dwelling in Him. By the way, when I read these words with all these different times in them, I think of a more famous psalm (one we have not gotten to yet). In Psa. 121, we read these well-known words: "He will not let your foot be moved; He who keeps you will not slumber. Behold, He who keeps Israel will neither slumber nor sleep" (121:3-4). The point the author of Psa. 91 is trying to make is the same. It does not matter what makes you fearful; God is always on guard and ready to protect.

Closing out this section, we read that, no matter how bad things might get for those outside the Lord, the one with the Lord is safe. Verse 7: "A thousand may fall at your side, ten thousand at your right hand, but it will not come near you." Verse 8 explains this in literal terms, that the one who sees this happen is seeing the judgment of the Lord. We read of that many times in the Old Testament, where the Lord sent disease or famine or an army against people who were standing against His ways.

Today, we cannot always discern whether a hurricane or famine or war is God's way of waking up an unrepentant people. However, we can take any of these negative things in two ways. First, we can take them as a wake-up call. While that may not be their intent, horrific events like these serve as a very strong wake-up call to make sure we are dwelling wholly in the Lord.

Also, we can take them as a reminder that all will be dealt with in the end. God will make things right when the end of the world comes. While we may suffer through a flood or economic crisis or disease just like anyone else now, we can use those things to draw near to God, knowing that in the end those who have not followed Him will suffer far worse for being disloyal to the Lord.

While we may pray today to be delivered from negative circumstances, we need to remember David's famous words in the 23rd Psalm. He did not say that the Lord, his Shepherd, was going to take him on some circuitous route around the valley of the shadow of death. Instead, he made the faithful statement, "Even though I walk through the valley of the shadow of death, I will fear no evil, for you are with me; your rod and your staff, they comfort me" (23:4). Bad things will happen, but through them all, God provides deliverance for His people by showing His protective wings and reminding us that He will make all things right in the end.

Demonstration (vv. 11-13)

Verses 11-13 likely contain the words you know best from this psalm. Of course, vv. 11-12 were used by Satan when he tempted Jesus to jump off the temple and let the angels catch Him, which would prove He was the Messiah (Matt. 4:6). Satan, however, took these words way out of context. Psalm 91 was not written to give us permission to test the Lord and have Him shoot lightning from heaven, as it were, to prove Himself or His prophecy in some way.

So, what are these words supposed to mean? These words are further assurances of God's protection. We have already studied vv. 9-10, but if you look back up at them, these words remind us of the need to dwell in the Lord, and that God will protect His people when we do that. Verses 11-13 are simply continuing that line of thinking by stating certain things that the people could picture in their minds as illustrations of God's protection.

Verse 11 makes it clear that angels have a hand in this. I do not believe (as some have said) that this is teaching that we have a guardian angel, with one angel assigned to each person to provide protection. In fact, the lesson being taught is even more powerful. All of God's angels are under the command of the Lord and are used as a major part of God's means of protecting His people.

Verses 12-13 are simply poetic ways to demonstrate how powerful God's protection is. It is as if we can walk on top of a lion or a snake when God is protecting us. We are safe enough that it is as if we won't even cut our foot on a rock. These things are not literal, but rather are meant to give us a picture of how strong the Lord's protection is for His people. Listen to how Spurgeon summarizes the power of these pictures in vv. 11-13:

> To men who dwell in God the most evil forces become harmless, they wear a charmed life, and defy the deadliest ills. Their feet come into contact with the worst of foes, even Satan himself nibbles at their heel, but in Christ Jesus they have the assured hope of bruising Satan under their feet shortly.[1]

Defense (vv. 14-16)

As the psalm ends, we once again see the "voice" of the psalm change. The final three verses are written from the perspective of God. It is almost as if the poet is writing this, showing that the Lord Himself is giving His stamp of approval on what has been said. We can claim that God protects and helps all we want, but now God is saying these things to verify that He will, in fact, provide defense for those who are dwelling in Him.

But I want you to notice that God also "verifies," if you will, something else. Three times in these verses, the Lord makes it clear that this promise of His protection is not for everyone. These three phrases "Because he holds fast to me," "Because he knows my name," and "When he calls to me," show that, although God loves every person, He holds a special place of protection for those who are truly near Him and honoring Him as their place of protection.

As we can expect from the Lord, He also is able to do more than

---

1. Spurgeon, *Treasury of David*, 2.2.93.

we ask or think. For 13 verses, the poet has spoken of the amazing protection of God but has basically left it there. It is just a way to get through the negative times. But God is able to do more than that! Start reading in v. 15: "When he calls to me, I will answer him; I will be with him in trouble; I will rescue him and honor him. With long life I will satisfy him and show him my salvation."

Now, if that description had stopped in v. 15 with the phrase "I will rescue him," it would sound about like the rest of the psalm, written from man's point of view. But as God goes further, we begin to see just how strong the defense of our Lord is. Not only will He be with us through the difficulty, He will honor us and bring salvation through it! God does more than give us a defense against negative things. He brings satisfaction and salvation. That's the God we serve.

Conclusion

Where do you go for protection? Maybe a better question to ask would be: Are you staying near God or do you wander back and forth, near and far from Him, and then wonder why you do not feel His protecting hand? The songwriter put it in words that we often sing:

> There is a place of quiet rest:
> Near to the heart of God.
> A place where sin cannot molest,
> Near to the heart of God.

I love the peace that song teaches, and I love it because I know it is real when I am remaining near to the heart of Jehovah. He provides all we need, but we must remain near to Him. He will not move, but we often move away and pull ourselves further from His protecting hand. Let's be resolved to dwell in God, who is our shelter, and know the full peace and protection that only comes from our loving and all-powerful God.

Let Us Worship!

PSALM 95

"Reverent honor." "Homage." "Adoring reverence." "Regard." Looking up the word "worship" in a dictionary reveals these as some of the words that try to describe what we are doing when we worship. The word as we have it today came from a Middle English word, "worthship," which basically meant to ascribe or describe the worth of something or someone. Songs have tried to capture for us the idea that worship is about more than cold and unfeeling acts; rather, it is to be filled with both mind and heart.

An older song begins, "Lord, we come before Thee now, / At Thy feet we humbly bow." A newer song words it, "Here I am to worship, / Here I am to bow down; / Here I am to say that You're my God." Old or new, these hymns help us focus on both the right mindset and the right heart. In reality, they are reflecting what Jesus stated in the most foundational verse concerning worship in all Scripture: "God is spirit, and those who worship Him must worship in spirit and truth" (John 4:24).

But the concept of worship is not limited to the New Testament, of course. One of the recurring themes in the Old Testament, and clearly in the Psalms, is that of devoted worship to the Lord. While these poems are spread throughout the book, there seem to be more praise psalms in latter portions of the book.

Psalm 95 is one that is not attributed to any poet, but Heb. 4:7 quotes from vv. 7-8 of this poem and says it is from David. What is most interesting to me about this psalm is that it is clearly intended to be a worship psalm, but there are two parts. The second part goes against what we usually think of when we consider worship as the poet issues a very stern reminder/warning. Worship cannot be done by just anyone or in any fashion and still be acceptable to the Lord.

The desire of our heart should always be to worship our Lord and Creator, and Psa. 95 is a wonderful poem to turn to when we are preparing to come before Him in reverent praise and adoration. In this chapter, with our mind centered on God and worshiping Him, let's walk through this psalm in just two parts.

True Worship (vv. 1-7a)

The majority of this poem is spent as an invitation to worship the Lord. Twice (vv. 1, 6), the phrase "O come" opens a verse, and the rest of this section fleshes out that invitation with words of praise and reason. There are two major things discussed in these verses, both of which need to be constantly on our mind when we worship the Lord.

What to do. First, phrase after phrase in the opening seven verses gives us the mindset as to what we should be doing in worship. While we may not literally do these same actions, they certainly fill our minds with a deep desire to worship God.

Sing to the Lord. Singing is nearly universal in worship of deities, so it is no wonder that David would include singing, but he makes sure to note that we are singing "to the Lord." There are few things so closely associated with worship as singing. But we must always remember that we are primarily singing praise to God. We are present to worship Him, and that includes the songs we bring to Him.

Make a joyful noise. This phrase is most likely meant to reflect the type of singing David had in mind. While there are occasions for songs that may be more doleful and reflective, our singing should mostly be filled with joy. And even when we sing songs that are more somber (e.g. "Night with Ebon Pinion"), there should still be a joy in our heart because we are singing about things that brought about our eternal salvation. Joy should fill Christian worship because we are "always" to "rejoice in the Lord" (Phil. 4:4).

Come into His presence. I separated this out from the verse because of what a powerful reminder this is. When we come together for worship, we are in God's presence! That should imply that we are prepared because we are coming into the presence of deity, but it also should imply that we take this very seriously. He allows us to come into His presence, and we need to see that as a wonderful honor.

Be thankful. David writes that we are to come "with thanksgiving." What is interesting about this concept is that, under the Law, "common" worshipers could not really be in God's presence. A priest had to bring a sacrifice before the Lord on their behalf. Still, that was enough to know the forgiveness and sanctification of God and should have built within the people a gratitude for all the Lord had done for them. Today, considering what Christ has done to bring us near to God by breaking down "the dividing wall of hostility" (Eph. 2:14), we should be filled with thanksgiving each time we come before God in worship.

Worship. Verse 6 contains the last three things we should do when we worship, and they are very difficult to translate. David was trying to build a strong picture of more than just physical action, but he uses physical pictures. The word "worship" is a Hebrew word that can mean "to prostrate" or "bow." It carried with it the idea of humility. We must remember this when we worship: we are not here to build ourselves up; we are here to lift God up! Worship should be a very humbling experience, but that begins before we ever worship, as we humble our hearts before Him.

Bow down. The word here was one that basically meant "to bend low," and could mean to bow or to kneel. It was a word that carried the idea of reverence for someone else.

Kneel. The final word had a duel meaning: to kneel and to bless. It originally had the idea of "breaking down" and is the final step in the heart that is prepared to worship.

Put all of these together, and you have a heart that is ready to worship and understands what worship is all about. It isn't about me getting everything for myself and just "feeling better" after having come to worship. It is about humbling myself before God and bringing Him praise. But why? That's what else is found in these first seven verses.

Why to do them. We worship God because He is worthy of such. In these verses, there are seven attributes of God that show us reasons why we should worship the Lord.

He saves. Verse 1 calls God "The rock of our salvation." A rock cannot be moved, just like the salvation of the Lord. Our salvation is safe in Him, and that should be enough for us to praise the Lord! David may have had in mind physical salvation in the history of Israel (such as the Red Sea or his own salvation from Goliath), but we know that those in the Old Testament also believed in the true salvation of the Lord. God will never stop being the One in whom salvation is found, and we should praise Him and thank Him constantly for that.

He is Lord. Verse 1 and v. 3 both simply refer to Him as "Lord." This is the word "Jehovah," which was the name God gave Himself. It refers to His eternal nature and is the same idea behind what He said to Moses at the burning bush: "I AM." God is always present and will always be in the present tense. We should worship Him in awe for that eternal nature because it reminds us of how much greater He is than we are, and that He is always near.

He is a great God. Verse 3 gives the wonderful description: "For the Lord is a great God." No doubt, the people of Israel in the time of David still knew of the many gods of the nations around them. Some may have been tempted to worship those other gods during that time. But only Jehovah can truly be described as "great." Other gods have to be built by human hands, but God is great. He needs nothing in order to exist. He is great in every way imaginable.

He is King. The end of v. 3 speaks to the majesty of God by describing Him as "a great King above all gods." Is David saying there are actually other deities? Of course not. He is asking the people to compare other gods to the One God of heaven. If (and only if) there were other gods, Jehovah would rule over them, for He alone is King.

He is Almighty. We are using the word "Almighty" here to summarize the power of v. 4. David writes about the depths, mountains, sea, and dry land and puts all of them under the power of God. He owns it all and controls it all. Contrast that with other gods. In so many other religions, you have "a" god of the sea and "a" god of the mountains, and so on. Not Jehovah. He is powerful enough to rule and control it all. Wouldn't you rather worship that One God who is over it all?

He is our Maker. The end of v. 6 makes clear that God is not just over the natural world, but that He made us just as He made the seas and mountains. We should worship God because He fit us together, and we are His. That is why this verse contains such powerful pictures of humility. We should worship, bow down, and kneel because we are coming before the very One who made us in the first place.

He is our Shepherd. Of course, David wrote famously, "The Lord is my Shepherd" (Psa. 23:1), but now he states that everyone who would worship God is part of that same flock. God leads and guides His people as a shepherd leads and guides sheep. It is always for the good of the flock and always done with care for what is best.

Knowing all that, how could the people turn down the invitation to worship? When we honestly consider what God has done, our heart should be ready to worship Him. But tragically, sometimes we fail to remember, and our hearts are not ready to truly worship Him.

So in the remaining lines of the psalm, David gives a very strong warning about not worshiping as God has prescribed.

Terrible Warning (vv. 7b-11)

The warning begins at the conclusion of v. 7 and contains that extremely powerful two-letter word "if." There are some who will hear the voice—the call—of the Lord but who will not respond as they should. To illustrate that and to warn us against it, David turns to one of the most infamous accounts in the history of Israel. Verse 8 speaks of Meribah and "Massah in the wilderness." Before we get to the actual event the Lord is using here, look at how God felt about the event. In v. 8, He said it was a place where the people hardened their hearts. In v. 9, the Lord called it a place where He was put to the test, even though the people had already seen His amazing work. And it led to punishment, as God "loathed that generation" (v. 10) and took away the rest He had promised.

What event was God using as the illustration of what it means to hear His voice but not be humble? It was in Num. 13-14, the story of what happened after the spies returned from scouting out the Promised Land. God had already shown His amazing power through the ten plagues in Egypt, as well as through leading the people across the Red Sea. They had seen His power on Mt. Sinai, and the Lord had sustained them through this journey; they were now ready to take the land that God had promised to give them.

But when the spies returned, ten of them gave a bad report of the land, saying the people were giants and the land devoured the inhabitants. They turned the hearts of Israel away from trust and obedience. In reality, they took the focus off the Lord and put it squarely on themselves. Due to that lack of trust and their selfish nature, the Lord said, "None of the men who have seen my glory and my signs that I did in Egypt and in the wilderness, and yet have put me to the test these ten times and have not obeyed my voice, shall see the land that I swore to give to their fathers. And none of those who despised me shall see it" (Num. 14:22-23).

Why would David use that account as his basis for a warning in a psalm about worship? It is because false worship—even by those who claim to be people of God—has at its heart the very same root problem: selfishness. It goes back to the warning in v. 8: "Do not harden your hearts." Notice that this is a choice! When I know about worship, I have a choice to remain selfish and think only of myself, or to humble myself before God and honor Him for who He is.

Now, you may think, "I'm reading a book about God. How could I possibly be hardening my heart and not worshipping as I should?" That's a fair question, but go back to the emphasis of the first half of the psalm. Ask yourself and give an honest answer: "Who is at the center of my worship?" Is it God, or is it you? Too often, we come to worship only out of selfish interests. My friends are there. It's just what I've always done. I like the singing. The preacher is great.

Is it wrong to enjoy the social interaction? Of course not! The church is a family, and we do come together to encourage and strengthen each other. We surely gain from the songs and prayers when we are engaged in those things with our fellow Christians.

But the center of our worship cannot be these things! It must be on God. He is the object of our worship. He is the reason we worship. He directs what we do in worship, both in action and in attitude. Anything less is selfishness; it is hardening our hearts because we have made the choice to do things the way we want or for our own purposes instead of what God has set forth.

Conclusion

Worship should be a true high point of our lives. We are allowed by the Creator of the universe to enter His presence. He could, if He so chose, cut us off and never let us near Him. In His love, however, He allows us to come near Him, which should be the deepest desire of our heart. Do I make sure that God is at the very center of worship, or do I make worship more about me and what I want?

Consider what God has done, both in history and in your own life. When you do, how could anyone keep you from coming before God in humility and reverence, and how could anyone keep you from joy and thanksgiving? When you honestly reflect on what the Lord has done for you, worship will never be a chore, and it will never be selfish. It will be the strongest desire of your heart.

True Thanksgiving

PSALM 100

At least two commonly sung hymns, which both use the same tune, are based loosely on the words of Psa. 100. In fact, for a number of years, people used the tune and simply called it "The Old Hundredth." The one I've sung more often is "All People That on Earth Do Dwell," which was arranged by William Kethe in 1560. About 150 years later, Isaac Watts reworded the poem slightly and gave us "Before Jehovah's Awful Throne," which took Psa. 100 and made it more sermonic, adding more teaching to the actual words of the poem.

In Psa. 100, we have another great psalm of praise. So many psalms deal with the praise of God that it is difficult to pick and choose ones to discuss, but this one is not only brief, it places our mind right on the place of God in our praise. However, it is interesting that the superscription to this short poem reads, "A Psalm for giving thanks." We are calling this chapter "True Thanksgiving" because we want to walk through this psalm with this idea in our mind: you cannot separate praising God and being thankful to Him. Only when we are truly thankful for what He has done can we praise Him as we should.

The great thing about Psa. 100 is its power and simplicity. The psalm can be divided into two halves, each of which does the same thing: Verses 1-2 speak of what we are to do, and v. 4 repeats those ideas. Verse 3 speaks of why we are to do those things, and v. 5 does that again. What you have in Psa. 100 is Hebrew parallelism on a grand scale. Instead of just one line repeating the previous line for emphasis, this entire psalm repeats itself (in its basic concept) to emphasize that we are to express gratitude to God in worship.

While we want to dig into this psalm and see what is there, we dare not miss the forest for the trees. Whoever the inspired writer of this psalm was, he did not write anything deep, but he certainly penned words of power. May we use them to help us be more mindful of our gratitude toward the Lord.

Gladness (vv. 1-2)

The first two verses comprise one of the best calls to worship found anywhere in Scripture. As we have noticed before in the psalms, the call is for people in "all the earth." We need to realize the universal, global scope of God's message. People in every land should worship the Lord, and we dare not just hold the message for ourselves.

It is the attitude of these first two verses that make this such a powerful call to worship. Not a negative word is said, not only in this section, but in the entire psalm. Instead, the focus is clearly on how wonderful the Lord is. Three times in these two verses, we are reminded of what we are to do when we enter worship.

"Make a joyful noise." The opening line of this psalm is a repetition of the first part of Psa. 98:4: "Make a joyful noise to the Lord, all the earth." The call here is for us to return to God, not only what He has given to us, but also His very nature. God's love demonstrates itself in delight and joy. While God is wrathful and will punish, love delights in joy and gladness. We should return that joy to God. Our hearts should not be able to contain the joy we feel for who God is and what He has done, so we should make a "joyful noise." Wor-

ship should not be a drudgery, but a time when what we do is filled with the joy of our hearts.

"Serve...with gladness." It should not be a difficult thing to serve our God, but the service we render should be filled with gladness. More famously, David wrote, "I was glad when they said to me, 'Let us go to the house of the Lord!'" (122:1). That attitude of gladness should fill our soul each time we are privileged to worship the Lord and serve Him as He so deserves.

"Singing." If there is anything closely associated with the worship of God, it is singing. But put this in the context of the rest of this verse, and we get a great reminder that singing should be filled with joy and gladness. God delights in such singing because it is expressing joy at what He has done for us and in our lives. Certainly, there are other things we do in worship besides sing, but singing is the clearest example of what worship is to be about. It is through singing that our expressions are most easily seen. How do we treat all of worship?

Grasping (v. 3)

Verse 3 gives us a very important aspect of our worship that is easy to overlook, or at the least to deemphasize. That is, our worship needs to involve our mind focusing on the Lord. The first line of the verse spells that out clearly: "Know that the Lord, He is God!" Look at that word "know." While this is a general word, it carries with it the idea of perception and becoming acquainted with something.

When we come to worship God, we cannot leave our minds at home. We must use our minds to center our thoughts, but that centering needs to be on God, not on ourselves. To help us with that realization, the rest of the verse gives four ways in which we need to think of God.

Source. "It is He who made us." God is the source of our life; He is our Creator. Some translations go on to state, "And not we ourselves." God is the only One who can create life, and we need to acknowledge that. We can extend our lives and improve them with wisdom and medicines and other discoveries, but only God can create life, and He created our life.

Sustainer. The ESV continues v. 3 with, "We are His." As we said, some translations have "and not we ourselves;" in other words, we did not create ourselves. The emphasis seems to be on trusting God, not only to create life, but to sustain life. Every time you take a breath, it is a gift from the Lord. Each time we eat, drink, have joy, or any other good thing, it is because God is giving that to us. If God so desired, He could end every life at any time He wanted. That realization should bring great humility into our minds as we worship the Lord.

Sovereign. "We are His people." We like to talk about being our own man and having things our own way, but the Christian is not one who is his own anymore. Under the Law, the people had a legal code that governed, not only their religious lives, but also their day-to-day activities. That served as a strong reminder that they belonged to the Lord. Today, we still have a law to follow in the New Testament, but it can be more difficult for us to get past our selfishness and submit in humility to the One who rules over us as God. Yet Jesus is Lord, and we must recognize that and submit ourselves to Him in humility when we worship.

Shepherd. Verse 3 ends with another strong reminder of the humility we need that we are not just the people of God, but we are "the sheep of His pasture." It is nearly impossible to read these words and not think of Psa. 23 which begins with the timeless words, "The Lord is my shepherd." But that thought should build within us a reminder that God leads and loves. If we are His people, we are privileged to have Him as our Shepherd.

Let me ask: when you come to worship, is it to worship God? Of course, we gain something from worship for our own lives, but our minds must be focused on Him. Our heart must desire to serve Him, and our thoughts need to put Him at the very center of all we do.

Do I realize what He has done, and who He is? Does that fill my mind with thoughts of thanksgiving when I come into His presence? By the way, this one realization—who God is and what He has done—would completely remedy any struggles I might have regarding a lack of desire to attend worship. When I come to a full realization of what the Lord has done for me, I will want to come into His presence every time I possibly can!

Gratitude (v. 4)

Turning back from the reasons to praise God, we have another verse (v. 4) that speaks of what we are to do. As we have said, this entire poem is one of praise, so the emphasis is on praising the Lord. The verse gives us two pictures of entering the presence of the Lord. First, we are to enter "His gates." This probably was used to signify the security of the Lord. But note that we are to enter with "thanksgiving." This is, of course, where we get the title for this chapter. Thanksgiving should accompany us every time we come into the presence of God, and that thanksgiving is because we are secure where He is.

We also are to enter "His courts." The picture here is not of a modern-day courtroom, but of the courtyard areas that surrounded the tabernacle and later the temple. These were areas where preparation was made and where people were constantly coming and going with sacrifices to bring to the Lord. These areas were often filled with people, but the emphasis here was not on filling those areas with lots of people for some social setting. After all, they are "His gates;" they belong to God. And we are to enter them with praise on our lips.

With that as the setup, the writer ends v. 4 in typical Hebrew poetic fashion by stating the same emphasis in two different ways: "Give thanks to Him; bless His name!" These are parallel thoughts because they both speak to giving God what He is due. He is due our thanks, but we also bless Him. This does not mean that we bless Him out of our goodness. Instead, we are simply trying to return to the Lord a blessing because of the way in which He has blessed us.

It may seem as if we are repeating ourselves a lot in this lesson, but that is, in some ways, the point of Psa. 100! The poet is so filled with gratitude for the Lord that he is calling on everyone else to express that same gratitude to God.

When I worship, I need to ask myself: where is my mind? Is it only focused on me, or do I realize I am entering the very presence of God? Do I come before Him with thanksgiving? Am I doing all I can to return in some way a blessing to the Lord for all the ways in which He has blessed me?

There is no way to worship properly if we are not cultivating a heart of thanksgiving, and that must start with gratitude to the Lord. We may show up, and we may sing some songs, but if our heart is only focused on what I can get out of this time, that speaks more to the lack of gratitude in my heart than it does anything else. My worship should be flowing out of a deep sense of gratitude for what God has done for me throughout the years of my life. He certainly has been good, and there is no way I could ever thank Him enough. But that should not stop me from trying to express my thanks through constant praise.

Goodness (v. 5)

As this short poem comes to an end, we return again to more reasons to bring praise and thanks to the Lord. But the emphasis of v. 5 is different than that of v. 3. The emphasis of v. 3 was on God's ruling power over us. The emphasis here in v. 5 is on God's eternal love for us. The poet lists three qualities of God that overlap somewhat, but give us a powerful portrait of the love our Lord has for His people.

He is good. The first line is one that is so simple that it is easy to miss how powerful it is. "For the Lord is good." We use the word "good" so often and for so many things that it has little meaning to us. Jesus understood the power of this description of God, though. In Mark 10, we have the account of the rich young ruler, who asked Jesus, "Good Teacher, what must I do to inherit eternal life?" (v. 17). Before answering the question directly, Jesus said, "Why do you call me good? No one is good except God alone" (v. 18). That is the power of this word in Psa. 100. While a lot of people, and many things, may be good to some degree, only God is perfectly "good."

He has steadfast love. Many translations use the word "mercy." This is the famous Hebrew term *chesed*, which is almost impossible to translate because it is so rich in meaning. It was a word of covenant. God would remain steadfast in His loyalty and love for His people, showing them mercy throughout their generations, and in spite of themselves. The fact is, God never breaks a covenant. We may, but He will not, and that is true eternally. Note the use of the word "endures." It is not a simple thing that God keeps His covenant and shows this mercy, but He endures.

He is faithful. The KJV has "truth," but the word here is one for something that is steady and solid. In fact, the same Hebrew word is found in Exod. 17:12 where Aaron and Hur held the hands of Moses up, so the Israelites could remain victorious in battle. The verse ends by saying, "So his hands were steady until the going down of the sun." The word "steady" is the same word used in Psa. 100:5. God is always steady in all His attributes; thus, He is faithful to His people. In a world that is constantly unstable, isn't that reason enough to praise the Lord?

Conclusion

What is worship to me? Maybe a better question would be:

What does God mean to me? That will express itself in my worship because the mindset that focuses on Him and what He has done will express itself each time I have the honor of coming before Him in worship. I should be filled with thanksgiving each time I have the opportunity to express this honor in praise.

The same tune used for the two adaptations of Psa. 100 mentioned at the beginning of this chapter has also been adapted into one other song, and it is one we sing quite often. In fact, the song is just a couple of lines long, but it expresses well what our mindset should be when we worship.

> Praise God from whom all blessings flow;
> Praise Him all creatures here below;
> Praise Him above, ye heavenly host.
> Praise Father, Son, and Holy Ghost!

God's Goodness in Spite of Ourselves

PSALM 106

We often sing the very simple but profound words, "God is so good." The song, through its short verses, shares a few reasons why that is true (e.g. "He answers prayer," "He sent His Son"). Each of those verses ends with the simple refrain, "He's so good to me." Sometimes words like those can be so simple that we fail to see just how deep their meaning is. God truly is good, and that is true whether we ever enumerate all His traits and gifts or not. He is innately good. That goodness demonstrates itself in countless ways and has throughout the ages.

But one thing we need to focus on even more deeply is that God is good, and so often shows that goodness, in spite of ourselves. That's not to say that we are always bad, but God is good to us despite the fact that we often fail to be good. We fail Him individually, and we fail Him collectively, more often than we like to consider. In spite of that, God remains good and continues to shower us with His goodness.

Psalm 106 focuses clearly on that concept. This psalm begins and ends with "Hallelujah!" (or "Praise the Lord," vv. 1, 48), and is the first psalm to do that, but it is not the last. In fact, ten more will both begin and end with a "Hallelujah" (Psa. 111, 112, 113, 117, 135, 146-150). In between those lines of Hallelujah in our psalm, there is a powerful reminder of the goodness of God, but also of our own sinfulness. Spurgeon suggests that it is good for us to begin and end with praise when our sin vs. God's patience is the subject.[1] Using this psalm, let us consider just how good God is, despite times when we fall short of His glory (cf. Rom. 3:23).

Reverence (vv. 1-3)

The poem begins with words of praise and reverence for the Lord. The opening verses share both reasons to offer the Lord reverence, as well as a blessing on those who do.

Verse 1 gives the familiar refrain, much like the song we referenced earlier, that God is good and "His steadfast love endures forever!" Those words and qualities are found often in the Psalms and, as with the hymn, if we are not careful, they can lose their meaning on us because the words seem so simple. That God is good is unquestioned, and that He is wholly good needs to be remembered. The Lord is good through and through, and there is nothing that fails to be good in His nature.

"Steadfast love" (KJV = "mercy") translates the well-known Hebrew word *chesed*, which is a very deep word. It includes the idea of being so zealous in love and care for another that you draw that person to yourself. It is a powerful word that aptly describes just how deeply God feels for each person. Knowing that, v. 2 asks a rhetorical question showing that none of us could ever list all the good things the Lord has done. While we should do all we can to speak for the Lord and make His deeds known to others, it would be impossible for us to list every good and powerful thing the Lord has done. The song reminds us to count our many blessings, and ends with the simple reminder, "It will surprise you what the Lord has done."

As this first part of the poem ends, a blessing is pronounced on

---

1. Spurgeon, *Treasury of David*, 2.2.363.

those who realize the goodness and mercy of the Lord and show that in their own lives. In reality, there is no way to have true justice or righteousness without knowing those same attributes in their perfection from the Lord. We reverence Him when we live out His traits as best we can in our life because we are letting others see Him through us.

Remembrance (vv. 4-5)

With a reverence for God as the backdrop, the poet next asks God to remember him. Keil and Delitzsch help us see this transition when they write, "In v. 3 the poet tells what is the character of those who experience such manifestations of God; and to the assertion of the blessedness of these men he appends the petition in v. 4, that God would grant him a share in the experiences of the whole nation which is the object of these manifestations."[2]

Notice the end of v. 4 where the real emphasis is given: "Help me when you save them" (i.e. Israel). Whoever the inspired author of this poem was, he clearly understood that deliverance and salvation are only given by the Lord. He is the only One who can truly bring salvation, so the poet seeks that from God alone. This is a concept we need to remember—salvation belongs only to the Lord. While the poet was probably referring more to some kind of earthly deliverance, he still understood that only God brings that about.

We live in a time where we are seeking a better country, which is heaven, and we need to understand that only God brings about the way for us to enter that place of rest. Salvation is His alone to give, which is why we do our best to stick strictly with His Word. In it, He reveals the way to be saved, and that is the only way (cf. John 14:6).

When we have that salvation, though, the poet writes that there are great blessings attached to it. Verse 5 shares some of those blessings: prosperity, joy, gladness, and an inheritance. Again, he was

---

2. Keil, *Commentary*, 5:669.

probably writing about an earthly deliverance from some kind of trouble, but we can make a very clear spiritual application of his words.

In Ephesians, we are again reminded that God has given us "every spiritual blessing in the heavenly places" (1:3). If we were to attempt to list each and every one of these spiritual blessings, the list would be inexhaustible. We never need to fail in remembering that God alone gives these gifts. We are blessed by them, but God alone gives them. Ephesians makes it clear (as does the remainder of the New Testament) that these spiritual blessings are only for those who are "in Christ Jesus." God gives, but we must be willing to humble ourselves to His will in order to receive.

Our prayer needs to be the same as the poet, that God will remember us when He is giving His good gifts. Of course, God never forgets, so instead we are basically praying that we will be found in the will of God so we can know the blessings only He can bestow. He truly is good!

Review (vv. 6-46)

As we said from the outset, God is good, but He shows that goodness despite our times of failure. In the major bulk of this psalm, the poet takes his readers on a little history tour. For some 41 verses, he writes of time after time when the people of Israel had failed God in various ways. Throughout it all, though, there are reminders of how God had continued to love His people and had been patient with them.

We do not have the space to write in full about everything in this list, but Harold Willmington, in his *Outline Bible*,[3] breaks the verses down into two lists, which we will borrow for our purposes.

Israel's corruption. At least ten different things are listed in these verses to remind the people of the sins of their ancestors.

---

3. Harold L. Willmington, *The Outline Bible* (Wheaton, IL: Tyndale, 1999), 276.

1. **Forgetfulness of God's miraculous hand** (vv. 7, 13, 21-23). As an example, note v. 7: "Our fathers, when they were in Egypt, did not consider your wondrous works; they did not remember the abundance of your steadfast love."

2. **Rebelliousness** (vv. 6-7, 33). Also mentioned in this same verse (v. 7) where the end says, "But rebelled by the Sea, at the Red Sea."

3. **Refusing to listen to the counsel of God.** Notice v. 13: "But they soon forgot his works, they did not wait for His counsel." Not only did they refuse to listen, they simply didn't wait for the words of the Lord. How often is it tempting for us to do the same, to run ahead of God and not wait for what He would have us to do?

4. **Testing the patience of the Lord** (vv. 14-15, 32). The end of v. 14 plainly states that the people "put God to the test in the desert." All their rebellious ways tried the patience of the Lord, but He remained loving, though He would punish them for their sins.

5. **Envious of leaders** (vv. 16-18). Mentioning specifically Abiram, vv. 16-18 show us that the envy toward Moses and Aaron was still remembered. The end of v. 16 reminds us that Aaron, as the priest, was put there by the Lord, but the people were jealous of that position.

6. **Idol worship** (vv. 19-20, 28-31). Specifically mentioning both the golden calf at Sinai and when the people later worshipped Baal in the Promised Land, this shows the depth of depravity the people had reached. They were exchanging the God who had led them and given then all things for something made by the hands of men.

7. **Fear** (v. 24). The night when the people refused to enter the Promised Land is often used in the Psalms as a reminder of how the people did not trust God. Verse 24 mentions it in this way: "Then they despised the pleasant land, having no faith in His promise." The opposite of faith is not non-faith; it is fear, which dis-

played itself that night in clear and shameful ways.

8. *Lack of trust in the promises of God* (v. 24). That same verse tells us what the people thought about the promises of God. Though He had followed through on all His promises, they refused to trust Him about this land and thought only of the human aspect of things.

9. *Grumbling* (vv. 25-27). Verse 25 begins by stating, "They murmured in their tents," as if to say that they were grumbling out of the way, thinking God wouldn't know about it. But the Lord knows and hears all. Grumbling against God and His appointed leaders will not be tolerated.

10. *Adaptation of sins* (vv. 34-43). Starting in v. 34, the poet writes about how the people did not drive out the nations from the Promised Land but (v. 35), "They mixed with the nations and learned to do as they did." For the next several verses, a litany of sins will be listed that were all adapted from the people the Israelites were supposed to drive out. Instead, they simply adapted the sins of those nations and turned further away from the Lord.

Now, that's an awful list. If we were to dig more deeply into each of these things, we would be appalled, but the power of the list is how long it is. It is a complete corruption by the people who were chosen and protected by the Lord.

But despite all that, in these verses, you also see God's compassion. Yes, in these verses you read of God punishing His people. But quite a few times, there is a beacon of hope because God is good and His mercy endures forever. He was compassionate with His people in spite of all the corruptions they brought upon themselves. At least six different ways are shown in these verses:

- "He saved them for His name's sake" (v. 8).
- "He rebuked the Red Sea, and it became dry, and He

led them through the deep as through a desert. So He saved them from the hand of the foe and redeemed them from the power of the enemy" (vv. 9-10).

- "Many times He delivered them" (v. 43).
- "He looked upon (literally, considered with perception) their distress" (v. 44).
- "For their sake He remembered His covenant, and relented" (v. 45).
- "He caused them to be pitied by all those who held them captive" (v. 46).

What an amazing God! Despite all these sins throughout the years, the faithfulness of God was always there. Yes, He often punished His people, but not out of spite. He was using punishment as a way to bring Israel to the holiness He demands. And how often did the people sin and rebel, yet God was steadfast in His patience and compassion? He was always ready to forgive.

Before we leave this long list of review, I want to return to the very beginning. The poet is not writing this historical poem just to give a dry history lesson. He is actually writing it to those of his own day to show that their people had been sinful in the past, and that people continue to be sinful. Notice v. 6: "Both we and our fathers have sinned; we have committed iniquity; we have done wickedness." In reality, the remainder of this long section is an illustration and a warning. Before you shake your head at how awful these people were, remember we are also God's chosen people, and how often do we fail Him? But praise God—He is good in spite of ourselves!

Requests (vv. 47-48)

Having reviewed the sins of the people and the goodness of God, the poet makes two closing requests. The first is a request of God

Himself, and it should not surprise us. Verse 47 begins, "Save us, O Lord our God, and gather us from among the nations." We have said throughout this chapter that we cannot be certain who the human author is. However, we may have a clue elsewhere in Scripture, and if we do, then this verse takes on even more meaning. In 1 Chron. 16, the Ark of the Covenant is brought up and is presented by David. In celebration of that, David penned some words. At the end of that poem, David wrote, "Say also: Save us, O God of our salvation, and gather and deliver us from among the nations, that we may give thanks to your holy name, and glory in your praise. Blessed be the Lord, the God of Israel, from everlasting to everlasting!" (1 Chron. 16:35-36).

If Psa. 106 is written by David, then what could he mean by the phrase "gather us from among the nations?" At this time, the Israelites were not in exile as they would be later in their history. Instead, David could have in mind God reclaiming His people from sinful ways, as He had done before. If that is done, the people will again turn to the Lord and give Him thanks. Sometimes, it takes God bringing His people back (even via harsh measures) for them to truly bring Him praise. Maybe we need to pray in that manner today.

The other request is for the people, and it is a call for them to agree with the entirety of the poem. The end of v. 48 states, "And let all the people say, 'Amen!' Praise the Lord." "Amen" is often thought of as just a way to end prayers and has come in some of our minds to mean something like "the end." But the Hebrew word carries with it the idea of truth. It can literally be translated "so be it," and it is a statement of agreement with all that has been said.

The poet of Psa. 106 is calling for all the people to speak in agreement with everything that has been stated in this poem. That would include agreeing that not only their ancestors had sinned, but that they also had sinned. That would include the goodness and patience of God. It would include agreeing that it could be good for God to punish people at times. Would we ever say "Amen" to a prayer like that? Would we desire that all these things be so?

Conclusion

"God is so good." Sometimes, those simple words are easier to say and to believe than others. When life is easy and things are going well (at least from our perspective), we praise God and give Him the glory. But when the tide turns and life takes a downward spiral, we must remember that God is still good.

Corrie Ten Boom wrote:

> Often I have heard people say, "How good God is! We prayed that it would not rain for our church picnic, and look at the lovely weather!'" Yes, God is good when He sends good weather. But God was also good when He allowed my sister, Betsie, to starve to death before my eyes in a German concentration camp. I remember one occasion when I was very discouraged there. Everything around us was dark, and there was darkness in my heart. I remember telling Betsie that I thought God had forgotten us. "No, Corrie," said Betsie, "He has not forgotten us. Remember His Word: 'For as the heavens are high above the earth, so great is His steadfast love toward those who fear Him.'" There is an ocean of God's love available–there is plenty for everyone. May God grant you never to doubt that victorious love–whatever the circumstances.[4]

May we be not only able, but willing to say that God is always good because His mercy endures forever! And, with that as our mindset, may our thoughts, our days, and even our life begin and end with "Hallelujah! Praise the Lord!"

---

4. http://www.sermonillustrations.com/a-z/g/god_goodness_of.htm.

Who Is Like the Lord?

PSALM 113

There are certain texts in the Bible, including in the book of Psalms, where we must dig very deeply to mine the meaning of the text. I love those, and we have tried to have some of them as we have gone through the various psalms so far. We will at times find a great nugget of truth in the translation of a word or in a historical setting that sheds great light on the poem itself. Then there are some passages of Scripture that, when you finish reading them, you are lifted up, and you wonder if there is any real need to dig deeply into the text because you are quite certain you can grasp it without trying to uncover some type of hidden truth or difficult meaning.

And that is the case with Psa. 113. Reading these nine verses gives us not just the words, but the sense of the words. As Charles Spurgeon so eloquently said, "This Psalm is one of pure praise, and contains but little which requires exposition."[1] This thought leads us to the natural follow-up question: if a passage is fairly easily understood, then why study it at all? Wouldn't we muddy the waters by trying to break down a text that is so straightforward?

I will say this: if we do that in this chapter, then I have failed in my task. Our goal through these words is to simply use the natural flow of this psalm to gain meaning for our life of faith. While we can

---

1. Spurgeon, *Treasury of David*, 3.1.28.

get the major thrust of the words of the poet by reading these nine verses, there are also some points of application we need to make sure we gain from this wonderful poem of praise. So together, let's consider this poem under just two points, both of which offer great praise to our God.

God's Glory (vv. 1-6)

The opening three verses share the praise of God in two ways.

An Invitation. Verse 1 begins with the Hebrew word *halal*, which is repeated three times in the verse and is translated "praise." The idea behind this word seems to be that of something that is brilliant or shining. There is no way to miss that this is a word meant to be a positive word, as something shone forth from one toward another.

The invitation was to praise the Lord, and v. 1 repeats that three times. The first and third lines of the verse ("Praise the Lord," "Praise the name of the Lord") basically mean the same thing, since a "name" carried with it all the attributes of someone. Praising the name of the Lord is the same as praising the Lord Himself.

The middle line may seem to narrow who should follow this command, but it brings to our minds a realization. Everyone is—or should be—a servant of the Lord. In reality, this is a universal invitation. Everyone who walks on the earth is indebted to God for all He has done; thus, we should all desire to praise Him for His goodness to us. Do I follow that invitation? Is the praise of God constantly in my mind and on my lips?

An Invocation. Verses 2-3 follow up this invitation to praise God with more of a prayer to Him. It is an invocation honoring God for what He so richly deserves. The poet says that the name of the Lord is "blessed." The word translated "blessed" can also be translated "kneel." The idea is that someone is showing homage to another. The name of God—and thus God Himself—is the One worthy of all our homage. We come before Him, kneeling in our hearts, as it were.

And that blessing is to be forever (i.e. "from this time forth and forevermore"). The inspired poet is not seeking a one-time action. Instead, he is trying to invoke the praise of God for all people in all times. Since God is eternal, He deserves praise forever.

Specifically, v. 3 states that the praise should last throughout the day. There are at least two different ways to interpret this verse. The first is simply a straightforward reading that is meant to be personal in nature. From the moment I wake up with the rising sun until I retire in the evening with the setting sun, I should praise God. The other possible meaning is that the sun is a symbol of God, and just the fact that God lets the sun shine on those who are sinful and rebellious should be enough to lead us to praise Him. Whatever the meaning, our days and our life should be filled with God's praise.

In vv. 4-6, the poet expands upon this praise to the Lord and speaks to how much greater God is than mankind. To describe this, the poet lists two things we think of as great, of which the Lord is greater than.

Society. He is "high above all nations." The term "nations" could be used here to speak of those who were Gentiles and did not know the Lord, or it could include both Jew and Gentile (notice "all"). Whichever is in view, we often think of our society as something that is great and powerful. Nationalism can tempt us to turn our attention and trust away from the Lord and more toward a government or army. But God sits above all things and is greater than the strongest of all societies. He is sovereign over them all and rules in the affairs of all people.

Skies. God's "glory [is] above the heavens." Spurgeon wrote, "The clouds are the dust of His feet, and sun, moon, and stars twinkle far below His throne."[2] We often stand in amazement at the beauty and power of what is above us: the power of the sun,

_____

2. Ibid., 3.1.30.

the brilliance of a clear summer day, the strength of rain and snow that fall from the clouds. But God's glory is above all that. And, by using the plural ("heavens"), the poet is saying God's glory is more brilliant than anything beyond the solar system, galaxy, and further. With what we now know about the vastness of our universe, these words should have even greater significance.

Verses 5-6 try to describe for us the position of our Lord. From His place above the greatness of society and the skies, God is compared with anyone else. The key question is at the beginning of v. 5: "Who is like the Lord our God?" The remainder of these two verses fleshes out that question. The poet is basically asking the reader to think of the greatest people—the greatest leader—they can consider. Who would it be? Then compare that person to Jehovah. As good as the human leader might be (as wise, as caring, as visionary), all will fall far short of the power and majesty of God. If nothing else, no human leader can know all that happens under his/her watch.

The word picture in v. 6 of God looking "far down" carries with it two important reminders. The first is that God is high above us, and nothing escapes His view. But the other is that God sees all and is willing to look upon us. He doesn't have to look down upon us in compassion, but He does.

The glory of God is amazing, and the poet of Psa. 113 brings us face to face with His glory and how it is a total contrast with even our greatest leaders. As good as we might be, or as great as some of our leaders might be, they pale in comparison to the glory of God. He is perfect, mighty, and great. For that, we should praise Him.

God's Goodness (vv. 7-9)

As if the previous few lines were not enough to encourage people to praise the Lord, the poet continues. In vv. 7-9, he lists for the reader several specific things the Lord does, and they all demonstrate His goodness. Think about the wisdom of doing that in the context of this poem. After stating that God is a leader who looks down on us, we could get a very cold view of the Lord. After all, when we speak of leaders "looking down" on their subjects, the image conjured up is often very cold and uncaring. But God's looking down is not like that of human leaders. When God looks down, He is not looking down in some condescending way. Instead, He is looking down upon us to care for us out of His love. What an amazing God! To illustrate that, the poet uses two examples.

The poor. Verses 7-8 describe the Lord's amazing power, as He "raises the poor from the dust," but does more than just give them a little money. No, indeed! The Lord makes the poor "sit with princes!"

Psalm 113 was commonly used at Passover, and this reference is one reason why. The poet likely had in mind the way in which the Lord lifted His people from literal dust when they were slaves in Egypt. He brought that lowly nation up and was able to cause their people to become equals on the world stage with the greatest peoples of the time. When we look at these words, we see strong spiritual overtones. We could never have saved ourselves from the mess we were in, but the Lord lifted us up and made us clean and right.

Listen to Spurgeon as he waxes eloquent on this concept:

> How wonderful that power which occupies itself in lifting up beggars, all befouled with the filthiness in which they lay! For He lifts them out of the dunghill, not disdaining to search them out from amidst the base things of the earth that He may by their means bring to nought the great ones, and pour contempt on all human glorying. What a dunghill was that upon which we lay by nature! What a mass of corruption is our original estate! What a heap of loathsomeness we have accumulated by our sinful lives! What reeking abominations surround us in the society of fellow men! We could never have risen out of all this by our own efforts, it was a sepulcher in which we saw

corruption, and were as dead men. Almighty were the arms which lifted us, which are still lifting us, and will lift us into the perfection of heaven itself.[3]

To those words, all I can answer is "Amen! Praise the Lord!"

The barren. Verse 9 goes beyond the poor to something that only the Lord could do. We might argue that a poor person could pull himself/herself up by the bootstraps and end up in a higher economic level of society. That person may even reach to the level of being a great leader and get all the credit for themselves. However, to give the woman who is barren the ability to have children is something only the Almighty could ever do.

In the age of miracles, giving children to the barren was rare, but it did occur. Scripture records the accounts of Sarah, Rachel, the unnamed wife of Manoah, and Hannah in the Old Testament, and Elizabeth in the New Testament. To these women, the impossible became possible through the power of God. Today, the age of miracles has ceased (see 1 Cor. 12-14), but these accounts from Scripture are there to remind us in a vivid way that the Lord can "do far more abundantly than all we ask or think" (Eph. 3:20; cf. Rom. 15:4). Working through His providential power, the Lord still does things today that open our eyes to the wonders of His amazing power.

Look back over these two examples written by the poet. For sure, these are not things that an ordinary human leader could do. But they are also not the type of thing most human leaders would do, even if they had the power. Most human leaders are concerned primarily with holding others down and making sure their own power is preserved. Too many are ruthless, but even many of those who are not ruthless in their heart still have a certain level of selfishness that is very difficult to overcome. If they raise up the poor, it is not usually to make sure that the poor have the same rights or abilities as the

---

3. Spurgeon, *Treasury of David*, 3.1.31.

leaders do. For example, what member of Congress is working on a program to pretty much guarantee the poorest member of his/her district earns a salary equal to that of members of Congress?

In contrast, God raises us far higher than we could imagine. We will not become God, of course, but He places us at levels that the rest of society never would. That's how good He is to His people.

Conclusion

Coming full circle, and knowing both the glory and the goodness of God, the poem ends as it began: "Praise the Lord." *Halel! Yahh.* Hallelujah! Is the praise of God continually on our lips? The words of Psa. 146:2 inspired a hymn that has a bit of a connection to our psalm. That verse opens with the words, "I will praise the Lord as long as I live." Using that idea, Isaac Watts wrote a hymn that he called "I'll Praise My Maker." Interestingly, when the words were put to music by a man named Matthaus Greiter, the name of the tune was "Old 113th." I want to close with two stories about this hymn, then let you know the lyrics.

John Wesley was about 21 years of age when he went to Oxford University. He came from a Christian home, and he was gifted with a keen mind and good looks. But in those days, he was a bit snobbish and sarcastic. One night, however, something happened that set in motion a change in Wesley's heart. While speaking with a porter, he discovered that the poor fellow had only one coat and lived in such impoverished conditions that he didn't even have a bed. Yet he was an unusually happy person, filled with gratitude to God. Wesley, being immature, thoughtlessly joked about the man's misfortunes. "And what else do you thank God for?" he said with a touch of sarcasm. The porter smiled, and in the spirit of meekness replied with joy, "I thank Him that He has given me my life and being, a heart to love Him, and above all a constant desire to serve Him!" Deeply moved, Wesley recognized that this man knew the meaning of true thankfulness. Many years later, in 1791, John Wesley lay on his deathbed at the age of 88. Those who gathered around him realized how well he had learned the lesson of praising God in every circumstance. Despite Wesley's extreme weakness, he began singing the hymn, "I'll Praise My Maker."

The second story is of an elderly Christian man, a fine singer, who learned that he had cancer of the tongue and that surgery was required. In the hospital, after everything was ready for the operation, the man said to the doctor, "Are you sure I will never sing again?" The surgeon found it difficult to answer his question. He simply shook his head no. The patient then asked if he could sit up for a moment. "I've had many good times singing the praises of God," he said. "And now you tell me I can never sing again. I have one song that will be my last. It will be of gratitude and praise to God." There in the doctor's presence, the man sang softly the words of Isaac Watts' hymn, "I'll praise my Maker."[4]

These are interesting stories, but why are they significant? Read carefully the opening lyrics of Watts' song:

> I'll praise my maker while I've breath,
> And when my voice is lost in death,
> Praise shall employ my nobler powers;
> My days of praise shall ne'er be past,
> While life, and thought, and being last,
> Or immortality endures.

The words remind us of exactly what the inspired poet of Psa. 113 was stating, "Blessed be the name of the Lord from this time forth and forevermore! From the rising of the sun to its setting, the name of the Lord is to be praised!" So, Hallelujah! Praise the Lord!

---

4. Both stories from http://www.sermonillustrations.com/a-z/p/praise.htm.

The Heart of God's Child

PSALM 119:129-136

It is the answer to one of the first Bible trivia questions many of us learn: "What is the longest chapter in the Bible?" Assuming we classify the psalms as chapters, Psa. 119 is by far the longest in Scripture. Containing 176 verses, this poem has either touched the hearts of Bible students or scared them off due to its length.

I don't have any obvious reason why, but when I was a teenager I frequently read parts of this psalm. I'm embarrassed to admit, but I think it was just because it was long, and I wanted to see how much I could read in certain amounts of time. Even if my reasons were not the noblest, I'm glad I have that background in this amazing poem. This great poem is more than just long; it is beautiful.

If you think this poem is long, consider some of the literature written about it. Charles Bridges wrote a book on this singular psalm. One hardback copy of his exposition fills 512 pages. But that is child's play compared to what Thomas Manton produced on this one poem. Manton, who was a preacher for the Puritans, wrote a 190-chapter book, filling 1,677 pages over three volumes, all on this one psalm! And if you ever want to complain that your preacher goes too long in a series, remember that these 190 chapters were originally 190 sermons Manton preached on this single psalm.

There are a couple of other things, besides the length, that make this psalm very interesting from a literary standpoint. The first is something the translators have tried to help us see. You may notice as you look over the psalm that, every few verses, there is a little break with a weird-looking word above it (*Alepth, Beth, Gimel,* etc.). These come every eight verses. Those words are the names of the 22 letters of the Hebrew alphabet. When David wrote this psalm, each of the eight verses in that section began with that same letter, so the poem is actually a giant montage of sorts, containing 22 shorter acrostic sections. While that does not come across very well in English, it tells us something of the amazing literary talent of David in writing this poem.

The other aspect is the subject of this psalm. For 176 verses, David does not for a moment move away from the subject of the Word of God. About 171 times in these 176 verses, words such as "law," "testimonies," "precepts," "commandments," and "statutes" are used, in addition to "word." The emphasis is always on how these are from God. While there are many places in the Bible we can go to for an emphasis on Scripture, there is no other place where the emphasis is so concentrated in one passage. It is interesting that the longest chapter in the Bible deals with the importance of God's Word.

When we look into the Word of God, it tells us a great deal about ourselves. In this lesson, we want to look at just one portion of Psa. 119 and see what it tells us about our own heart. If we have a heart that is seeking after God—if we are one of God's children—then there are certain things that should be true about that heart. From vv. 129-136, we want to notice eight traits present in the heart of God's child.

Reverential (v. 129)

We could use almost any verse from this psalm to make this point, but notice the emphasis of v. 129, that the testimonies are

God's testimonies. Nearly every one of the 171 times God's word is mentioned in this psalm, it is "your" Word (here, "Your testimonies").

David goes on to state that these testimonies are wonderful. The idea behind this word is not quite the same as our word "miraculous," but it is close. The emphasis here is that the testimonies of the Lord are superhuman. They are something above what mankind or nature could ever give. We must come to the realization, as Paul did, that "all Scripture is given by the inspiration of God" (2 Tim. 3:16). It is something greater than what we could ever produce. Knowing that, David writes, "My soul keeps them." There is a submissiveness in these words that many of us often fail to have.

Do we see that the Word of God—all of it—is to be kept? David was submissive in heart and wanted to do God's will. Only by having a reverence for God and His Word will that ever be part of our lives.

Respectful (v. 130)

We get this from the very end of each line of this verse, where words are used to show a great deal of humility by David. By stating that God's Word "gives light," there is an implication that light is needed. Here, of course, light is being used to describe that someone needs information. We still speak that way when someone does not know something, claiming they are "in the dark." David does not want to be in the dark, but he knows that true light only comes from the Word of God. To further emphasize that idea, he writes that those who do not have the words of God are "simple." The word is one that was used for someone who was naïve, or someone who was easily enticed. Again, there is serious humility in knowing and being willing to state that one does not know everything.

The respect of this verse is found in that David does not claim to have all the answers for how to be one who is in the light, or one who is no longer easily enticed. He understands that only the words of God can bring light and help him have a foundation of faith.

Do I really believe the same thing? Too often, we can feel as if we are the answer to all our problems, even though we often caused the problems in the first place! At other times, we are like those of Isaiah's day who call dark, "light" (Isa. 5:20). God's Word is the only true standard that can help us call things as they are and be able to see the light in the midst of a very dark and corrupt world. Do I have that kind of respect for all of God's Word? And do I have that kind of respect for it, not just because of the darkness I see in others, but for the need I have to walk in the light?

Ravenous (v. 131)

One of the most interesting word pictures in the entire poem is found in this section. In v. 131, David writes, "I open my mouth and pant, because I long for Your commandments." That is a powerful word picture, and it is one we cannot fail to get in our minds. Even the word "open" is a very strong word. In Job 29:23 the same Hebrew word (*paar*) is used to describe those who open their mouth to drink rain as it falls after a long dry season. Couple that with the idea of panting, and the picture here is of a ravenous beast who is thirsty and showing that in a visible, unmistakable way.

It certainly leads to a strong point of application for me to ask in my own life. Do I have that same ravenous desire to hear and read the commandments of God? Could I describe my desire to hear from the Lord through His Word as insatiable?

Consider for a moment what the poet was longing after—the "commandments" of the Lord. While there might be certain biblical accounts or even some of the psalms that I long to hear because they sooth my soul and build my faith, do I have this same attitude for the commandments of the Lord? What God demands, I must seek after with that same insatiable attitude.

Step back for a moment to consider the whole of the Bible. What is my desire for what God says? Many of us treat the Bible as a snack. We get just enough to sooth ourselves for a little while—almost like appeasing our "sweet tooth"—then we go on to other things that we desire more. Hearing from God through His Word should be something we are longing after. Our thirst for what God has to say should be ravenous!

Resigned (v. 132)

One of the great temptations of our hearts can be to be righteous so that others will take notice. We can follow the rules and then have a "look at me" attitude. But such is not the right attitude of a follower of God. No matter how much good we might do, we still must have a humble attitude. Jesus would state it this way: "Blessed are the poor in spirit, for theirs is the kingdom of heaven" (Matt. 5:3). Isaiah would remind us that, if we piled up all our righteous deeds, they would still be "like a polluted garment" (Isa. 64:6).

Obviously, we are to do good works (Matt. 5:16), but our focus should never be on doing those good works just to build up our own reputation. Instead, we must have the attitude of v. 132. Before reading the verse, remember that these are words written not as a statement to another person, but as a prayer to the Lord. "Turn to me and be gracious to me, as is your way with those who love your name." That needs to always be our attitude. We must seek the graciousness of God. Our attitude needs to be one that seeks to do God's will in a humble way, realizing we could never do enough to "prove" our worth to the One who is perfectly holy and right.

When we begin to think too highly of our own good works, we will start to think less of God. Instead, be poor in spirit and seek the graciousness of the Lord. That's the heart of one who is God's child.

Right-seeking (v. 133)

This may be the most obvious trait of our study, but it still needs to be pointed out. With all the temptations in the world, it is not enough to "happen" to do things that are right. We need to be intentional about seeking to do what is right. Our heart needs to be one that has that as its desire. In v. 133, David wrote, "Keep steady my steps according to your promise, and let no iniquity get dominion over me." That is a powerful prayer! Notice the little word "no"—not a single bit of iniquity.

It can be easy for us to have certain sins that we do not see as a big deal, and we sort of hide them over on the side. We don't do any "big" sins, so we don't mind something more private that isn't really hurting anyone. But Paul wrote, "Do you not know that if you present yourselves to anyone as obedient slaves, you are slaves of one whom you obey, either of sin, which leads to death, or of obedience which leads to righteousness?" (Rom. 6:16). Jesus famously reminded us that you cannot serve two masters (Matt. 6:24).

The whole of our heart needs to be on seeking to do what is right, and not allowing any single iniquity to keep hold of our heart. Am I seeking what is right, and am I seeking God's help to steady my steps in His way? That's the heart of one who is a child of God!

Redeemed (v. 134)

David makes a direct request of God in v. 134, that God would "redeem [him] from man's oppression." While what man can do to us may pale in comparison to the power of God, the oppression of man is still difficult for us to endure. We are human, and being turned away by our fellow man is hard to take. Concerning this phrase, Spurgeon wrote,

David had tasted all the bitterness of this great evil. It had made him an exile from his country, and banished him from the sanctuary of the Lord: therefore he pleads to be saved from it. It is said that oppression makes a wise man mad, and no doubt it has made many a righteous man sinful.[1]

But notice David's conclusion. He was not just asking God to get him out of a tight spot. There was a higher purpose: "That I may keep your precepts." While we can, and must, obey God no matter our external circumstances, there is nothing wrong with praying that God will help us have a better path to follow. That is especially true when the way seems too hard to bear. However, we must also be willing to uphold our end of things. If (or when) God does provide deliverance, it can be easy for us to turn away from Him in our newfound ease. We must continue to follow His ways, whether times are good or bad.

Of course, as New Testament Christians, we should know the real and full meaning of redemption. Instead of being redeemed merely from the harmful ways of man, we are redeemed from the eternally damning ways of sin. When we let our mind dwell on that, it should fill us with joy and give us strong motivation to always obey the precepts of God.

Ready (v. 135)

The end of v. 135 shows humility yet again, but in a different way than before. Instead of asking again for God to show graciousness to him, David says, "Teach me your statutes." The heart of God's child is one that desires to know the way of God, but is humble enough to admit there are things unknown to him/her.

In the midst of this great psalm, this request is even more interesting. As we said in the introduction, this entire psalm is built upon

---

1. Spurgeon, *Treasury of David*, 3.1.379.

praising the Word of God. Throughout the poem, there are dozens of statements that show that David knew the Word of God well. Just notice four well-known verses as examples:

- "I have stored up your word in my heart, that I might not sin against you" (v. 11).
- "I will delight in your statutes; I will not forget your word" (v. 16).
- "Oh how I love your law! It is my meditation all the day. Your commandment makes me wiser than my enemies, for it is ever with me" (vv. 97-98).
- "Your word is a lamp to my feet and a light to my path" (v. 105).

But even with that intimate knowledge of the Word of God, David was ready to know more. The more he knew, the more he realized there was more to know.

Each year, I try to read through the Bible. As a preacher, teacher, and Christian, I try to take in as much of the Bible as I can for each aspect of my life. But the more I read and study, the more I come to realize I have a long way to go in my knowledge of the Bible. The main things in Scripture are easy to understand, but there are passages that have such depth that mining them is a lifelong pursuit. God's child must always be ready to take in more of God's Word.

Reflective (v. 136)

The final verse in this section of the psalm begins in a way that might make us think less of David since he writes about shedding "streams of tears." Our culture does not like the idea of someone who is overly emotional, and that is especially true of males. However, notice the reason for David's emotion in this verse: "Because people do not keep your law." How powerful is that! David had such a strong desire for people to know and obey God that he wept when he knew they were not doing as God directed.

We are giving this verse the heading "reflective" because it takes both the willingness to look into the hearts of others and the willingness to care enough for their soul that we are emotionally touched by their obedience or disobedience to God's will.

Too many Christians see others in sin and just think it's no big deal. Or we look forward to the day when they will "get what's coming" to them by way of God's punishment. We need to see the act of following God's Word as the most important thing anyone could ever do. It should lead us to sorrow when we know that people are not following what God would have them do. Have you ever shed tears because someone was not a Christian? Have I? To do this, we must have a heart willing to reflect on what God has said and a heart that is reaching out to others in a way that shows a strong desire for them to know God's will for their life.

Conclusion

All of Psa. 119—176 verses in total—focus on the Word of God. If we focus on it also, yet fail to make it part of our lives of faith, we have missed the entire point of what the inspired poet was trying to write. After looking at just this short section, my prayer is that we all seek to look more deeply into the Bible and let it penetrate our heart, so that we, too, can have a heart that reflects what it means to truly be a child of God. As Lloyd O. Sanderson wrote:

> How precious is the Book divine,
> By inspiration giv'n!
> Bright as a lamp its precepts shine,
> To guide my soul to heav'n.
>
> It sweetly cheers my drooping heart,
> In this dark vale of tears;

Light to my life it still imparts,
And quells my rising fears.

This lamp, thro' all the tedious night
Of life, shall guide my way,
Till I behold the clearer light
Of an eternal day.

Holy Bible, book divine—
Precious treasure, thou art mine.
Lamp to my feet and a light to my way
To guide me safely home.

Looking Up for Mercy

PSALM 123

They are fifteen in number and begin after the well-known 119th Psalm. They are usually called the psalms (or songs) of ascent, but they can also be called the songs of degree. These poems, which run consecutively from Psa. 120-134, were sung by the people of Israel as they came to the city of Jerusalem for feasts. As they walked up the incline toward the city, these songs filled the air with joy and praise. While there are words in some of these poems that express difficulty or fear, the vast majority of lines in these fifteen poems are filled with praise and glory to God.

In 1 Chron. 13:6, we are told, "And David and all Israel went up to Baalah, that is, to Kiriath-Jearim that belongs to Judah, to bring up from there the ark of God." The phrase "bring up" is a form of the same word in the superscription of these psalms: "ascents" or "degrees." Some suggest that since there is a connection with the ark, these poems were sung by the priests as they walked up the steps of the temple. Others believe that all the people sung them as they neared the city of Jerusalem. The key, though, is that these were songs that were lifted in praise, and even used the imagery of walking "up" to underscore the praise of God.

If you look at the fifteen poems individually, you will also notice they are quite short. The longest (Psa. 132) is just eighteen verses, and most of them are five to eight verses in length. The psalm at the center of our attention is Psa. 123, which is just four verses in length, but fits perfectly within the concept of the people being lifted as they go up to God to praise Him.

In Psa. 120 (the first of the Psalms of Ascent), the people cried out to God from their distress but knew that the Lord would answer. In Psa. 121, the worshiper is lifting up his eyes to the hills and seeing the Lord and finding assurance in Him. In Psa. 122, there is now joy, and that poem begins with the famous words, "I was glad when they said to me, 'Let us go to the house of the Lord!'" So his eyes are now on the city of Jerusalem and the temple. And now, in Psa. 123, the ascent continues, and the worshiper looks only to the Lord. As Spurgeon wrote, "The eyes are now looking above the hills, and above Jehovah's footstool on earth, to His throne in the heavens."[1]

As the praise has now built to its height, looking fully to God in heaven, this psalm is one that is filled with praise and trust. We will examine this poem in just two points, but notice that both of our thoughts focus solely on the Lord above.

Raising Eyes to God (vv. 1-2)

The key to the opening two verses is found in the second line of v. 1: "O you who are enthroned in the heavens." Whenever we need help, we need to know where to look, and the psalmist reminds us that our eyes need to go directly to the Lord. Also in speaking this way about God, there is a clear indication of respect for the Lord. By writing about the throne of God, we are reminded of at least two attributes of God that we never need to lose sight of.

His majesty. The Lord is a majestic king. Even in the final book of the Bible, we are reminded many times of the majesty of the Lord. In Rev. 4, John is given a glimpse into the throne room of God in

---

1. Spurgeon, *Treasury of David*, 3:39.

heaven. The appearance of God is represented by light and precious jewels, and everything surrounding the throne is glorious and praising Him. All of it has to do with the majesty of God as the very center of praise. As the praise goes up to Him, we are told that the continuous words offered are, "Worthy are you, our Lord and God, to receive glory and honor and power; for you created all things, and by your will they existed and were created" (4:11). The words we sometimes sing are quite simple, but express what needs to be stated to our God: "O Lord, our Lord, how majestic is Your name in all the earth!"

His justice. Speaking of the Lord on a throne reminds us that He is the great judge, and He sees all that happens. His throne being in heaven helps us to remember that even the strongest of earthly leaders is under the Lord's watchful eye. He will judge all, and He is a perfect and righteous Judge.

The rest of the first two verses provide a comparison for us, and it may be one that makes us a bit uncomfortable. The poet writes about a servant (or slave) who looks to the master and a maidservant to her mistress, then compares that to how we should be looking to the Lord. If we did not have the end of v. 2, this could be somewhat confusing or almost degrading. We do not like the idea of being compared to a slave with someone over us. And considering U.S. history, we have every right to feel quite uncomfortable with that comparison. But since none of us was alive when slavery was part of American culture, these pictures lose something on us, but we know the point the poet is trying to make.

However, the end of v. 2 says that we keep our eyes on the Lord in that way "till He has mercy upon us." Think for a moment about the implications of that. God is a God of mercy, and it is one of the traits we appreciate the most. His mercy is something we rely on in greater depth throughout our lives. But the psalmist is saying that there may come a time when we have to wait to know that mercy. While the Lord's mercies are "new every morning" (Lam.

3:23), there may be instances in our lives when it takes some time to realize or recognize His mercy. Still, we keep looking to the Lord. Our eyes remain on Him for this reason: He is the only One who can truly provide mercy, and we so need it in our lives.

Place this concept back in the overall picture of the Psalms of Ascent, and you get an even more powerful idea. In Psa. 121, the poet needed to know the assurance and protection of the Lord, so he looked to the hills since the Lord made them. In Psa. 122, the poet wanted to praise God and be near Him, so he was glad when it was time to go up to the temple in Jerusalem. Now the poet recognizes that he needs the mercy of the Lord, and that can only be found from One who is in control, so the poet goes to the throne of the Lord in heaven. In faith, that is where he will find mercy.

Are we looking for God everywhere? Too often, we can see God in creation and be in awe of His design or His eternal intelligence. But when we seek God's mercy, we must look beyond the world and realize that mercy can only be extended when we realize who is in control. So we must go before God's throne by faith.

Requesting Mercy from God (vv. 3-4)

In the second half of the psalm, that is exactly what the poet does. Now that he has made the realization that he needs to raise his eyes to God's throne to seek mercy, he pleads for that mercy in the latter half of the poem. The plea is simple enough and breaks naturally into two parts.

The request. Twice in v. 3, the request is given in exactly the same words: "Have mercy upon us." Before continuing in this lesson, we need to define what is meant by the idea of "mercy." The Hebrew word (*chanan*) is translated many ways in the Bible. Some of those ways include "graciously given" (Gen. 33:5), "gracious" (Exod. 33:19), "be favorable" (Judg. 21:22), and even "supplication" (2

Chron. 6:24). When you put all those together, you get a clearer picture of the request the poet is making.

He is asking God to give gracious favor to the people. He is not stating that they have the right to anything. Instead, he is leaning on the grace of God to pour out favor upon them since the Lord alone is the only One who could grant it. Now you see why the pictures of a slave and a maidservant could be used in v. 2. Just as only the master could grant mercy in those situations, so God alone can grant this type of gracious favor to us.

Notice that we are calling it a "request." This is not a demand. There is still a great deal of respect, as you see the words "O Lord" in between the request twice being made. The poet knows to whom he is making this request, and he is coming before the Lord in reverence and respect. Remember that God is majestic and seated upon a throne of judgment, so there must be respect.

The reason. This is not some hollow request. The poet goes on to share the reason why he would raise his eyes to heaven and make this request of the Lord. The end of v. 3 states, "For we have had more than enough of contempt." The remainder of the psalm restates the same thing in more words, adding to our understanding of what is going on. Others had been scornful, though they were the ones at ease and had shown contempt even though they were arrogant (or proud).

Aren't you glad those in the Bible write or talk this way at times? Here was a poet in the midst of a time of praise who still poured out his soul and said, "We have had enough!" These writers were people just like you and I. There are many times when we praise God and love Him, but we have had enough of what people are doing to us because of our faith.

The KJV says, "We are exceedingly filled with contempt." There are times when our cup overflows from the goodness of God (cf. Psa. 23:5), and there are times when it is as if our cup overflows with the bitterness of others. Both are real, and the Bible addresses both. And, we need to note, God desires to hear both.

Here you have an inspired poet writing about some situation (we do not know the historical background of the psalm) and is willing to state to the Lord, "We are overflowing with contempt from other people." To make matters worse, the contempt was coming from people who, from an earthly standpoint, had it all together because they were "at ease" and "proud."

Conclusion

"That's all well and good," someone is thinking, "But this is an Old Testament passage." Today, we still get filled up with difficulties and need somewhere to turn. Can we have the same attitude as the poet of Psa. 123? We can actually have something far better if we will just follow the New Testament! The people of the Old Testament had to go through all sorts of ritual in their prayers and feasts, and only then could they really feel any sort of connection with God. Even then, they were tethered to a priestly system and never truly felt as if they had access to the Lord in a personal, direct way.

But we do! Because of the work of Jesus Christ, we have access to the very throne of God through our perfect High Priest, Jesus. The book of Hebrews was written to Christians who had been under the Old Testament law and were considering returning because they were being persecuted for their faith in Christ. The writer reminds them over and over of how much better they have it through the blood of Jesus and how much better the way of the Lord is now.

While we may not be tempted to return to Judaism, there are times when we are filled up and may consider walking away from the faith because there has to be something better. If you are ever tempted in that way, keep Psa. 123 in your mind and listen to these famous words from Heb. 4:14-16:

Since then we have a great high priest who has passed
through the heavens, Jesus, the Son of God, let us
hold fast our confession. For we do not have a high
priest who is unable to sympathize with our weaknesses, but one who in every respect has been tempted
as we are, yet without sin. Let us then with confidence
draw near to the throne of grace, that we may receive
mercy and find grace to help in time of need.

Look at what we have today! Where did the psalmist look? To
the throne in heaven where God is. Where is Jesus? He is right
there, having passed through the heavens and is now seated at the
right hand of God. What was the reason for the plea in our psalm?
They were filled up with contempt from those who did not believe.
What do we have? We have a high priest who understands all that
because people were contemptuous toward Him to the point of putting Him to death for His teaching. And what was the psalmist seeking? Mercy—gracious favor. What can we find when we have need?
"Mercy and ... grace to help in time of need."

What an amazing Lord we serve! We need mercy many times in
our lives because people will not like what we teach or what we do.
But we can lift our eyes to the majestic throne of justice where God
is, and find the gracious favor only He can provide. Then, we can face
this world of contempt and go on ascending in praise to our Lord.
Where are your eyes?

The Wise Man Built His House Upon the Rock

PSALM 127

If Solomon is the inspired author of the fascinating book of Ecclesiastes, then this wise king gives us an amazing look at a life that most in the world would consider to be perfect. From the world's perspective, Solomon had it all. He was rich beyond accounting, was able to build a harem with an unthinkable number of women, and had power that monarchs still dream of. If Solomon were alive today, he would be the most famous person on earth (which tells us more than we might want to admit about our society). However, after chronicling that lifestyle, Solomon ended the book of Ecclesiastes with extremely profound words: "The end of the matter; all has been heard. Fear God and keep His commandments, for this is the whole duty of man. For God will bring every deed into judgment, with every secret thing, whether good or evil" (12:13-14).

Here was a man who tried to build his life on everything earthly and sensual, and only after knowing the short-lived and bitter fruits of it all did he come away with true wisdom: an eternal perspective. Why all this talk of Solomon? Because we are told in the superscription that Psa. 127 was penned by this amazing individual. Rather than writing about the huge pleasures of this life, Solomon pens words that are about something far simpler: having a home that is blessed. Don't you find it interesting that this man who tried it all would pen a poem that focuses instead on what we might call the simpler pleasures?

About 950 years after Solomon, One greater than Solomon would talk about a wise man being the one who built his house upon the rock. When the storms came, that person's house continued to stand (Matt. 7:24-25). In Psa. 127, we read words that are completely countercultural because they are not what you will read in magazines about how to have a good home. Instead, what we are reading here are inspired words that will help us be wise: those who build homes upon the rock of the Word of God. In this chapter, let's notice how to do that by walking through this simple psalm.

Building a Godly Home (vv. 1-2)

As Solomon begins this great poem, he shares some countercultural ways to have a proper home. As expected, they focus attention away from self, and toward God.

Needed trust. First, Solomon writes that, for a home to be what it needs to be, it must be grounded in God. "Unless the Lord builds the house, those who build it labor in vain." Do you not find it interesting that the man who is so renowned for building the house of the Lord—the temple—would tell us how to build our own house?

There is also a tie here with Solomon's other writings. Again, if he is the author of Ecclesiastes, he often used the phrase "vanity of vanities." Three times in the opening two verses of this psalm, including here, he tells us what is vain in our homes. We must let the Lord build our house, or our efforts are in vain. That is not to say that a non-Christian home cannot last, but it is not all it could be. Simply by not allowing the Lord to be the true Builder of that relationship, it will be lacking in joy, peace, and other wonderful blessings, in good times and in bad.

To further emphasize that, Solomon expands on the picture of a house and adds walls, making it a city with watchmen. But notice the trust in the Lord implied in these words. We can have all the watchmen we want in place, but it is ultimately the Lord who looks out for His people.

In an earlier psalm, Solomon's father, David had, said, "Some trust in chariots and some in horses, but we trust in the name of the Lord our God" (20:7). The same is true of too many nations. We are thankful for our military, but we can put too much trust in them and fail to put our real trust in the Lord.

Too often, this happens in our homes as well. We know there are temptations and barriers in our homes, but we decide we will take care of everything ourselves. If we are not careful, we can put so much emphasis on our own strength and protection that we feel as if we no longer need God. But our homes need God's protection! We need to seek His wisdom in watching over our homes and helping avoid true disaster—the infiltration of sin into our hearts and minds.

Needless toil. In v. 3, Solomon wrote words that every American family needs to hear. "It is in vain that you rise up early and go late to rest, eating the bread of anxious toil; for He gives to His beloved sleep." Was Solomon saying that we are not to be diligent in caring for our homes? Not at all, but He was saying that we put too much stock in what we can do. We are running from early morning until late at night trying to do all we can to build up our home. We think the more we do, the more protected we will be from bad stuff. But if we are honest, we too often think that the "bad stuff" is not having enough material things. So we run harder and try to get more stuff, thinking that will protect us from anything that could harm our home.

How does the verse end? Speaking of the Lord, we are told, "He gives to His beloved sleep." Why are we running the rat race all the time when we have a God who will provide just what we need? We must do some work, and we are to do our work unto God. The Lord never excuses laziness, but He also does not excuse us destroying ourselves in the name of a lack of trust in His helping hand.

Solomon's father also wrote words along this line. In Psa. 37:25-26, he said, "I have been young, and now am old, yet I have not seen the righteous forsaken or His children begging for bread. He is ever lending generously, and His children become a blessing." Does that mean God will give us a 60-inch flat screen TV? No, but it should also provide us with a great deal of peace that God will give us what we need throughout our lives. In our homes, we need to work hard, then leave the rest in God's hands and trust that He will provide what we most need in this life.

Put these together, and you have the formula for having a godly home. Realize there are certain things you must do, but recognize that God is the head of it all. Solomon does not say we should never labor in building a home, but it is vain if we try to build it without God's leadership. It is not wrong to watch over your house and protect it from danger, but make sure the Lord is the true guide in how you watch. It is not wrong to work, and in fact that is required, but we must ultimately trust in the Lord for what we need.

Blessing a Godly Home (vv. 3-5)

If trusting in the Lord to have a good home is countercultural, then Solomon has saved something truly different for the second half of his poem. After reminding us to trust in God, he turns to the blessings that come when we do, and he claims these blessings are children. This is not to say that families who do not have children have sinned or are being punished by the Lord for some gross immorality. Instead, Solomon is linking one generation to the next. If one generation is trusting in God and builds a faithful home, then if that family has children, those blessings are likely passed on. But there is also a blessing for the family itself. And that's where Solomon begins.

The reward of children. "Behold, children are a heritage from the Lord, the fruit of the womb a reward." The word "heritage" can also be translated "inheritance" and may indicate a bit of a play on words from the previous part of the psalm. If a person has built a house and toiled in the way God has provided, who will he leave things to? Who will get an inheritance? God is saying that, if children come into the family, the inheritance from the Lord will get that inheritance.

Notice that children are clearly called a blessing by Solomon. While most of us would agree with that, if we are not careful, we can say things that betray us. How often do we act as if children are a nuisance; something that prevents us from being able to climb the corporate ladder or get more of what we want out of life? Of course, the ultimate extreme of that mindset is seen in those who support the notion that a baby in the womb should just be done away with if it doesn't match up with what you want in life. Each year, Americans kill over a million children in the womb out of sheer selfishness.

Children are a blessing. Yes, they might frustrate at times, and they might make certain things in life more difficult, but they are given to us by God. The children we are given should be treated as His reward given to us.

The rearing of children. The picture of v. 4 speaks to the aging process. You can see the skilled warrior reaching for an arrow and hitting the target. For that to happen, an arrow must be both aimed and released. It must be aimed through proper training, but the training needs to be godly for it to be proper. Children can be aimed anywhere, but they can also be aimed nowhere. What are we aiming our children toward? Our prayer as parents needs to be that we aim them toward God, but also toward faithful, sacrificial, strong Christian service. We want them to set the target toward heaven and realize that, to reach that target, they must honor God here.

An arrow must also be released to be effective. If we aim and aim and aim and never shoot the arrow, it is ineffective. Eventually, the warrior has to release the bowstring so the arrow sails toward the target. As parents, we must do the same. And while we will continue to pray and help as we can, the decisions at that point will be up to our children. Too many parents never release their children, so they just remain "children." They do not mature and grow. They do not sail toward the target. It is a blessing to a family to know that they have reared their children in such a way that they are now able to sail toward the target of heaven, straight and true.

The return of children. The final verse of the psalm is about as countercultural as we could get. Not only does Solomon state that it is a blessing to have children, but he also says (continuing the imagery of a warrior), "Blessed is the man who fills his quiver with them!" In other words, Solomon felt it was a blessing to have many children.

On the other hand, today we see the cost of children and how they hinder us from gaining economic ground in this world. But the Bible doesn't treat it that way. It is a blessing—not some type of freak reality show—to have several children. And in a practical way, Solomon writes that there is a return when this happens. The man gains a level of respect. The one who has many children is said to be respected even by his enemies when he speaks with them in the gate.

Notice that these conversations occur at the gate. This was the place where business commonly occurred. It was where judgments were rendered and transactions took place. It was a place of honor. Solomon is clearly stating that the one who has children is able to stand in respect, either because he is respected or because his children are carrying his legacy into the future, and they are standing strong. Either way, that's a pretty good return on an investment!

Conclusion

How do you want to build your home? I think it is key that Solomon is the one who wrote Psa. 127, since he is the one who built the house of God. Recall that, regarding the temple:

He had preparation. David, his father, laid out instructions, but

Solomon was wise enough to take those instructions and make sure they were correct. If we want to have a godly home, we need to prepare for it. If you are not yet married, do not just think of getting married. Think of how you can insure that you have a godly home.

He had comprehension. Solomon's wisdom is legendary, but we know that God has promised to grant us wisdom if we will just ask Him. Do we ever pray for His wisdom in leading our families?

He had moderation. It took seven years to build the temple. Some of that was simply because it took a long time to build things in those days. But for seven years, Solomon led this work. Having a home built on a godly foundation is not going to happen in a matter of days or weeks. It needs to be a constant, patient pursuit.

He had a celebration. The dedication of the temple is a landmark event in Old Testament history. It contains the longest recorded prayer in the Old Testament, and it is a prayer that honors and glorifies God. When our homes have a moment of victory in our spiritual life, we need to celebrate. This is not done in an arrogant way, but in a way that brings glory to God for what has been done.

What you really have in Psa. 127 is an application of Jesus' great statement that the wise man is the one who builds his house on the rock. Are you wise?

Lifting an Aching Soul

PSALM 130

Have you ever been down? Has your soul ever ached for help? If you answered "yes" to those questions, that makes you one thing: human. We've all gone through a time when it seemed as if the world was against us, when it seemed as if darkness was our only companion. It is in these times that people often find the most comfort and help in the book of Psalms.

There are several biblical narratives that speak to these times in life. You might think of Elijah under the juniper tree. We might think of Esther, upon realizing what could happen to her people if she didn't stand before the king. We could look to Job's suffering that seemed to never end. And of course, we could travel in our mind's eye to Gethsemane and see Jesus in the depths of despair. Those accounts help us see that others who were faithful to the Lord went through awful times of darkness and confusion.

When we go through these difficult times, we come to the psalms because they express in raw and clear ways how we are thinking and feeling. I find it a testament to the grace of God that He would have these poems included in Scripture. It shows us that He knows the cries of our heart, not only when we are doing well, but also when life is seemingly completely against us.

Psalm 130 is a short poem that has touched countless lives

throughout the years. It has done so, in part, because of the setting. The poet is crying to God from "the depths," and as the poem goes on, it becomes clear that this is a symbolic word. He is crying to God out of the depths of difficulty. But this poem has also touched many lives because of the tone. While the poet is struggling, he is focused on God and willing to let Him control the situation. It is a poem that expresses a profound perspective, even in the midst of struggle.

In this chapter, we will walk through this great psalm and see if it will help us keep a proper perspective when we, like all people, go through a time when our soul aches for something better.

Hearing (vv. 1-4)

As the poet begins this powerful psalm, he speaks directly to the Lord, seeking a hearing from Him, but also recognizing that no one is worthy of coming before God of his own accord.

The Cry (vv. 1-2). As we've stated, there are times when we are about as low as we can be, and it is from that state that the poet cries to the Lord, calling it "the depths." When I read those words, I can't help but think of Jonah, the prophet who cried out to God from the literal depths. After he was thrown into the sea, the prepared sea creature swallowed Jonah. An often forgotten part of the short book of Jonah is chapter 2, in which the prophet pours out his heart to God from the belly of that sea creature. He repents, and he cries out to God. Even from that very odd place, God heard the cry of the prophet.

Of course, the phrase in Psa. 130 is not meant to be taken literally, but the story of Jonah serves as a great foundation for us to consider. God will hear us from literal depths, but He will also hear us from emotional depths.

The rest of vv. 1-2 are simply the poet restating his cry to God, asking for a hearing. This is not meant to imply that God would not hear. Instead, it is meant to show the depths of depression from which the poet is writing, and an understanding of who God is.

But key in for a moment on the end of v. 2: "Let your ears be attentive to the voice of my pleas for mercy!" It is here that we see the real heart of the poet. The writer is sharing, not just out of some difficult circumstance, but obviously has some sin in his life that he knows needs to be dealt with. Thus, he pleads to God for mercy.

I don't want to overstate this, but too often we can pray to God for forgiveness without really meaning it. We sin, and we know it's the "right" thing to do to pray for forgiveness, but even those prayers can seem half-hearted. Our sin needs to be so real to us, and our desire to please God so strong, that we beg and plead with God for mercy. That's the cry of the heart of the poet.

The Condition (vv. 3-4). After making that cry, the poet admits that sin is the separator, and that God is perfectly holy. If God kept some sort of scoreboard of sins, there would be no one worthy of even considering entering the presence of the Lord. Of course, God does see and know every sin we commit, whether an outward sin or a sin of thought and attitude. But God does not call us to account for every sin we commit in the moment. If he did, we would spend basically all our time repenting and would never be justified. Instead, God forgives and allows us to stand in His presence out of His abundant mercy.

The first word of v. 4 is one of the most powerful words in Scripture. "But!" We are sinful and need to understand that we are unholy compared to a perfectly holy and pure God. But with God, forgiveness is found. "Free, full, sovereign pardon is in the hand of the great King: it is His prerogative to forgive, and He delights to exercise it."[1]

We need to recognize that it is only because God forgives that we are able to stand in His presence. Without His forgiveness, not a person alive would be able to come before Him. So even the simple fact that we are allowed to pray to the Lord should stand as a stark reminder that we are forgiven by a great and merciful God. But we

---

1. Spurgeon, *Treasury of David*, 3.2.119.

also need to petition Him to change our condition through His mercy, so the cry of our hearts can come before Him. Aren't you thankful God hears our prayers? Aren't you grateful that, in His mercy, He allows us to enter His presence, even from the depths of our soul?

We see that spelled out for us by Jesus in the Sermon on the Mount: "Ask, and it will be given to you; seek, and you will find; knock, and it will be opened to you. For everyone who asks receives, and the one who seeks finds, and to the one who knocks it will be opened. Or which one of you, if his son asks him for bread, will give him a stone? Or if he asks you for a fish, will give him a serpent? If you then, who are evil, know how to give good gifts to your children, how much more will your Father who is in heaven give good things to those who ask Him!" (Matt. 7:7-11).

As parents, we could just cut our children off and never allow them to seek things from us. While that would be bad parenting, we could make that choice. In our love and mercy, though, we allow them to come to us with whatever is on their heart. In a far greater way, God allows us to enter His presence. He does not cut us off, but gives us the good things we need in this life.

Hoping (vv. 5-8)

With that reassurance in his mind, the poet breaks out in praise to the Lord, and shares how God is lifting his aching soul. Based upon the mercy of God, the poet writes that he will wait upon the Lord. But notice that he says, "My soul waits." Just as he has been in the depths of inner despair in his life, so he is quieted within by the knowledge of the mercy of God. His soul is resting in the Lord. The poet writes two facts about this waiting.

Through what. It may seem like a throwaway phrase, but the end of v. 5 is very important: "In His word I hope." It is through the word of the Lord that the poet had learned to trust in God and to put his hope in Him. While God's Word is always true, sometimes it does not give us the answer we might want right when we might want it. But through continually looking into Scripture, we can gain hope.

Paul, speaking of the Old Testament, would write, "Everything that was written in the past was written to teach us. The Scriptures give us patience and encouragement so that we can have hope" (Rom. 15:4, NCV). Notice: patience and hope—exactly what the poet of Psa. 130 is talking about! If we would spend more time in the Scriptures, we would be better able to wait on the Lord in hopeful expectation of what He will do. We would be reminded of how He has done great things at just the right time in the past, and we would find comfort and encouragement for times when we must wait.

How. Twice in v. 6, the poet compares his waiting to that of watchmen who are looking for the morning. It is said twice merely for emphasis. It was a way to show the poet was now eager to wait upon the Lord and know His good works.

The picture of a watchman looking for the morning brings us a great picture of expectation in a time of fear. In ancient times, before artificial lighting, nighttime attacks on a city were often very effective. You might think of Gideon's tiny band of 300 destroying an entire army in the middle of the night. Because there was no artificial light back then, the watchmen would welcome the first light of the sun because it made their job so much easier. We can only imagine what those last couple of hours before dawn must have been like if the thought of an impending attack was great.

It is with that same intensity that the poet is willing to wait on the Lord. He is still struggling in the depths, but he is going to seek the Lord's will and watch closely for it. He is also trusting that, just as day certainly follows night, the Lord's goodness will follow this time in the depths.

As is so often done in the Psalms, the poet ends by turning from speaking only about himself to speaking words to the nation as a whole. The same principle that is true in his own life is true across the nation, if they will just recognize and follow the goodness of the Lord.

Just as he is stating that he will hope in the Lord, that is also his call to the nation. But in case the people of the nation are not as convinced as is the poet, he shares two traits of God that the people need to keep in mind to place their hope in Him.

First is steadfast love. Here again is that famous Hebrew word *chesed* that we have pointed out so many times in the psalms. God's love is covenantal; it cannot be broken. It draws people due to its amazing depth and power. Israel saw that love demonstrated over and over again, but she often failed to bring it to mind. A very quick reflection over their own lives and over the history of the nation, however, should have been enough to bring this great attribute of God clearly into their minds and overwhelm them with God's amazing covenantal mercy and love.

Second is redemption. The end of v. 7 speaks of God having "plentiful redemption," which is a beautiful picture. God is not just powerful enough to redeem the poet from the depths. He can redeem anyone willing to call out to Him. The word "redeem" carried with it the idea of "loosing" or "setting free." When God forgives, we become truly free. So the poet writes that God forgives "from all … iniquities." He is not going to partially forgive. When the Lord forgives, it is complete.

Where is your hope? It is easy to place it in all the wrong places because we can often see more tangible results. Sometimes, we place our hope in people or things because we see the results our flesh wants. Instead, the poet of Psa. 130 reminds us to place our hope in the Lord and realize the great blessings only He can provide.

Conclusion

When you look at Psa. 130 as a whole, you see something very powerful. The psalmist began with an aching soul, crying out in fear. His sin and his circumstances led him to the depths of despair, and fear gripped him. However, by the end, the psalmist was calling for the entire nation to put their hope in the Lord.

What changed? What can change us from having a soul in despair to coming to help others know the Lord? It is recognizing who God is. Only when we see His holiness and forgiveness will our souls truly cry out to Him and seek His forgiveness.

On June 22, 2008 another poet took pen in hand after looking around at distressing circumstances. Though not as inspired as was the poet of Psa. 130, her words share a look at a nation that needs to realize the hope that only God provides.

> Society seems in a mess
> Mothers cry, while Fathers stress
> to be polite is a disgrace
> as children mock you to your face
>
> every day the papers show
> that crime and rape did upward go
> the things done in laboratories
> are stashed away in lavatories
>
> drugs and sex aren't hard to find
> it seems as if the worlds gone blind
> for what the people fail to see
> is messing up society
>
> as Dads no longer head their home
> and kids all sit, and chat by phone
> what once to all has been a home
> is looking like a war torn zone
>
> no longer do you find that kids
> are playing in the park
> for it's become a hideout place
> for gangsters after dark

what once was right now seems so wrong
no more joy and no more song
as what this all was meant to be
lies buried in a cemetery

by telling you these things my aim
is not to make you mad
it's just to tell another truth
which soon will make you glad

amidst the chaos of this world
of hurt, despair and pain
and hate along with treachery
all done for selfish gain

there's this one thing I know of
believe with all my heart
that when I bend my knees to pray
my God will make a way

Lydia Preston[2]

Do you realize that God can and will make a way to provide you hope? Whether it is the ills of society or the despair of your own soul, cry out to God and trust Him to deliver.

---

2. http://www.familyfriendpoems.com/poem/god-will-make-a-way#ixzz3DV9JmKfz

How Great Is Our God

PSALM 135

A relatively new song of praise begins with these great words:

> The splendor of a King
> Robed in majesty;
> Let all the earth rejoice, all the earth rejoice.
> He wraps Himself in light
> And darkness tries to hide,
> It trembles at His voice, trembles at His voice.
> How great is our God.

What a wonderful sentiment. But if we are honest, as great and powerful as those words might be, they still fall short of offering to God the praise He is due. There is no way we could ever bring before God what He fully deserves, but that lack of ability should not preclude us from bringing the best we can offer. After all, that is what God requires. And that is what we see in Psa. 135. As amazing as the psalms are, they still fall short of bringing God all He is due. Poems like this psalm give us an amazing template to follow when we praise God.

That template is simple: use the Bible to find ways to praise the Lord. Psalm 135 has been called a "mosaic" because it seems to take portions of other passages and weave them together. We do not know who wrote Psa. 135, but considering some of the references are from later Old Testament books (such as Jeremiah), it seems that this is one of the later psalms chronologically.

If you were to walk through Psa. 135 and find all the quotations or allusions from other passages of the Bible, you would be amazed. Just as an example, vv. 2-3 are closely related to Psa. 116:19, while v. 4 seems to allude to Deut. 7:6. Verse 7 is almost word for word the same as Jer. 10:13, and vv. 8-12 are repeated in the very next psalm, Psa. 136. This is just a sampling of how many other passages are at least alluded to in this great poem, but it is enough to remind us that if we wish to praise our God, we should spend time searching the mind of God through the pages of Scripture. So, using Psa. 135 as our template, let us think of the greatness of God and how we can praise Him.

The Call to Praise (vv. 1-3)

As with many of the psalms, the poem opens with a call to praise the Lord, and as is quite common, the call is made more than once. It is interesting that this call includes words specifically written to those in the house of God. The end of v. 1 is directed to the "servants of the Lord," then v. 2 speaks of their work: "Who stand in the house of the Lord, in the courts of the house of our God!"

It would be easy to overlook calling for those who are near to the Lord's work to praise Him. After all, they are close by. It is sometimes easier to talk about all the needs "out there" and how people not near the Lord, in fact should be. Sometimes, however, those who are nearest to the service of the Lord need to have their spirits renewed. They need to be reminded to praise the Lord and have their hearts revived in his service.

As the poet ends the call, he gives two attributes of God that should begin our praise. First, the Lord is good. As we have said many times in looking at the Psalms, this can be a trait of God that is easily overlooked simply because the word "good" is so common. But the Lord is truly good, and He is good through-and-through. There is nothing that fails to be good about His nature or actions. As good as a person might be, there will be something about that person that is not good. So we struggle to understand true goodness. But God is perfectly good, and that alone makes Him worthy of our praise.

The other trait is in v. 3, where we are called to "sing to [the Lord's] name, for it is pleasant." The question is, "What is pleasant?" It could be (1) the name of the Lord, or (2) singing. It could also be that the poet has both in mind. When we sing praise to the name of the Lord, that should be pleasant! That pleasant nature should be seen both by us and by the Lord. Surely as those who serve the Lord, we can see that the name of the Lord is pleasant.

This is one reason it should truly eat away at us when we hear the name of God used in a demeaning fashion. His name is not lowly. It is not a byword. It is not something that just fills in spaces in our sentences when we aren't thinking straight. On the other side of the coin, when we hear the name of the Lord reverently spoken or praised in song, there is nothing sweeter to the ears of those who serve the Lord. That is the opening call.

The Causes to Praise (vv. 4-12)

As the poem continues, the writer begins to do what is often done in the Psalms. He begins to list item after item of what God has done. Sometimes, we will see poems where the things God has done are personal in nature. At other times, as is the case here, the poet will take a grander view and look at the history of Israel to remind his readers of what God has done throughout the centuries for His people.

Three things are used in these verses to speak of why we should praise God. Interestingly, though just three in number, each one focuses on a different attribute of the Lord.

His passion. Verse 4 speaks of God choosing "Jacob for Himself, Israel as His own possession." In that one verse, you see a thumbnail sketch of the overall picture of the Old Testament. Through Israel, God would show His divine planning and would demonstrate His love in unmistakable ways. Israel was nothing special, so far as size or wealth was concerned. But God chose that nation to be the conduit of His great plan for saving mankind. That nation became the clearest picture of God's love, patience, and even His wrath. It was all from the passion that God showed for this nation of people.

His power. Verses 6-7 speak to God's amazing power. In fact, the opening line of v. 6 could be the clearest statement in the Psalms of God's truly infinite power: "Whatever the Lord pleases, He does." And that is true no matter the place, since His power is not limited by space or sea. God controls the weather and knows the ins and outs of it all. It does not matter how powerful a bomb we can create or how much processing power we can put in a computer; it is child's play compared to the awesome power of our God. Our young people sometimes sing a song that I love. One of the lines makes me think of this part of our psalm, as they sing, "Every time I watch a storm, I know the awesome power of my Lord." Amen to that.

His preeminence. Verses 8-12 end this section with a quick walk through the history of Israel and show that God's hand was over it all. He was more powerful than Pharaoh and completely brought Egypt to its knees. Further, he was more powerful than the kings in the wilderness and those in the Promised Land, and simply "gave their land" to His people. Those earthly kings certainly had power and might, but God's power was infinitely greater and His will was to be done. It does not matter what type of government a nation has or how much power is consolidated into one person—a president, a king, a queen, etc.—that person is still subject to the Lord above. He is "a great God, and a great King above all gods" (95:3).

You may have noticed that we skipped over some verses. In the midst of giving this amazing description, the poet simply bursts forth with his own personal praise and provides for us the key to the section. Verse 5: "For I know that the Lord is great, and that our Lord is above all gods." Whenever we think of any—or all—of these traits of God, our reaction should be the same. We should recognize the splendor and greatness of our God.

The Contrast in Praise (vv. 13-18)

Starting in v. 13, the poet draws a clear contrast. At first, it looks as if this is going to be another section of pure praise. If we just read vv. 13-14, that is exactly what it would be. Notice that the poet speaks of how God endures forever and that the knowledge of God is permanent. The way that will be seen throughout the generations goes back to what the poet had just been talking about. Just as the Lord had delivered His people from Egyptian bondage and given them a land they never could have taken on their own, so He will continue to vindicate His people. While things may look bleak at times for God's people, they will always be proven right in the end, not because they are something special, but because they are following the only true God.

After those words, though, the poet enters into a strong contrast. Standing completely on the other end of the spectrum from the God of heaven are the idols of other nations. Simply put, they are "the work of human hands" (v. 15). Verses 16-17 remind us of something concerning idols and false worship that should have our attention. Notice that, when humans make idols, we make them like us. While they may be shaped like an animal, they still have mouths, eyes, and ears. We cannot think beyond what we know, so we just make our own gods to be somewhat like us.

However, those mouths cannot speak, and those ears cannot

hear, and those eyes cannot see. In fact, v. 17 tells us that there isn't any breath whatsoever in these idols. They are, at the end of the day, just statues or carved images, no matter how much power we might attribute to them.

In the closing part of this section, the psalmist reminds us of a very important truth: we become what we worship. He says, "Those who make them become like them, so do all who trust in them!" Have you ever noticed how sensual and grotesque idol worship often is? Since we think with carnal minds, we simply ascribe to the false gods those same traits and become increasingly sensual and carnal. We do not aspire to anything higher and greater.

May I point out here that this does not have to be an idol of gold or silver? How many of us worship the god of entertainment? We revel in all the latest shows and just accept whatever is put before us because it calms our nerves for a few moments or gives us a few laughs. But we are not aspiring to anything greater, and we are letting our lowest and basest thoughts be our guide.

What is the poet saying? When we do that, we still have mouths, but we don't speak. We still have eyes, but we don't see. We still have ears, but we don't hear. In other words, those who worship false gods—including those who worship at the altar of entertainment—become fools. We are made idiots by what we let control our minds.

Contrast that with the greatness of Jehovah. How many gold or silver idols worshiped back then are still worshiped today? Their relative influence is small and short-lived, but God endures forever and will be known forever. When we worship God, we are worshipping One who is higher and greater than we are. We are worshiping One who causes us to aspire to loftier, grander goals. We are worshiping One who takes the emphasis off ourselves and places it on the good of others. That's a serious contrast in what we praise.

The Closing Praise (vv. 19-21)

As the poem comes to a close, it travels full circle. Verses 1-2 called for praise by those who were servants of the Lord. In the closing verses, we see more specifically who that is. Verses 19-20 start with the larger picture and quickly come closer. All Israel is to praise the Lord. But the microscope closes in, and we see that the house of Aaron was to bless the Lord. Aaron was the first high priest of Israel, and those who served as priests came from his lineage. Then the microscope becomes broader, and those who are of the house of Levi are to bless the Lord. Levi was the priestly tribe, and his descendants worked constantly in the service of the temple.

But then, it is as if the microscope is taken off and the poet makes a general statement: "You who fear the Lord, bless the Lord." That could be viewed as if the microscope were getting closer still. What if there were only a handful of those Israelites in the house of Aaron of the tribe of Levi who were truly following God? Maybe this statement is meant to say that not even all those of the priestly tribe are following God. Or, it could be a return to the opening call for the entire nation of Israel to fear the Lord. Maybe the microscope is pulled back, and the people of God as a whole are in view. No matter their tribe or lineage, if they fear the Lord, they need to express it.

Whichever is in view, the command is the same. If you have a reverent awe for God, it needs to be more than just a view held in your mind intellectually. It needs to be expressed explicitly. If someone fears the Lord, they need to be willing to speak for the Lord and bless His name no matter who might hear.

To close, the poet shows that he is one who fears the Lord because he follows his own statement from v. 20 and states a blessing to the Lord. "Blessed be the Lord from Zion, He who dwells in Jerusalem." Just as he had said that the fear of the Lord should lead to pronouncing a blessing, he follows his own advice. We do the same today when we sing.

> All praise to Him who reigns above
> In majesty supreme;
> Who gave Himself for man to die
> That he might man redeem.
> Blessed be the name,
> Blessed be the name;
> Blessed be the name of the Lord.

With that in mind, the poet ends as he began: "Praise the Lord."

Conclusion

The song with which we began may fall short of fully praising God, but it nonetheless does a great job of helping us express our praise today. The other verse of that song says:

> And age to age He stands,
> And time is in His hands;
> Beginning and the end, beginning and the end.
> The Godhead three-in-one:
> Father, Spirit, Son,
> The lion and the lamb, the lion and the lamb.
> How great is our God,
> Sing with me, how great is our God.
> And all will see how great,
> How great is our God.

The only way "all will see" the greatness of God is if we share His greatness with them. Words like Psa. 135 remind us that this praise of God starts with us. We cannot just keep our love and admiration for God bottled up inside. It must be something that is openly expressed. After all, He is certainly worthy, not only of our mental appreciation, but of our open praise. How great is our God!

A Time to Shout Praise

PSALM 138

O ne of the most difficult psalms to figure out is Psa. 137. While it is not the focus of our study, we need to notice something about it in order to get to the heart of Psa. 138. Psalm 137 begins with the heart-wrenching words, "By the waters of Babylon, there we sat down and wept, when we remembered Zion" (v. 1). As the poem goes on, we read that the captors were poking fun at the people, tormenting them by asking them to "Sing...one of the songs of Zion" (v. 3).

The poet of Psa. 137 goes on to write a tearful question: "How shall we sing the Lord's song in a foreign land?" (v. 4). Much of the remainder of Psa. 137 is a cry for God to exact vengeance against these enemies. In fact, in one of the most confusing verses in the entire Bible, the psalm ends with the poet saying, "Blessed shall he be who takes your little ones and dashes them against the rock!" (v. 9). Of course, this action would not be the will of God. The poet is ending that way to express his extreme anger and frustration.

Chronologically, it is obvious Psa. 137 was written during the time when the people of God were taken into captivity for their constant sin against the Lord. It is unusual, then, that the psalm we are focusing on should come next. You may notice that the superscription of Psa. 138 simply says "Of David." Of course, David died several centuries before the people were carried into captivity. So chronologically, this poem doesn't fit here.

However, it does fit perfectly in a thematic way. Psalm 137 is one where the people do not want to say anything. They are being tormented by their captors to sing words or praise and devotion. They will not do so; at least not with any real heart behind it.

Immediately flipping to the other side of the coin, you come to Psa. 138, which is one that bursts forth with praise. It is a reminder of Solomon's maxim—there is "A time to keep silence, and a time to speak" (Eccles. 3:7). It seems as though David is not going through a perfectly smooth time in his life when he composed Psa. 138 (see v. 7), but he knows that praise to God is the only proper way to handle life, so that is what he offers.

I want to challenge us through this psalm to consider that we should always work at shouting praise to God. No matter what might be going on around us, let us be people who are thankful. Using this psalm, let's notice how David was able to do that.

Praise (vv. 1-3)

As David opens the psalm, he speaks about this praise, and he does so by answering several questions.

With what? David states he will praise God "with my whole heart." Notice how the poem begins by connecting thanks and praise. These two should always be connected. When we remember that God is the giver of every good and perfect gift (Jas. 1:17), we will not only thank Him for those gifts, but that gratitude will express itself in praise. And David's praise is from his whole heart. There really is no such thing as half-hearted praise. We are either praising God fully, or we are not giving Him what He is due.

Above what? The end of v. 1 has David saying he will sing the praise of God "before the gods." It is possible that this is hinting at a time when either foreign influence was taking hold of the kingdom, or when David was on the run and in a pagan land. Whichever was the case, David was seeing idols, but he was not about to let that keep him from praising the true God of heaven. No matter what might seem to hold sway in our world, nothing should ever be able to seize our heart of praise. It may not be a carved image in our society, but it could be a green piece of paper or the gratification of fame. Instead, we must always praise God above all else.

Toward what? Verse 2 begins by stating David would "bow down toward [God's] holy temple." Now this is a bit confusing because David lived before the time of the temple. Remember, he was not allowed to construct it because he was a man who shed blood. So is this a discrepancy in Scripture? No, because, in the mind of David, the temple was where the ark of God was, even if the building was not actually constructed yet. The point here was that David's heart was turned toward God, just as ours must be. Today, we do not have to face Jerusalem (or any other earthly location) to worship acceptably, but we "must worship...in spirit and truth" (John 4:24). Our hearts need to be always pointed toward heaven.

For what? As David ends this first section, he does something so typical of the psalms: he lists reason after reason for which God is worthy of praise. There are two different kinds of traits listed here.

First, there are traits of omnipotence. God's amazing power is mentioned over and again in the psalms, and here David lists several traits that again picture for us the great strength of God. He has "steadfast love," "faithfulness," and God's name and word are "exalted above all things." There is nothing greater or more powerful than God! Notice that these traits are for people and for position. "Steadfast love" and "faithfulness" demonstrate themselves to people, while the exaltation of God is true to all.

Then there are traits of omni-benevolence. Verse 3 is so tender, as David writes that God not only answered him, but strengthened his soul. Note that this happened "on the day I called." God did not make David wait. He gave what was needed right when it was needed. That's God! While we may not know His gifts in the very moment, we can trust that, through his perfect benevolence, God will give just what we need just when we need it. For all that, David gives thanks and praise to God.

Power (vv. 4-6)

To share God's power, David takes the time to contrast the rulers of this earth with the rule of God. Think about that for a moment. David was a king, so this was not written by someone thinking out loud. Instead, David was speaking as one who knew the vast difference between even his own power and the power of God. Verse 4 makes it clear that "all the kings of the earth" are under consideration. "Kings have usually small care to hear the word of the Lord; but King David feels assured that if they do hear it they will feel its power."[1]

Again, was David wrong? We know there has never really been a time when every monarch has followed God's ways. So was David speaking of something that would never happen? No, he was speaking of the way things *should* be. Should any monarch, no matter how powerful, come to hear even a word from God, he or she would stop singing their own praise, and would "sing of the ways of the Lord." That is true because of both who God is and what He does.

God is greatly glorious and also described as "high" or "lofty." Every king desires glory. It is only natural for someone with all the power of a nation resting upon his shoulders to feel the majesty that comes with such a position. Seemingly, everything associated with the position is built around pomp and glory. The thrones of kings were typically at the top of a staircase or up on a stage, and they were carried through processions to symbolize their loftiness. But God is higher than any of that. He is naturally glorious and lofty. Even if we

---

1. Spurgeon, *Treasury of David*, 3.2.245.

never recognized that about God, He would hold that lofty position.

Notice that David also writes about what God does, and it is very different from the ways of earthly kings. Verse 6: "For though the Lord is high, He regards the lowly, but the haughty He knows from afar." God's heart is not on encircling Himself with the best and highest in society, for those people are usually too full of themselves to care about others. God knows their heart, and He will be certain that the lowly are regarded. However, even above that He will not allow those who are arrogant to have their way because He knows their motivation without needing some sort of vetting. "[God] has shown Himself to be the Exalted One who in His all-embracing rule does not leave the lowly unnoticed, but on the contrary makes him the especial object of His regard; and on the other hand even from afar He sees through the loft one who thinks himself unobserved and conducts himself as if he were answerable to no higher being."[2] Psalm 113:5-6 put it in the form of a rhetorical question: "Who is like the Lord our God, who is seated on high, who looks far down on the heavens and the earth?" Then the answer is given: "He raises the poor from the dust and lifts the needy from the ash heap, to make them sit with princes, with the princes of His people" (vv. 7-8).

God set up governments, but He warns over and over that the power of being a leader is hard to overcome. Our selfishness can easily take over, so it is difficult for one in power to remain humble. God is greater than all leaders, and that realization should keep a leader humble if he will just look to the Lord.

Preservation (v. 7)

Some of my favorite words we sing are these:

Though I, thro' the valley of shadow,

---

2. Keil, *Commentary*, 806.

O'er mountain or troubled sea,
And oft in the darkness, have traveled,
The Lord has been mindful of me!

Lloyd O. Sanderson

Even though that great hymn was written centuries after Psa. 138, it expresses similar thoughts as what David wrote in v. 7 of our poem: "Though I walk in the midst of trouble, you preserve my life." One of God's greatest gifts to His people is that He preserves them through times of struggle and difficulty.

Does that mean God will remove all difficulties? Of course not. We understand that struggle will be part of our life, even if we are faithful. We also need to recognize that some of those struggles will come because there are some who are, simply put, the enemies of God. David here calls them his own enemies, but if people are opposed to the followers of God, they are, in reality, opposed to God Himself. Those who oppose the Lord will do what they can to make life a struggle for the faithful. David is writing from a real time of emotion and struggle, and that should help us realize that we will face the same, even should we be faithful to the Lord.

God knows, and God cares. So David writes that God was against those enemies and ultimately delivered him. God does not just make us suffer through every struggle. The Lord is right there with us. Though we will certainly have difficult times, God will not let evil stand forever. Deliverance will come. It may not come as quickly as we desire, or even in the way we may think, but it will come.

We should also keep in mind that deliverance implies there are some negative things that happen. One of the most beloved verses in all the psalms reminds us of that, too. "Even though I walk through the valley of the shadow of death, I will fear no evil, for you are with me; your rod and your staff, they comfort me" (23:4). Notice the words: "valley," "shadow," "death," "evil." There are bad things around, but where is the Lord? Right here with us, walking with us and delivering us in the end. He is a deliverer, and One who preserves us through the struggles of life. Do we ever thank Him for that? When we are looking at a time of difficulty, we will plead to God for His help through that season of life. But when we have come through that time with God's help, do we ever praise and thank Him for preserving us and walking with us?

Purpose (v. 8)

Sometime ago, I read through the Bible over the course of a year on my Kindle. As I read, there were certain verses that were marked as being highlighted by a large number of people as they, too, had read the book. One of them was this famous verse from the Old Testament book of Jeremiah: "For I know the plans I have for you, declares the Lord, plans for wholeness and not for evil, to give you a future and a hope" (29:11). There is a great deal of comfort in the fact that God has a plan or purpose for our lives, and that it is to our ultimate good. Here is David, obviously in a time of struggle, but look at his great confidence in God as the poem ends.

There is a forward-looking part of this: "The Lord will fulfill His purpose for me." David is going through a time of struggle, but he is able to look to the future and know with complete certainty that God has a plan for his life and will fulfill it in the end. What peace that had to bring to the life of David! To underscore that, David writes again of the steadfast love of God, just as he had done back in v. 2. Now, however, he writes that this mercy of God "endures forever." Again, note the forward-looking nature of this. God's mercy is not present only when we are going through a time of struggle. We can know it is ever present, in both good times and bad.

David is able to make this final request: "Do not forsake the work of Your hands." He is not saying this because he fears that God will leave him. Instead, he is using this request as a way to finalize his trust in the Lord. He knows God will stay with him through this struggle and through every day of his life. "Our confidence does not cause us to live without prayer, but encourages us to pray all the more."[3]

While it may not always be abundantly clear what the purpose of God is in the moment (Should I pick this college or that one? Should I move into this house or that one?), we can know God has an overall purpose for our lives. That purpose is to glorify Him with our whole being. We can know God will help us fulfill that purpose for our life if we will just look for His will in each moment.

Conclusion

I think there is a sense in which this psalm comes full circle. Notice again how the psalm began: "I give thanks to you, O Lord, with my whole heart." There is a fullness to the thanks David is offering to God. And now, as the psalm comes to a close, he states that "The Lord will fulfill His purpose for me" (v. 8). There is a purpose that will have its fullness in David's life. Those two things work together. When we are willing to give God our whole heart, we will know His full purpose. We will also know that we can live out that purpose in our lives, no matter where we might be or what might be threatening to lead us away from Him. For that, we should realize that every time in our life is a time to shout His praise.

---

3. Spurgeon, *Treasury of David*, 3.2.247.

God Cares for My Soul

PSALM 142

As you near the end of the book of Psalms, there are eight poems that may seem out of place. Earlier in Psalms, we stop reading poems that are clearly written by David and begin reading those by other authors or that are anonymous. However, as the book begins to wind down, we return to David, and eight poems (Psa. 138-145) are given to us from him. They again remind us of his struggles, but also of his unfailing trust in the Lord.

We are told in the superscription that Psa. 142 was penned when David "was in the cave." I find it interesting that there is the definite article there: "the cave." I find that interesting because David often fled to caves, and we do not know which of these would have been considered "the" cave. When David was on the run from King Saul, he often sought refuge and rest in caves, such as Engedi, Adullum, and others that are not named for us. We do not know which of these is in view, but we know David was on the run and was hurting from this exchange with King Saul. Spurgeon, in commenting on this setting for the psalm wrote, "Caves make good closets for prayer; their gloom and solitude are helpful to the exercise of devotion."[1]

But the gloomy location of a cave serves as a perfect backdrop for the mood David was in as he writes these words. He is running;

---

1. Ibid., 3.2.323.

he is scared; he is hurt. But his trust remains full in the Lord, and that is why we can title this psalm "God Cares for My Soul." If you have ever felt as if no one else cared for you in the deepest and most important ways, take heart from this poem and know what David knew: God cares.

A Hurting Plea (vv. 1-2)

David opens this psalm, as we have seen so many times before, by stating his intent to call out to the Lord. Sometimes a psalm begins by saying, "I call out to God," while at other times (as is the case here), we read more of a "report," stating that this plea is being made. There is something here, though, that may seem obvious, but needs to be pointed out. Twice in v. 1, David writes that this plea was made with his voice. Two things sound out about this plea. First is the audible communication. Again, that may seem like an obvious point, but I think it is interesting. Most of the time, when we think of calling out to God in a personal way, we think more of a prayer we "say," but only in our thoughts. We may not think of actually opening up our mouth and having words audibly come out.

When I read this, I think of the heartfelt plea of Hannah. Many of us have probably prayed as did this godly lady. First Samuel 1:12-13 tells us, "As she continued praying before the Lord, Eli observed her mouth. Hannah was speaking in her heart; only her lips moved, and her voice was not heard." The text goes on to tell us that Eli thought she was drunk because of this action. But we have all probably prayed at times where our hearts were stirred enough to cause our lips to mouth some words, though not make much—if any—sound.

In our psalm, David is saying that his plea was so deep that he was not concerned about being silent. He was not just thinking a prayer or mouthing some words. Instead, with his voice he cried out to the Lord. Can't you just hear the hurtful plea of David echoing throughout this cave he was in? He was about as distant and down as a person could be, and he just let it all out through a plea to the Lord.

The second thing that stands out about this plea is the ardent content. David uses three words to describe what he was praying about. The first is "mercy" (v. 1), and notice that he was pleading for that mercy. The KJV has "supplication," and the Hebrew word (*chanan*) is one that meant "to be shown favor or to be pitied". David was making a deeply felt request to know the pity of God in this situation.

The second word is "complaint" (v. 2). The word can also be translated "meditation," but it carries with it the idea of being anxious or in trouble. David knows his situation, and he has meditated on it with a great deal of anxiety. So he takes that before the Lord. New Testament Christians are told to do the same thing: "Casting all your anxieties on Him, because He cares for you" (1 Pet. 5:7).

The third word is "trouble" (v. 2), and David says it is "my trouble." He is not trying to pass this off as some generic problem. He has a personal struggle and will take that before the Lord. Today, are we not sometimes afraid to take things before the throne of God? We need to take specific troubles before the Lord and seek His counsel and help when times are rough.

After commenting on this section of the poem, Spurgeon wrote these powerful words about praying when we are in a time of trouble:

> Note that we do not show our trouble before the Lord that *He* may see *it*, but that *we* may see *Him*. It is for *our* relief, and not for His information that we make plain statements concerning our woes. ... Pour out your thoughts and you will see what they are; show your trouble and the extent of it will be known to you: let all be done before the Lord, for in comparison with His great majesty of love the trouble will seem to be as nothing.[2]

---

2. Ibid., 3.2.324; emphasis in original.

A Harmful Path (vv. 3-4)

As the poem continues, David writes what the plea actually was, and it concerned his path in life. The imagery here is fantastic, as David was likely running for his life and thus would have had to know the paths (even the rarely used ones) of the area. Using the imagery of paths that he would have known, David writes about the path where his enemies were. But even in the midst of that, there is a trust in God. David writes, "When my spirit faints within me, you know my way!" (v. 3). We are not yet to the truly hope-filled part of the poem, but David inserts these words to show his complete trust in God in the midst of a very difficult set of circumstances.

We do not know if the trap and path David is writing about in v. 4 is literal or figurative; it could very well be both. As King Saul was seeking the life of David, he no doubt tried to trap David on certain paths. But this could also be extended to mean that there were "traps" that could have caused David to stumble in his trust in God. There is also a spiritual application here. Notice that the trap set for David was hidden. It was not overt, or else David would have not needed to be concerned with it. Traps are not set out in the open.

Satan operates the same way. While some of his temptations may be overt, the temptation to sin usually starts in a much more subtle way, often with a very private "hidden" trap. The man who ends up addicted to pornography likely did not start down that path by walking into an adult book store in broad daylight. Instead, he started by clicking on a link while doing research for a business project or by watching "risqué" movies late at night. Those are more hidden, but they are also the traps that work.

David's situation seems even darker because he reveals in v. 4 that he feels as though he is walking this dangerous path alone. Verse 4 begins in a bit of an odd way. The ESV translates the opening line, "Look to the right and see," as if David is giving God a challenge. The KJV has "I looked on my right hand, and beheld," stating that David was doing the looking. The key to this part of the verse, though, is not on whether God was to look or whether David had already searched. It was where the look was that makes this powerful.

I think the KJV has this part right in stating "my right hand." Do you not find it odd that David would avoid looking in any and every direction for help in this situation? By looking at his right hand, David was looking for his most trusted people (his right-hand man, if you will), and even those people were not with him at this time. The right hand was one of honor and trust. David feels as if even those who would be in those very trusted places have deserted him.

That realization causes David to state, "No refuge remains to me." Matthew Henry summarizes this verse to this point:

> [David] looked round to see if any would open their doors to him; but refuge failed him. None of all his old friends would give him a night's lodging, or direct him to any place of secrecy and safety. How many good men have been deceived by such swallow-friends, who are gone when winter comes![3]

With all of that pressing on his mind and emotions, David states the most famous line of the psalm: "No one cares for my soul." What a pitiful state David was in. Not a person cared for him, not even for his inmost needs. Even here, though, there is a faint hint of faith. Notice that David did not state that people failed to care for his physical needs. Instead, he knew all this was a sign that people did not care for what really mattered: his soul.

When troubles come our way, and when those we thought were close to us run away, we might have physical pain or difficulty. In reality, what really suffers the most is our inner person. We are hurting in ways we cannot fully describe because it is a pain of our soul.

---

3. Henry, *Commentary*, 765.

What a sad state that is, but we need to recognize it for what it is. Our primary concern should not be on our physical suffering, but on the things that really matter through it all: the matters of the soul.

Thankfully, the psalm does not end with that plaintive cry!

A Hopeful Petition (vv. 5-7)

David ends the poem by continuing to state that he is in a time of great difficulty, but his hope is still strong in the Lord. We need to remember that hope is not really needed when everything is smooth sailing, nor does it mean we fail to state the truth. Our circumstances do not change just because we are hopeful; hope helps us define our circumstances, no matter how negative, in God-centered terms. That's exactly what David does in the final three verses. Four words define this hope in the final verses.

Refuge. David states that God is "my refuge," and adds that God is his "portion in the land of the living" (v. 5). He does not say that God changes all the circumstances, but that in the midst of the difficulty, the Lord is a place of safety. We all need a safe place to go in the midst of struggle, but thankfully, we can know that God is always present with us. He provides us a refuge, no matter the external circumstances. All we have to do is go to Him in our thoughts and prayers, and He will help guide us.

Realism. David does not mince words in v. 6, as he states, "I am brought very low." He also stated that his enemies were too strong for him. That is a realistic cry to the Lord. Too often, we take some struggle to God in a half-hearted way, basically giving God a report and then saying (in essence), "But I'll take care of this myself." David knows that whatever this specific situation is, it is truly too much for him. If the enemies catch him, he will lose. Remember that he at least feels that he is totally alone, so his enemies would not face much of a fight! Part of being hopeful is avoiding generalizations or being superficial. We need to be real and admit when something is too great for us to bear. When you come before God, admit when something is too much for you!

Release. Verse 7 begins, "Bring me out of prison, that I may give thanks to your name!" Again, I think the KJV does a better job here by stating that David is asking God to bring his soul out of prison. David may be using the cave he is in as a metaphor for a prison, but he is more likely saying that no one caring for his soul (v. 4) is like a prison from which he needs delivering. If and when God grants that release for David, he will give thanks.

Righteous. Though it seems no one cares for David, he ends by stating that those who are truly righteous will surround him because they will have seen God help David through this seemingly impossible time. There is a strength that comes to others when we see a fellow believer overcome a difficult time through faith in God. When one has been in a time of soulful prayer and comes through, the reaction of believers should be celebratory praise. God has helped again, and we should be giving Him thanks and praise for His faithfulness and power.

Conclusion

Even in the midst of a group of believers, you may feel as if no one really cares. You may, at least, feel that no one really cares for you on the deepest of levels: on the soul level. If that is how you feel, though, remember the Lord. He cares for your soul. He cares for you, and every worry and struggle can be brought before Him. He will help and deliver if you will just walk by faith with Him.

What cave are you in? Who cares enough to rescue you?

A young woman, her brother, and her father were once spending a day together diving at Merrit's Mill Pond near Marianna, Florida when the trip took a scary, and almost tragic, turn. The group's father was an open-water diving instructor, but they were warned to stay away from the entrance to the underwater Twin Caves located in the pond because they were not certified or prepared for that type of dive. They realized how dangerous cave diving could be when the group was separated and visibility was eliminated due to silt being stirred up in the cave.

Cave diver Andrea Rance was completing her first dive at Twin Caves when her group found the inexperienced divers trying to exit the cave. They were able to help the son out, and the father came out soon after, but they realized the daughter was still trapped in the cave. Fearful and anxious, they tried to quickly locate the girl, but they realized they needed an experienced cave and rescue diver if they had any hope of finding her in time.

A call was made to Edd Sorenson, who had been part of a Cave and Underwater Rescue Team for fifteen years, and he was contacted just minutes before leaving for a dive that would have made him unreachable. Through his efforts, he located the girl who had found a place to stand with an air pocket that she was using to breathe. "She had used well over two thirds of her breathing gas by the time Edd found her and she was probably only minutes away from drowning in the dark cold water." He confirmed she had enough air in her tank to make it out, and he told her not to let go of his arm as he led her out of the cave through lines he had established to follow. Because of the help of others, this girl was rescued to the relief and joy of her family and the others who were there.[4]

If you think no one else would rescue you, God will come and save you. When he does, you will realize, like the girl did, that others are there and cheering for you. The Lord cares for your soul.

---

4. "Rescue at Twin Caves—a Lesson for SCUBA Divers," http://www.floridadiveconnection.com/rescue-at-twin-caves-a-lesson-for-scuba-divers.

Victory!

PSALM 144

When victory comes in different areas of life, we have different traditions we follow to celebrate those times. Some are quite shameful, such as college stadiums filled with fans chanting obscenities or major league baseball teams spraying thousands of dollars of alcohol on one other (and consuming no telling how much more). Others are more playful, such as the tradition of telling the camera after winning a Super Bowl, "I'm going to Disneyland!"

No matter the type of celebration, victory is a wonderful feeling. From athletics to music to drama competitions to politics, everyone who enters a contest wants to win. The same is obviously true of those who enter battle. More is on the line, to be sure, but no one enters a battle just to take part in a spectacle. Each person involved wants to come out victorious. They have a cause in which they believe, and they want to fight for that cause through every means necessary.

David is often depicted as a gentle, almost effeminate character, due to his writing poems and hymns and his love of sheep. But David was a fierce warrior. Not only did he physically protect his sheep early in life, but he was later on a true warrior. From carrying Goliath's head as a trophy to living off the land for years while avoiding King Saul, David was no weakling. And the number of times David was defeated in battle is far and away outweighed by the number of times he was victorious. He knew strategy and how to wield a weapon. He wanted to win, and most of the time, he did just that.

In addition to being skilled in war, David knew from where his victory came. Psalm 144 represents a psalm of praise in honor to God. David knew that the victories he gained were not from his own hand alone, but were through the greatness of God. Personally, I believe this psalm is just one of many that David would have written or sung along these lines, but this one was inspired and, thus, is included in the canon of Psalms.

Through David's powerful words, we can learn more about how to handle times when victory is ours. Although we are not always victorious, the follower of God must know how to handle himself/herself in every situation, and Psa. 144 shows us how to handle times when pride could creep in. Instead, we focus on the Lord and His faithfulness in granting us victory.

Victory's Cause (vv. 1-8)

If you were to Google "how to win at..." (and fill in the end with nearly any topic), you would be inundated with articles, books, and videos showing you how to be victorious. You might want to be a more victorious chess player or win at a favorite computer game. There is no end, in our information age, to the tips and tricks to help you be a winner at nearly anything. But David, in the first half of Psa. 144, shares a much simpler formula for his victories. In fact, it consists of just two things, and even those two are related.

Cause #1: God is invincible. The first and last verses of this section are all about how God simply cannot be defeated, and how David had been strengthened by the Lord. Just in vv. 1-2, David describes the Lord in an amazing nine different ways.

1. *My rock.* This is a common image in the psalms because it would have meant the foundation for the

poet (in this case, David). God was the One on whom David built everything, including his battles. The KJV has "strength" here, but "rock" seems to fit better, as it is the foundation for everything else to follow not only in this list, but in the entire poem.

2. **My trainer.** God "trains" (KJV, "teaches") for battle and war. The Lord does not just lay the foundation for David, God provides the instruction for him. The Lord is behind and involved in every aspect of David's victory. Today, the Bible does this in a spiritual way for the Christian, as God has given us everything we need to fight off the Devil.

3. **My steadfast love** (KJV, "goodness"). The Hebrew word *chesed* is found again in the Psalms, as David is expressing his trust in God throughout the process. God's love and mercy draw David, even through times of battle and war. God is always present and always good, even when we are in a time of battle.

4. **My fortress.** Considering the battle imagery of this psalm, this is a beautiful picture. To be victorious, a fortress is extremely helpful. Also, considering that David had done a lot of his fighting while on the run, he probably longed for the luxury of a true fortress to regroup and have strategy meetings. God provides that walled place in our lives.

5. **My stronghold.** Similar to fortress, the stronghold is probably meant here to symbolize the watchtower. God not only gives us a safe place to go, but He provides further protection by watching out for us through the battles of life.

6. **My deliverer.** I love that, before the list is even over, David is already writing that God delivers! That's a level of trust that needs to be built into our character if we are to be people who fully trust the Lord. God is David's only real deliverer in battle, and He is the only hope we have of being delivered from our greatest battle, the one against sin and Satan.

7. *My shield.* The word here (*magen*) is one for a small shield, but even that may indicate a level of trust. David carried a shield, but he didn't feel as if it needed to be a huge shield. God provided all the protection David needed. Do we ever struggle to feel that way when times of battle are in our lives?

8. *My refuge.* Even if a soldier or battalion is making great progress, they must rest. David's trust in God is not just when the battle is raging; it is also there when it is time to slow down and take refuge. God is always there to help His people.

9. *My reason for victory.* The Lord is the one "who subdues people under me" (v. 2). When victory came, David did not take all the credit. Instead, he gave the Lord the credit because through training, help, and rest, the Lord had led David through every step of the battle.

With all of that in mind, David takes the time to write words of praise that express the absolute power and majesty of God. Verses 5-8 are filled with imagery of how God is greater, not just over armies ("send out your arrows and rout them"), but all creation ("touch the mountains so that they smoke"). David's trust in God is based in the fact that the Lord is greater than anyone or anything. Even though David was a great warrior, he understood fully that he needed the help of God to be truly victorious. "Stretch out your hand from on high; rescue me and deliver me from the many waters, from the hand of foreigners" (v. 7). What trust! What a wonderful God!

Cause #2: Man is inconsequential. Here is where the contrast comes into play. David was not saying that the enemies he was facing were not real. He needed God's help to win the battles. However, compared to the invincible power of Jehovah, whatever power man can muster is just child's play.

Interestingly, though, David does not write specifically about his enemies, but about all people. Considering not just his enemies, but himself, David asks, "O Lord, what is man that you regard him, or the son of man that you think of him?" (v. 3). David was nothing special, but God took care of him. David's enemies were surely nothing special, but God still knew who they were.

In his humility, David wrote, "Man is like a breath; his days are like a passing shadow" (v. 4). Even when we are victorious, we need to avoid thinking we will live forever on earth. Battles and competitions of all sorts can make us think more of ourselves than we should. Even if we are people of faith, we can begin to think we are invincible. Only the Lord is truly invincible. We will lose at some point, while God is always victorious.

Too often, we struggle in life because we mix these two things up. We begin to think we are the invincible part of the winning formula, that God is only there to cheer us on in our amazing abilities. While what people can do is remarkable, it is but child's play compared to how great God is. Only He is truly invincible, and we can only be victorious in this life if we walk under the power of God.

A Victory Cry (vv. 9-15)

It is rare to find a sports team that does not have some type of song. Nearly any school has an alma mater that might be played at the conclusion of every game, and most teams have some sort of fight song. Even the simple organ player leading the fans up to the cry of "Charge!" is meant to build a team up for victory. Some of these songs, though, are downright strange. The University of Utah's fight song does not exactly open with intimidating words: "I am a Utah man, sir, and I live across the green. Our gang is the jolliest that you have ever seen." I guess to find a word that rhymes with the name of their school, Bowling Green sings "Make the contest keen" after they score a touchdown. But maybe nothing is more confusing than the fight song of New Mexico State University, which ends with a cliffhanger: "We'll win this game or know the reason why." I want to know why!

Obviously, when we deal with things of greater importance, we take more care in what we say. In David's poem, he ends the psalm with a word of praise to the Lord. In a sense, it is his victory cry, written out of both experience and expectation. The cry of David falls into two parts.

Praise to God (vv. 9-11). As we might expect, David's victory cry is filled with words of praise to God. As one who often wrote poems and also music, David fills these verses with both. He "will sing a new song" to the Lord and will accompany that song "upon a ten-stringed harp." We do not know what this new song is, but David is sure of the victory, so it is as if he is already composing lines in his head.

The praise is based upon how God has delivered victory to kings in general, but then David focuses specifically on the way God has helped him. God "rescues David his servant from the cruel sword" (v. 10). The word "rescues" (KJV "delivereth") is in the present tense, showing that David was continuing to know and appreciate the deliverance only the Lord could give. While we do not know of any specific threat against David at this time, the scope of this psalm makes it seem as though he was facing some threat, but knew the Lord would deliver him through it.

As David ends this praise, he writes a request. He is not making this request in v. 11 because he suddenly doubts the Lord. He is not going to presume on God, and David wants to show his total reliance on the Lord. Though he knows God will deliver, he still wants to show honor to the Lord by making the request. Notice that David makes clear that these are not just people that he doesn't personally like; they are enemies of the Lord and show that through their actions. We need to be very careful that we do not ask God to act against people we have nothing more than a personality conflict with. But God's deliverance against truly evil people is worthy of our praise.

Prizes from God (vv.12-15). David makes requests, but trusts they will be given as a reward to the faithful. There are three types.

1. **Families.** His first request is for the children of the faithful to be safe and to grow to maturity. Even when they are young, David asks that his sons "be like plants full grown" (v. 12). He is basically seeking a maturity and a depth that is too often not seen in those who are younger. That strength, when it is present, helps sustain more than a family; it helps sustain a nation. The request for daughters is that they be "like corner pillars, cut for the structure of a palace" (v. 12). What a beautiful picture of a woman of strength! The request is not just for sons to be strong and influential, but for daughters as well. David knows the strength and influence of a faithful woman, and he wants that for future generations. The Lord can grant these, but it also takes a desire and a willingness to work to help cultivate this type of strength in future generations.

2. **Fields.** After seeking the well-being of the family, David seeks economic well-being in the form of good and full harvests. "A household ... must have its granary as well as its nursery."[1] From grain to sheep to cattle, David's request is for great harvests and future generations, again to continue the nation as well as the family. I do not believe David is seeking some sort of health-and-wealth gospel in this request, though he asks for huge amounts of sheep. Based upon all the other things he has written in this psalm, he is stating that God can do amazing things, and that is what he is seeking for his family and the nation.

3. **Freedom.** "May there be no cry of distress in our streets!" (v. 14) This is a picture of true delight and peace. When things are right in the family and when God grants the necessary food for generations to continue, people should behave in such a way that

---

1. Spurgeon, *Treasury of David*, 3.2.359.

not only praises Him, but that also is to the benefit and safety of others. Spurgeon again summarizes the thought here very well: "No secret dissatisfaction, no public riot; no fainting of poverty, no clamor for rights denied, nor concerning wrongs unredressed. The state of things here pictured is very delightful: all is peaceful and prosperous; the throne is occupied efficiently, and even the beasts in their stalls are the better for it."[2]

With all that in his mind, David ends the poem with words that are a combination of praise and invitation: "Blessed are the people to whom such blessings fall! Blessed are the people whose God is the Lord!" (v. 15) In those words, there is great praise. David is correct in that; it is a great blessing to be in the Lord and know the blessings that only come from His hand to His people.

In those words, there is also an invitation, for some who would have read these words then (and some who will read them now) are not following God as their Lord. They may give Him lip service, but He is not truly the Lord of their life. Those who are in such a state do not know nor appreciate the fullness of the blessings of the Lord. But those who do can join in the victory cry and know what it means to be ultimately victorious in the Lord.

Conclusion

I considered ending this chapter with a sport's analogy. I thought about trying to find a story of a team that was way behind in a game and came back to win. Or maybe the story of a team that was buried in the standings, only to make an amazing march to a playoff. Anyone who follows the world of sports knows these types of stories abound. They are some of our favorites to tell.

---

2. Ibid., 3.2.360.

Upon reflection, though, I decided against using that type of illustration for one reason: any such illustration pales in comparison to the ultimate victory of God and His people.

1. In how many of your favorite comeback stories has your team been "down" for centuries?

2. In how many has there been no word for 400 years?

3. In how many has the greatest figure been murdered during the game?

4. Moreover, in how many has your favorite team never really been behind?

You see, when it comes to following God, it may seem as if He is silent or that His way will not win. Ultimately, though, the Lord is always in total control. He is not really behind, no matter what our perception may be. No matter how dark things may be for His people, if they are with Him, we know we will be victorious in the end. It's not a matter of "if;" it's simply a matter of "when." And how amazing is this—God decides the "when!" The only question left for each of us to answer is, will I choose to be on His victorious team?

Hallelujah, Praise Jehovah!

PSALM 148

It may seem strange to include Psa. 148 in this collection, but the reason is best summarized by Spurgeon. In his entire work, *The Treasury of David* (from which we have quoted often), his introduction to Psa. 148 is one of the shortest. Here it is, in its entirety:

> The song is one and indivisible. It seems almost impossible to expound it in detail, for a living poem is not to be dissected verse by verse. It is a song of nature and of grace. As a flash of lightning flames through space, and enwraps both heaven and earth in one vestment of glory, so doth the adoration of the Lord in this Psalm light up all the universe and cause it to glow with a radiance of praise. The song begins in the heavens, sweeps downward to dragons and all deeps, and then ascends again, till the people near unto Jehovah take up the strain. For its exposition the chief requisite is a heart on fire with reverent love to the Lord over all, who is blessed for ever.[1]

Many people, who may have only read this poem a time or two, have sung much of it. For decades, a favorite hymn of praise for many Christians has been "Hallelujah, Praise Jehovah!" which takes

---

1. Ibid., 3.2.437.

many lines from this great psalm and puts them to soaring music. In fact, in just three verses, you will find almost the entirety of Psa. 148 in one form or another.

Singing that grand hymn may help us gain some appreciation for the heart and mind of praise that accompanied this psalm, even in ancient times when it was written. Still, we wonder what tune was used. The psalm soars with the heights of praise, and it is our goal in this chapter not to take away from the power of this great psalm.

This poem sits directly in the center of five psalms (146-150) that both begin and end with the words "Praise the Lord!" It is only fitting that this great collection of emotional poems should end this way. We will notice three things from this psalm that we have seen multiple times in the psalms already, but that this inspired poet obviously loved.

Praise (vv. 1-12)

"Hallelujah" both opens and closes this poem, and there is no way to miss that the praise of Jehovah is the overarching theme of this entire poem. Throughout the lines of this poem, "the psalmist designs to express his affection to the duty of praise" and "does all he can to engage all about him in this pleasant work."[2]

As Spurgeon said in his introduction, there is a flow to this psalm as we move from the heavens to the depths, to people. We could, if we chose, walk through each one of those and try to see some significance in all the things that are called upon to praise the Lord (angels, sun, waters, etc.). But the key to all these things is not what is found in the list, but the totality of the list. It is as if the psalmist is looking all around him and naming everything he can think of in the moment, calling on every part of creation to praise God.

Of course, we need to consider that creation itself brings glory

---

2. Henry, *Commentary*, 782.

to God simply by its order, beauty, and power. As a fellow psalmist famously said, "The heavens declare the glory of God, and the sky above proclaims His handiwork" (19:1). In New Testament times, Paul would tell the Christians at Rome that certain traits of God are evident simply from the power of creation (Rom. 1:20).

The strength of Psalm 148 is found in the sheer volume and breadth of things found in the list. From huge celestial bodies, such as the sun to things we might not consider powerful like mist (v. 8), everything the poet can think of in the moment is called upon to praise God. Also, when the poet gets to people, he doesn't list just one type of person: "Kings of the earth and all peoples, princes and all rulers of the earth! Young men and maidens together, old men and children!" (vv. 11-12). It simply does not matter if it is a king sitting on a royal throne or a maiden serving in the house—all are to praise God.

Before moving away from this part of the psalm, though, there is a concept that can be missed if we just run through the text. There is a part of this praise that is clearly meant to show that God controls the entire universe. Notice a few phrases:

- "Praise Him, all His angels; praise Him, all His hosts" (v. 2).
- "...stormy wind fulfilling His word" (v. 8).

God did not just create the world and let it go. He did not just wind it up and watch it all wind down. One of the reasons creation praises the Lord is because it is His. He still controls it, and it fulfills what He wants to be done.

God is truly worthy of our praise. The day before writing these words, I spent about an hour in a local park with my children. The beauty that was around us was evident. It was autumn as I was writing, and the leaves on some of the trees were stunning in their multi-colored beauty. Although the weather was getting cooler, the grass under the canopy of reds and yellows was still a strong green.

As I looked around, with this psalm in my mind, all I could think was "Hallelujah, praise Jehovah!" All creation cries His praise, and I am not just compelled, but motivated, to join in the praise.

Power (v. 13)

The idea of God's power permeates this psalm and is one of the clear reasons why the praise of creation flows to Him. As the inspired writer begins to draw the poem to a close, he focuses his words on that power of God: "Let them praise the name of the Lord, for His name alone is exalted; His majesty is above earth and heaven."

Considering how religions are put forward as plausible, this is a powerful statement. The exclusivity of praising God is one of the most controversial stances of the Christian faith, but it is one that believers must constantly hold to. That is true for one simple reason: Jehovah is the only true God. Others are made by the hands of men, or are put forward by man's imagination, but Jehovah always was, is, and is to come. The psalmist here even uses the word "alone" to describe the exaltation of the name of God. Yes, there are other deities (and even some people) who are lifted up in praise at times, but those will ultimately fail.

One clear example of a man failing is found in Acts 12. Herod decided to have a procession in his own honor (sort of a "Herod Day") in front of some of his subjects. To add to the splendor, Acts 12:21 tells us, "On an appointed day Herod put on his royal robes, took his seat upon the throne and delivered an oration to them." Everything about this day was meant to exalt Herod. The people were so amazed by what they saw that they began crying out, "The voice of a god, and not of a man" (v. 22). Here was a moment of truth. Herod could have silenced the people, asked for their respect as their earthly leader, but then given the ultimate glory to God. Instead, he "did not give God the glory" (v. 23), and his fate was awful. Herod "was eaten by worms and breathed his last" (v. 23). I will propose that was not the ending to Herod Day he had in mind.

While that may be an extreme case, consider how many deities and people have been hailed and worshiped throughout the centuries, only to see the religion or the movement falter. Zoroastrianism is a footnote in history. The Egyptian gods were all shown to be frauds through the ten plagues. All mythical religions (Norse, Greek, Roman, etc.) may have fascinating stories, but they have all been proven to be false. Still, over the years, people have fallen for these false religions. Through it all, the name of Jehovah stands. While God may not be popular in some places for long stretches of time, the belief in Him and the worship of Jehovah continues on. As other religions rise and fall, it only proves what the psalmist says: "His name alone is exalted."

Because of that, "[God's] majesty is above earth and heaven." This fits naturally with the rest of the psalm. All of creation that have been called upon to praise Jehovah are to do so, in part because He is above them all. Their beauty is truly amazing, but it simply cannot compare to the matchless power and glory of God. "There is more glory in Him personally than in all His works united. It is not possible for us to exceed and become extravagant in the Lord's praise: His own natural glory is infinitely greater than any glory which we can render to Him."[3]

Some are greater at appreciating certain aspects of nature than I am. I know some things that I think are beautiful, but I cannot understand those things on a scientific, biological, or physical level. I just don't have that kind of training. Yet the most powerful parts of creation—the explosions of volcanoes, the indescribable lamination of stars, the complexity of the atmosphere—still pale in comparison to the glory of God. He set it all in motion with nothing more than His voice. And He holds it all together, no matter how powerful it may

---

3. Spurgeon, *Treasury of David,* 3:440.

seem, out of His infinite power.

Protection (v. 14)

The incredible power God has is not just reserved for the powers of nature. As the psalm comes to an end, the poet states that the power of God is also given to His people: "He has raised up a horn for His people, praise for all His saints, for the people of Israel who are near to Him." The picture of a horn could mean different things, both of which make sense in the overall flow of both this psalm and the entirety of Scripture.

First, the horn could symbolize the type of horn that held oil and was used for healing and anointing (cf. 23:5). When Samuel anointed both Saul and then David, he anointed them as kings. The poet of Psa. 148 may have the idea of God anointing His people for healing or for some type of special service.

The horn could also symbolize more of a call of honor. When dignitaries were nearing a location, horns were blown to express the coming of one who was powerful and important. It could be that God Himself is doing something—pictured as blowing a horn—to show honor to His people. Whichever is in view, the picture here shows that God is protecting His people. He has not just left them to their own devices while He sits back and watches them try to solve the issues of life. God is always present, helping and honoring His people.

But we must keep in mind this key phrase of v. 14: "For the people of Israel who are near to Him." God is not going to heal and honor those who are far from Him. While His general goodness is evident to all people—"He makes the sun rise on the evil and on the good" (Matt. 5:45)—God has a special protection for His people. To know that protection, we must be near Him.

There are too many people who try to straddle the fence with God and then wonder where He is when difficulties come. These are the people who come to worship and many "look the part" of a disciple of Jesus, but they are only thinking of themselves when they are away from the people of God. Then when difficulty comes, they wonder where God is. The truth of the matter is that these people were never all that close to God, and He will not provide His special protection for those who are not truly near Him. He desires us to be close and to be seeking always to stay near. When we do, He raises up a horn for us. He heals, and He honors.

Conclusion

As I was writing this chapter, I tried to find the history of the hymn "Hallelujah, Praise Jehovah." Even though it is clearly from Psa. 148, and the composer, William J. Kirkpatrick, is well-known in musical circles, there is not much information on the actual writing of the hymn. I did run across one story, though, that I found stunning. It talked about Kirkpatrick's life and his willingness to lead in worship for years. The history also discussed that this poem and song showed a mature faith. It also detailed what each verse of the three-verse hymn expressed.

There was only one thing missing from this particular article. There was not a singular mention of Psa. 148! I don't know if it was an honest oversight, or if the writer of the article was just oblivious to the clear use of this grand inspired poem by Kirkpatrick for his hymn. Either way, to strip the psalm from the hymn is to do more than a disservice. It is to fail to consider the inspired text, which is far greater than even Kirkpatrick's wonderful hymn.

We do not know who the inspired author of Psa. 148 was. David, of course, is put forward as a possible author, but no scholar can say with certainty who wrote these words. Whoever the writer was, one thing is certain: the poet had a truly high view of God, one that all believers should have.

Too often, we want to bring God down to our own level and make Him more like something of our own experience. But God is not "one of us," no matter the mistaken philosophical thoughts of Joan Osborne's pop hit. We are not to bring Him down to our level. We look at His created order, and our souls thrill at His amazing glory. We know His power and soar with amazement. We feel His protection and are touched by His compassion. And so, with the poet, we cannot help but say, "Hallelujah!" We praise the Lord.

The Zenith of Praise

For dozens of pages in the Bible, a collection of poems captures our attention. Sometimes, the Psalms hold our attention simply out of the sheer volume. If you are reading through the Bible cover-to-cover, for example, you might spend nearly a month in this one book, longer than any of the other 65 books of the Bible.

If you take the time to read each of these grand poems, you are captivated by something more than that volume. You are captivated by emotion. Every conceivable emotion is captured in these poems, and every one of them is put before the throne of God. It simply does not matter if you are joyful, angry, sad, distraught, or confused, every one of those emotions (and more) is contained somewhere in this collection of inspired poems.

It is most appropriate that the final few psalms are all psalms of praise. While the Psalms capture us with their range of human emotion, they quickly turn our focus away from ourselves and place it clearly and unmistakably on the Lord Jehovah. He is the One who created every emotion, and He is the One to whom we can take every emotion. Realizing that, the final few psalms all are poems of praise.

The last poem, Psa. 150, is the zenith of the book. It is not just a quick ending, and it is not just put here because there was no other place to put it. This poem brings this entire collection of Psalms, and especially the final psalms of praise, to a close. It leaves us filled with wonder of God, and though we have read 149 poems already, the grand nature of this poem leaves us wishing there were more.

While it may seem as if we have read everything and—in this book, written everything—that can be said about praising God, Psa. 150 reminds us that our praise for Him should flow from us. We can never give full and complete expression to Him, but our awe of the Lord should lead us to express everything we can to His glory and praise. Using this final psalm, the zenith of praise, let's walk through Psa. 150 and consider our praise to the Lord.

The Scene (v. 1)

After giving the opening "Hallelujah," the inspired poet gives the location for the praise of God that he has in mind for this final poem. In reality, it is everywhere, but that is expressed with two phrases.

"In His sanctuary." The poet probably has in mind the most holy place of the temple, but of course, he could be speaking of Heaven. Either way, the picture is one of the very presence of God. This is a description of God's royalty because this sanctuary belongs to Him. When we come before God in worship, we need to keep clearly in our mind that we are in His presence. While we gain a great deal from worship, we are not the object. It is all focused on the One who is the divine King.

"In His mighty heavens (KJV = firmament)." Without belaboring the point, notice again that the firmament belongs to God. But the praise of God is pictured here as being spread throughout the sky and heavens. Since these belong to Him, this is a picture of the power of God. Even the powerful and beautiful skies belong to Him. Of course, the skies themselves praise God by their very existence (cf. 19:1). In our psalm, though, the poet is speaking metaphorically as if we could travel throughout the heavens and praise the Lord

from the clouds, the lightning bolts, or the stars. God created it all and holds it all together, thus He is worthy of praise. So the scene is set. The praise of God is to come forth from every place because of God's royalty and power.

The Sense (v. 2)

Why would we praise God? What reason do we have to go to these places (even through the eye of faith) and offer Him praise? In v. 2, the poet gives two reasons, sharing why it makes sense to praise the Lord.

"His mighty deeds." It may seem strange, but this is one of the few times in the psalms where the poet does not begin to enumerate some of the wonderful acts of God throughout history. But maybe that should not surprise us here. After all, list after list of God's amazing deeds has already been found in this book. There is no need to try to give a summary list, or to try to build some "master list" for this final poem. Instead, the poet wants the one praising God to consider whatever mighty deeds he wishes to bring about praise.

Sometimes, those mighty deeds are personal in nature. Throughout the psalms, for example, we see several times when David (and others) remembered ways in which God brought about deliverance and help. His mighty deeds sometimes involved overcoming armies, while at other times they involved simply being present in a time of trouble. At other times, the mighty deeds of God were more national in their scope. There are regular references in the Psalms to the Red Sea, entering into the Promised Land, and other concerns of Israel. Each of those was to remind the people of God's power and faithfulness.

In this final psalm, though, there is not a specific type of mighty deed given because the poet simply wants each reader to consider a reason—or many reasons—to bring God praise.

"His excellent greatness." Notice the supreme nature of this description. God is not just "great"—He is excellently great. There is nothing and no one greater than the Lord. He supersedes anything we can imagine. This is a clear picture of the majesty of our Lord. Would this realization not lead to greater worship? In commenting on this phrase, Spurgeon wrote:

> [God's] being is unlimited, and His praise should correspond therewith. He possesses a multitude ... of greatness, and therefore He should be greatly praised. There is nothing little about God, and there is nothing great apart from Him. If we were always careful to make our worship fit and appropriate for our great Lord how much better should we sing! How much more reverently should we adore![1]

Throughout the collection of Psalms, God's attributes have been listed numerous times. Sometimes, as here, there are just a couple mentioned; at other times, fuller lists are enumerated. Once again, this final psalm is not trying to give us a full list of reasons to praise the Lord. Instead, the poet gives two general reasons and lets the reader fill in his own reason to praise God. When you and I consider God's mighty deeds, we might list different things, but each list is no less meaningful. And when we consider God's infinite majesty, we might think of different traits of God, but each one is important and powerful. As the song says, "That's why we praise Him." It makes logical and emotional sense to bring praise to our God.

The Style (vv. 3-5)

The bulk of this psalm enumerates musical instruments and dancing in the worship of the Lord. Of course, under the New Tes-

---

1. Ibid., 3:463.

tament, nothing of the sort is to be found in sacred worship (cf. Eph. 5:19; Col. 3:16; cf. John 4:24). Still, there is something to be gained from these verses. It is simply this: worship is to be lively and emotional. While we understand there is a decency to worship (cf. 1 Cor. 14:40), too often worship is seen as cold and unfeeling. When we consider what God has done and who He is, there should be a clear emotion and a strong joy that fills our praise.

Some have called John 4:24 the foundational passage in Scripture concerning worship, especially New Testament worship. There, Jesus stated, "God is spirit, and those who worship Him must worship in spirit and truth." Before making our main point from that verse, we must always keep in mind that we are to be worshiping God, not ourselves. That being true, we have no right to change worship based on what makes us feel good or what sounds good to us. If we are going to please the Lord, we need to do exactly what He directs. Knowing that, we need to understand what Jesus commanded. There are two parts to our worship, both equally important. Notice them, in reverse order.

Truth. By stating this, Jesus made it clear that there are commands to follow when we worship. We cannot just make up the rules as we go along. Throughout the pages of the New Testament, God has made it clear that He delights in His people preaching and teaching His Word, observing the Lord's Supper, giving financially, offering fervent prayers, and singing praise to His name. Anything beyond these acts—or anything less than these—is not worship as properly prescribed in the pages of the New Testament.

Spirit. Too often, we can get so caught up in checking off those five acts of worship that we fail to incorporate our hearts and minds. Emotion—spirit—is just as essential to proper worship as is following the pattern of the New Testament. "Lifeless worship" is impossible because if our worship is lifeless, it is not proper worship. The spirit of worship does not trump truth, but it must be present.

As is always the case, the key here is balance. Jesus did not say "spirit or truth," but "spirit and truth." Both must be present, and both are important. When you come to worship God, are you coming to offer Him joy-filled praise? Or are you simply going through the motions and trying to fulfill some heartless obligation? The spirit of our worship needs to center on how great God is and why He is so worthy of our praise. Joy should permeate our worship when we reflect deeply on what God has done for us. Wonder should fill our minds when we consider how great and majestic He is.

If we think about these things and still fail to have life in our worship, we are doing something wrong! God is great and worthy of our very best. In considering v. 2 along with vv. 3-5, Matthew Henry wrote these powerful words about what praise should be in the New Testament church:

> Praise God with a strong faith; praise Him with holy love and delight; praise Him with an entire confidence in Christ; praise Him with a believing triumph over the powers of darkness; praise Him with an earnest desire towards Him and a full satisfaction in Him; praise Him by a universal respect to all His commands; praise Him by a cheerful submission to all His disposals; praise Him by rejoicing in His love and solacing yourselves in His great goodness; praise Him by promoting the interests of the kingdom of His grace.[2]

The Shout (v. 6)

There is no way this psalm could end with more appropriate words, but they are also words that are perfectly appropriate to bring to a close the entire collection of poems. So often, we have seen these poems end with a call for some group of people or a nation

---

2. Henry, *Commentary*, 788.

to praise the Lord. But as has been the case throughout this final psalm, the poet is not interested in giving a call to one group of people. Instead, he makes a call to all creation. "Let everything that has breath praise the Lord!"

Of course, the poet could be speaking of all animals and people, and certainly that is possible. Considering the rest of this psalm, though, it seems as if he is using the idea of all who have breath to mean every person. If someone is still in the land of the living, that person is being called upon to shout the praise of God.

Our goal is to help every person see the greatness and majesty of God so they, too, will use their breath to bring Him praise. We must make the same call for all to praise the Lord, but that is often considered unappealing in our world. In a time of political correctness, such an exclusive call is seen as intolerant and close-minded. If only people would open their eyes to see the truth of God and the greatness of God! Then they too would join in the praise that only Jehovah is due.

Conclusion

With one final Hebrew word, *Halel-Yahh*, the poem and the entire book of Psalms come to a close. But it is not an abrupt close because this entire six-verse poem has served as a close to the collection of poems. We might think that this poem should end with a short prayer of some type. Maybe we might think that "Amen" would be an appropriate ending to the book. However, it is quite appropriate, considering all that has come before, that the powerful ending is a call and a shout: "Praise the Lord!"

As we have Psa. 150 divided, it contains just six verses, and each verse is quite short. Still, in just six verses, you will notice a call to praise the Lord some thirteen times. In fact, in the original Hebrew, the greatest number of words between a call to praise the

Lord is just four, and that is only one time.[3]

I have never been mountain climbing. I have ascended a few hills and enjoy driving through the Smoky Mountains, but I have no desire to be strapped to the side of a mountain. Those who do climb mountains speak of the unexplainable rush of emotion upon reaching the pinnacle of a mountain. Although I do not know that feeling from climbing mountains, I do know it from this great book. When we read Psa. 150, we have climbed a great mountain. We have spent a great deal of time reading and considering 149 poems, each one designed to help us draw nearer to God. Then, in just a few moments, we read this final poem, and we are there at the zenith of praise. And there we are reminded once more:

God is worthy. Praise the Lord!

---

3. https://bible.org/seriespage/psalm-150-priority-praise

Epilogue

Hymns of the Heart. When I first started working on this project, there was no real "title." This was originally designed to be a set of sermons and nothing more. But as I continued to study and write, it grew within me to put this material out for more people to use. My prayer is that this is done not to my glory, but to the glory of the One written about in these great poems.

It has been quite a long project. When I first started studying and writing, the weather was cold and fairly nasty. As I write this final part of the book, about eleven months later, the weather is again cooling down, with temperatures in the 40s. I have read, studied, prayed, and written through all the seasons and an array of weather patterns. Those things have changed as they always will, due to the faithfulness of the Lord.

What has not changed—except for increasing steadily—is my sense of awe of God. Spending such serious time with these in-spired poems has filled my soul with a wonder of Him for which I am grateful. Knowing that these great poets expressed every possible human emotion to the Lord, and that He allowed every one of those emotions to be placed into the sacred canon, only increases my love for, respect for, and sense of awe toward God.

There is no way the 35 chapters that have preceded these final words have fully expressed everything to be found in the Psalms, or even in the selected poems discussed. That was never the intent. Though I wanted to dig deeper than I had ever done into these great poems, I never wanted to lose sight of the proverbial forest for the trees. My prayer is that this book has not caused you to lose the overall amazing picture of these poems. If it has, it is completely my fault.

If I may, I want to share one personal reflection on writing this book. In actuality, it is a combination of several reflections, one that will let you know what the Psalms have meant to me over the past few months. Quite a number of times—probably a dozen or more—I found myself simply staring out my window or looking across my office. If someone had happened by, they would have thought that I was doing nothing except waste time. What I found myself doing, though, was simply thinking about some insight I had gained from reading, re-reading, or studying some matter from one of these great poems. I might not have been praying, but I was simply reflecting and letting a new insight dig deeply into my mind. To say it was refreshing would be a grand understatement, as would saying that I need to do that more often. These great ancient poems have reminded me of that.

Ultimately, the one takeaway from this study is that God is above all I can imagine. He stands as the central Figure of every poem, and these poets—far greater writers than I will ever be—have put into words what my heart longs to express at all times of life to Him. From the remarkable descriptions of Him found in these poems (Shepherd, Rock, Fortress, Tower) to the listing of attributes (steadfast love, goodness, victorious, avenging), to His willingness to hear His people, I am humbled in amazement. He is. He is great. He is God.

The very first word and very last word of this collection of poems perfectly bookend my feelings about Psalms. They express what I am because of God, and what I desire to do.

I am blessed (1:1), and I desire to *halal-Yah* (150:6)!

Works Cited

Cloer, Eddie. *Psalms 1-50*. Searcy, AR: Resource Publications, 2004.

—. *Psalms 51-89*. Searcy, AR: Resource Publications, 2006.

—. *Psalms 90–118*. Searcy, AR: Resource Publications, 2013.

Henry, Matthew. *A Commentary on the Whole Bible*, vol. 3. Iowa Falls, IA: World Bible Publishers, n. d.

Keil, Carl Friedrich, and Franz Delitzsch. *Commentary on the Old Testament*, vol. 5. Peabody, MA: Hendrickson, 1996.

Keller, W. Phillip. *A Shepherd Looks at Psalm 23*. Grand Rapids: Zondervan, 2007.

Morgan, Robert J. *Then Sings My Soul*. Nashville: Nelson, 2003.

Spurgeon, Charles H. *The Treasury of David*. 3 vols. Peabody, MA: Hendrickson, 2014.

Made in the USA
Lexington, KY
02 June 2015